# Entrepreneurial Business and Society

# Entrepreneurial Business and Society

## Frontiers in European Entrepreneurship Research

*Edited by*

Friederike Welter

*IfM Bonn and University of Siegen, Germany and Jönköping International Business School, Sweden*

Robert Blackburn

*Kingston University, UK*

Elisabet Ljunggren

*Nordland Research Institute, Norway*

Bjørn Willy Åmo

*University of Nordland, Norway*

IN ASSOCIATION WITH THE ECSB

**Edward Elgar**

Cheltenham, UK • Northampton, MA, USA

Published by
Edward Elgar Publishing Limited
The Lypiatts
15 Lansdown Road
Cheltenham
Glos GL50 2JA
UK

Edward Elgar Publishing, Inc.
William Pratt House
9 Dewey Court
Northampton
Massachusetts 01060
USA

A catalogue record for this book
is available from the British Library

Library of Congress Control Number: 2013933498

This book is available electronically in the ElgarOnline.com
Business Subject Collection, E-ISBN 978 1 78254 602 3

ISBN 978 1 78254 601 6

Typeset by Columns Design XML Ltd, Reading
Printed and bound in Great Britain by T.J. International Ltd, Padstow

# Contents

*v*

# Contributors

**Bjørn Willy Åmo**, University of Nordland, Norway

**Fabio Bertoni**, EM Lyon, France

**Mattia Bianchi**, Stockholm School of Economics, Sweden

**Robert Blackburn**, Kingston University, UK

**Malte Brettel**, RWTH Aachen University, Germany

**Davide Chiaroni**, Politecnico di Milano, Italy

**Jill Collis**, Brunel University, UK

**Annalisa Croce**, Politecnico di Milano, Italy

**Philipp Eckerle**, RWTH Aachen University, Germany

**Federico Frattini**, Politecnico di Milano, Italy

**Jorunn Grande**, Nord-Trøndelag University College, Norway

**Massimiliano Guerini**, University of Pisa, Italy

**Jarna Heinonen**, University of Turku, Finland

**Leila Hurmerinta**, University of Turku, Finland

**Ulla Hytti**, University of Turku, Pori Unit, Finland

**Eva Kašperová**, Kingston University, UK

**John Kitching**, Kingston University, UK

**Elisabet Ljunggren**, Nordland Research Institute, Norway

**René Mauer**, RWTH Aachen University, Germany

**Tommaso Minola**, University of Bergamo, Italy

**Örsan Örge**, Bilkent University, Turkey

**Eriikka Paavilainen-Mäntymäki**, University of Turku, Finland

**Rakesh K. Pati**, University of Minnesota, USA

**Eeva Vuorinen**, University of Turku, Finland

**Friederike Welter**, IfM Bonn and University of Siegen, Germany and Jönköping International Business School, Sweden

**Shaker A. Zahra**, University of Minnesota, USA

**Liman Zhao**, University of Minnesota, USA

# Foreword

Dear reader,

As President of the European Council for Small Business (ECSB), I am pleased to welcome you to the latest volume in the series 'Frontiers in European Entrepreneurship Research'. The volume contains selected papers presented at the 25th Research on Entrepreneurship Conference (RENT XXV). The RENT, which is jointly organized by ECSB and the European Institute for Advanced Studies in Management (EIASM), represents the most important pan-European conference for entrepreneurship scholars and experts. The conference is also an ECSB signature event, a 'product' of which we are extremely proud.

The growth of the RENT conference in terms of its volume and quality of activities and outputs is such that I am very confident that the RENT anthology offers a representative overview of the latest and most cutting-edge developments in entrepreneurial and small business studies in Europe. The chapters are based on a selection of the best papers presented at the Conference. The chapters were drawn from nominations by the Conference Scientific Committee and the session chairs; they then went through a review process, of two or more stages, until they achieved the high quality standard that is required to be included in the volume.

In 2011 the RENT conference celebrated its 25th anniversary. We have asked Professor Dr David Smallbone, one of ECSB founding fathers and distinguished ECSB fellow, to offer his thoughts to celebrate this particularly important anniversary. You will find a reflection from David in this volume. We have also commemorated the anniversary by publishing a book containing the history of the conference, its main achievements and the many colleagues that have contributed to its success. The book is available on the ECSB website, www.ecsb.org.

ECSB has worked hard to make the RENT more and more attractive. Today the RENT conference is surrounded by several pre-conference events including the PhD and postdoctoral workshop, the policy forum, the case study workshop, special interest groups meetings and the ECSB mentoring programme in which young participating scholars have the opportunity to meet their mentors and network with their peers.

Luca Iandoli
President, ECSB

# Some personal reflections on RENT

I am delighted to have this opportunity to reflect on my participation in the Research on Entrepreneurship Conference (RENT) over the years, because I speak of an event which has become an immovable fixture in my professional calendar. My first visit to RENT was in 1993 when the conference was held in Budapest at a time when Central and Eastern Europe still held a certain mystique for most of us in the West. Since then I have been fortunate enough to attend all RENT conferences to date. Personal memories include Piacenza, where NATO airmen took over the town's accommodation, resulting in us decamping to hotels some 20 miles away. To list the venues since then sounds like a cultural tour of Europe, but in the words of an old cliché, people are more important than places and one of the lasting features of RENT, as it has grown in size, is the friendliness and approachability of all participants, which is something that I hope will remain a permanent fixture.

One reason why I kept coming back to RENT in the early days was because it offered exposure to different European traditions in the field of small business including rich methodological diversity. Face-to-face contact gives the opportunity for discussion and questioning rather than just absorbing new ideas and new approaches. As a young(er) researcher I was attracted by being able to meet and talk to people who would otherwise have remained as just names on papers and books.

One of the remarkable achievements of RENT has been to maintain quality at a time when the conference has been rapidly growing in size. This is an important characteristic because it would be too easy to increase the number of participants in the conference to boost revenue for the organisers. Fortunately this temptation has been avoided.

Ultimately, the future of professional organizations and events depends on their ability to attract younger people who can provide vitality and future sustainability. In this regard, the European Council for Small Business (ECSB) is to be congratulated for developing the postdoctoral writing workshop and maintaining the doctoral consortium initiated by the late Jose Veciana. Both of these events have proven to be hugely successful, supported by the recently introduced mentoring programme.

The financial imperative is never far away, which suggests that in the future we can expect a growing proportion of professional activity that is virtual. Whilst this offers opportunities for conference materials to be made available to a wider audience, there is no substitute for face-to-face debate in the development of ideas. In this context, RENT has come a long way in the last 27 years and with the current level of support and attendance the future looks healthy. For many of us RENT provides a shop window for the best of European research in the field, highlighting the diversity and richness that attracted people like me in the first place. Long may it continue.

David Smallbone
ECSB Fellow

# PART I

# Introducing the Theme

# 1. Entrepreneurial business and society: introduction

## Friederike Welter, Robert Blackburn, Elisabet Ljunggren and Bjørn Willy Åmo

### INTRODUCING RENT XXV IN BODØ

This volume represents a selection of best papers from the ones presented at the RENT XXV conference, hosted by Bodø Graduate School of Business and the Nordland Research Institute in Bodø in Norway, in November 2011. The anthology presents a window on contemporary European research in the field of entrepreneurship and small business. Its overall theme, entrepreneurial business and society, highlights the interplay between the entrepreneur, the entrepreneurial firm and the society. Part II puts an emphasis on promoting entrepreneurial businesses, while Part III focuses on entrepreneurial people and entrepreneurial sectors, thus drawing our attention to that entrepreneurship also may contribute to social change and welfare and success could be measured in terms of the effect on the society.

RENT XXV emphasized how new firms are a result of entrepreneurs interacting with stakeholders in their environment, not only in the market but also with wider stakeholders such as interest groups and government institutions. As the book itself demonstrates, the themes of the conference span a wide range of contemporary issues. These include how governmental support programmes supporting entrepreneurial activity are reasoned, the red tape burden of small and medium-sized enterprises, how venture capital is offered and the role of technology transfer offices, through to issues in entrepreneurship education, intrapreneurship in public healthcare, how resources and capabilities shape the entrepreneurial opportunity and how the entrepreneurial opportunity itself is identified, evaluated and capitalized upon.

## AN OVERVIEW OF CHAPTERS

Chapter 2, authored by Shaker Zahra, Rakesh Pati and Liman Zhao, focuses on counterproductive entrepreneurship. Entrepreneurship generally is seen as contributing to social, economic and technological change, whilst entrepreneurship research has focused mainly on formal, productive entrepreneurial activities. The authors argue that having a more accurate appreciation of the value of entrepreneurship for a society requires us to consider counterproductive entrepreneurship that occurs with the formal and informal parts of a nation's economy. They identify its types, the forms it takes, the origins of these forms, and the potential effect on society. Thus, the authors highlight areas worthy of attention by public policy makers as they map their strategies to reduce the dysfunctional effects of counterproductive entrepreneurship. They also identify areas that require attention in future research, aiming to curb the dysfunctions of entrepreneurship and make it truly an important means of economic, technological and social transformation, progress and development.

Part II discusses approaches to promoting entrepreneurial business and society. In Chapter 3, Örsan Örge analyses entrepreneurship policy in Turkey, drawing on the example of a support programme, introduced in 2009, that was to provide seed financing to young entrepreneurs with technology-based venture ideas. In applying a discourse-based approach, the author goes beyond a quantitative analysis of costs and effects, emphasizing how power relations impact upon entrepreneurship policies. Empirically, the chapter draws on an extensive analysis of programme material, official documents and interviews with politicians, keynote speeches and press statements. A discourse-based approach serves to highlight the actors involved in supporting entrepreneurship as well as their respective agency and power relations. With this, the author emphasizes that the policy discourse not only helps to define the problem to be solved and offer solutions, but that at the same time it may restrict the means, or in other words, the support approaches, used by governments. The author shows how the policy discourse contributes to justifying and legitimizing the existence of specific policies. Young high-tech entrepreneurs in Turkey are seen as a 'vulnerable' and 'weak' group, which urgently needs particular policy support. By portraying the target group as dependent and passive, the discourse negates their entrepreneurial agency, while at the same time reconstituting government as 'heroic' political entrepreneur. This consequently serves political interests, because the discourse endows policy makers with much-sought-after qualities such as vision, courage and benevolence. The author further suggests that the versatile nature of the concept of 'entrepreneurship' allows the Turkish government to put entrepreneurship forward as national imperative for progress without an alternative, and this in turn secures the political power of the ruling party. Here, the author's analysis draws attention to the geopolitical context of entrepreneurship policy illustrating that, in countries where the institutional framework is less developed, powerful actors can influence the discourse to serve their own interests.

Chapter 4, by John Kitching, Eva Kašperová and Jill Collis, takes a fresh look at administrative burdens in relation to small firms. The chapter explores whether and how regulation, governing the public disclosure of financial information and allowing for abbreviated accounts, influences small business performance. Most research studying the impact of regulation on small businesses emphasizes regulation as an entry barrier, due to its administrative and psychological costs, and it is this view which is underpinning the current approach of the United Kingdom (UK) government in implementing facilitated reporting rules for small and medium-sized enterprises (SMEs).

The authors draw on empirical research conducted in the UK, consisting of 12 interviews with small business respondents (most of them micro firms) who are preparers and users of abbreviated accounts, and complemented by expert interviews with account users from 18 intermediary organizations such as banks, credit insurance companies, professional bodies, public sector organizations and a small business membership organization. Their results illustrate that, on the one hand, it is less 'administrative burdens' that result in small companies filing abbreviated accounts, but rather administrative ease, and in particular also suggestions made by their accountants for whom abbreviated financial reporting appears to be the default option in the case of a small firm. On the other hand, stakeholders presented varied opinions, with some believing that abbreviated accounts are, up to a point, useful to support credit risk assessments and abbreviated credit decisions, and others favouring more comprehensive information. The empirical results presented emphasize that abbreviated accounts provide only limited financial transparency, with important consequences for users, small companies themselves and the wider economy. With their analysis, the authors provide a more comprehensive perspective on regulation and its effects, by both studying the direct impact of regulatory burdens, in the form of the responses of small enterprises as well as analysing indirect effects, namely stakeholders' responses to abbreviated financial regulations.

In Chapter 5, Fabio Bertoni, Annalisa Croce and Massimiliano Guerini study the effectiveness of public venture capital in supporting young high-tech companies in Europe. Young high-tech companies face severe financial constraints because of information asymmetries and the mismatch in their investment and revenue cycles. It is here that venture capital may contribute both directly, through expanding the capital base of the firm, and indirectly, through reducing information asymmetries. In an effort to stimulate the development of high-tech industries, many governments in Europe have introduced public venture capital (VC). In contrast to independent venture capital, public VC often focuses on a broader (and less clear-cut) set of goals, including political aims such as developing links between universities and the private sector, supporting the development of the VC industry and fostering employment. It is surprising, however, that public VC has received but little attention in research. In this regard, the authors ask whether public venture capital is as effective as independent venture capital in closing financial gaps for young firms.

The authors study the effectiveness of public VC based on a sample of 1312 European high-tech companies from the manufacturing sector, of which 74 are backed by venture capital. Their results show that independent venture capital can help to alleviate the financial constraints faced by young high-tech companies in Europe: companies which had received independent VC were able to invest more in the long term and their investment policy was unaffected by shocks in their current cash flows. The picture on public venture capital is more bleak: direct support is limited to the financing round and its immediate aftermath; financial constraints of high-tech companies persist, also because public VC invests smaller amounts per round and is active in fewer subsequent investment rounds. Moreover, there is little evidence that public VC conveys a positive signal to other potential investors, thus generating an indirect negative effect. It may be that public VC lacks the credibility or networks of contacts that are required to attract other, independent VC into the syndicate or to provide follow-on investment. The authors point out that while they evaluated the effects of public VC on high-tech companies, there may be other, more indirect effects, such as contributing to a regional venture capital culture, that their study has neglected.

High-tech companies are also discussed in Chapter 6, co-authored by Mattia Bianchi, Davide Chiaroni, Federico Frattini and Tommaso Minola. The authors study the role of technology transfer offices (TTOs) for entrepreneurial universities, applying a dynamic capability view to be able to identify determinants of superior performance of such offices. In particular, they focus on the management and organization of technology transfer activities as key levers to overcome market failure and increase the productivity of TTOs. Technology commercialization is complex, it requires a wide range of diverse competencies and skills, and it occurs in conditions of high uncertainty; therefore, managerial and organizational aspects of TTOs gain importance. In this context, the authors suggest a framework which attempts to identify those managerial antecedents that underlie superior capabilities in commercializing academic research, as well as allows studying the complex set of tasks and actors involved in technology transfer at multiple levels.

Empirically, the chapter draws on the case of two TTOs at Italian universities, which have been active in technology transfer for many years, albeit with very different degrees of success. Their qualitative approach allows an in-depth exploration of the micro-foundations of the commercialization and transfer process, thus generating new insights into a topic which has been dominated by quantitative studies. The cases demonstrate sensing, seizing and reconfiguring as important dynamic capabilities of TTOs and the people employed there. Their findings suggest that processes and organization need to move between standardization, systematization and flexibility in order to successfully support technology transfer, while as regards people, a strong scientific background together with an entrepreneurial mindset and business skills are required.

Part III of this anthology moves to entrepreneurial people and entrepreneurial sectors. In Chapter 7, René Mauer, Philipp Eckerle and Malte Brettel discuss entrepreneurship education, attempting to add pieces to the entrepreneurial intention puzzle. The authors set out to study the factors that play a role in the formation of entrepreneurial self-efficacy and entrepreneurial intentions of students. They argue that entrepreneurship education research still lacks detailed knowledge on the drivers of entrepreneurial self-efficacy. Therefore, entrepreneurship education researchers should focus on the development of entrepreneurial self-efficacy, because we need a deeper understanding as to the effects of entrepreneurship education, pedagogies and methods on students' self-efficacy and entrepreneurial intentions.

The authors draw on social cognitive theory in order to study the antecedents of entrepreneurial self-efficacy. Their empirical sample includes 211 responses from non-business students, most of them industrial engineers in machinery constructions, at RWTH Aachen University. Their study is among the first to simultaneously measure all main antecedents for entrepreneurial self-efficacy, derived from social cognitive theory: mastery experiences, vicarious experiences, social and verbal persuasion and judgements of one's own physiological states. Findings from the empirical study show that, with the exception of social persuasion, all antecedents significantly contribute to the emergence of entrepreneurial self-efficacy. In other words, all sources of self-efficacy identified by social cognitive theory are important within the entrepreneurship environment.

The next three chapters focus on entrepreneurship in less-researched sectors. Jarna Heinonen, Ulla Hytti and Eeva Vuorinen, in Chapter 8, shift our attention to public healthcare and intrapreneurship. In an era of ageing population, shrinking public budgets and increasing competition from private sector clinics, public healthcare faces enormous challenges in attracting competent personnel, finding new ways to customer-oriented services, to renew organizations and to develop new, innovative services. In this context, the concept of intrapreneurship gains importance, referring to the practice of developing new ventures and strategic renewal within an existing organization in order to exploit new opportunities and generate economic value. So far, little is known about intrapreneurship in public sector healthcare organizations, which also have a social mission shaping key processes and their outcomes. In this regard, the authors explore intrapreneurship in the context of a public healthcare organization.

Empirically, the chapter draws on an ethnographic study of a large Finnish public university hospital, and particularly its eye clinic. The authors combined a survey of all staff members with several interviews, participant observations of everyday activities within the clinic, feedback sessions and other workshops. The case selected for this particular chapter, a nurse's account of her daily activities within the clinic, highlights the difficulties and opportunities of intrapreneurship in a public health organization, where intrapreneurial risk taking goes hand in hand with challenging existing boundaries of supervisors, the clinic organization and the sector of healthcare. The findings helped to identify five boundaries which could constrain intrapreneurship. With this fine-grained understanding of intrapreneurship within a public health organization, the chapter adds to our knowledge by complementing previous research on intrapreneurship and corporate entrepreneurship.

Chapter 9, by Jorunn Grande, studies resources and capabilities that are deemed as critical for successful entrepreneurship in agriculture. The author is especially interested in exploring entrepreneurial efforts, the ability to change and resources that are of critical importance to new value-added ventures on farms. In light of the declining agricultural sector, diversification of farm businesses and other efforts to increase entrepreneurship at farms are seen as means to increase income and employment as well as sustain economic development in rural communities. Farm firms may encounter specific difficulties in adding new entrepreneurial activities, due to type of industry, traditions and their liability of smallness.

The chapter draws on an in-depth and longitudinal study of three Norwegian farm businesses engaged in new, value-added businesses. A case study research design was set up with the farm business as the unit of analysis. The cases selected represent different firm sizes, type of operations, farmer's background, location and resource endowment. The empirical findings illustrate that a simultaneous focus on resources, entrepreneurial orientation and dynamic capabilities is needed to provide a more complete picture on how a firm's internal factors may leverage competitive advantage in new value creation processes. This is of interest for policy makers, emphasizing that a focus on building entrepreneurial skills may help rural business owners in exploring and expanding the uniqueness of new activities.

In Chapter 10, Leila Hurmerinta and Eriikka Paavilainen Mäntymäki revisit the entrepreneurial opportunity process. The authors set forth to study the process of how entrepreneurs identify, evaluate and capitalize on opportunities. They apply a novel approach, namely diaries, aiming to provide some fresh insights on opportunities. Diaries are time-sensitive, and informants in diary research are active data providers and creators instead of passive participants. In particular, diaries capture emotions, feelings, attitudes and impressions that informants may not be able to or may hesitate to describe in retrospective interviews or narratives.

The empirical context is Finnish small enterprises operating in the food industry, where in recent years opportunities were essential to create new inputs and changes in a traditional industry. During recent years, Finnish food SMEs strived to increase their competitiveness, growth and international market share, while at the same time international food chains and imported produce and groceries have gained a firmer foothold in Finnish food markets. This chapter draws on diaries of three small-scale entrepreneurs from the food industry.

Results highlight the complexity and dynamics of opportunities as well as their contextual dimension. Opportunities do not emerge outside a social context; the opportunity process is a contextually bound iterative learning process, stimulated by a range of events. Moreover, there is a temporal dimension to the opportunity process, with time being a scarce resource that influences the nature of the opportunity process, although opportunities as such are not bound by time or place. The authors also conclude that the diary method proved a fruitful and rich data source as well as a means for the entrepreneurs themselves to reflect on their business and management practices.

Overall, this anthology offers new insights to our understandings of the conditions for entrepreneurship and entrepreneurial behaviour. The chapters represent a rich variety of topics and research methods reflecting the multidimensional nature of the entrepreneurship construct. Clearly, the conditions for entrepreneurship and entrepreneurial activities differ across time and locations, and entrepreneurship research is inspired from other research disciplines and streams in order to understand and explain this complex social phenomenon. As this collection of recent research indicates, there is a multitude of analytical levels in entrepreneurship research. The many aspects of entrepreneurial activity and the many societal arrangements that affect such activities necessitate different lenses for investigating the entrepreneurship phenomenon. The diversity and creativity in utilizing scientific methods reported here may act as a basis to inspire others to find new ways to build new knowledge and hence enrich our joint understanding of the forces that shape our economy and society.

# 2. How does counterproductive entrepreneurship undermine social wealth creation?

## Shaker A. Zahra, Rakesh K. Pati and Liman Zhao

## INTRODUCTION

The study of entrepreneurship has advanced rapidly over the past decades. A vast body of literature now exists on the nature, antecedents and outcomes of the entrepreneurial act. This literature touts the varied contributions entrepreneurs and entrepreneurship make to a community and society. This rich stream of research has invited communities and governments to craft policies to stimulate and promote entrepreneurship. One glaring gap in the literature is systematically ignoring the dysfunctions of entrepreneurs and the socially undesirable by-products of the entrepreneurial process. The pervasiveness of these dysfunctions and their potentially negative effects on individuals, families, organizations, communities and societies are the focus of this chapter.

To be sure, entrepreneurship is a powerful source for good. Yet, it can be a socially costly activity in terms of the use of human and natural resources, wealth distribution, access to institutions, amassing political and other types of powers, and controlling the direction of a nation's development trajectory. The field's tendency to accentuate the positives of entrepreneurship has had several drawbacks, specifically ignoring the associated social costs of entrepreneurship. Social cost is defined as the harmful consequences to communities, societies, and even individual citizens of a nation (Kapp 1950). Entrepreneurs, for example, have contributed to a wealth gap that has magnified a sense of social injustice; they have abused labour, and damaged natural resources and environment without being held accountable. Even though a few scholars have acknowledged that entrepreneurship might have negative influences on entrepreneurs and their families, the social costs and ills have not been subjected to careful study (Zahra and Wright 2011). Baumol (1996) has also argued that not all entrepreneurial activities are productive; some are underproductive and others are counterproductive.

In this chapter, we ask: Is entrepreneurship always economically productive for society? What are the social costs associated with entrepreneurship? Besides the economic cost born by individuals, organizations and society at large, are there other side-effects of entrepreneurship? Are there different types of dysfunctional entrepreneurship? If so, how do they differ and what are their effects? Currently, our understanding of these basic issues is limited, perhaps because of the international acceptance of entrepreneurship as a means of economic growth and job creation. Appreciating the 'dark side' of entrepreneurship, however, can provide a more realistic and accurate accounting of entrepreneurship's real contributions.

Ongoing discussions of the social contributions of entrepreneurship (Larson 2011) also require us to pause and consider the dysfunctional effects of entrepreneurs' behaviours. These behaviours may result in the loss of value to society, disrupting and corrupting national and local institutions, directing national and regional economic development plans in ways that serve the needs of the few at the expense of the majority, and undermining a country's political process in ways that ensure that the minority controls and usurps disproportionate powers. By examining these issues, we believe we offer a more 'balanced scorecard' of the net value added by entrepreneurs to society. In so doing, we highlight areas of concern where society might have to safeguard against these excesses, providing an opportunity for a more balanced and sustainable growth.

## ENTREPRENEURSHIP AND SOCIETY

There is near universal agreement that entrepreneurship is the engine of economic, technological and social progress. These powerful contributions have drawn worldwide attention of governments, foundations and universities across the world towards strongly encouraging entrepreneurship. Today, entrepreneurship is considered a critical driving force of the economy by establishing new firms, industries and institutions, and creating many new jobs (Birley 1987). It also enhances federal and local tax revenues, increases exports and helps in improving national productivity (Low and MacMillan 1988). Entrepreneurship develops new products, conceives different and efficient means of economic exchange, and creates new wealth by stimulating innovation and discoveries (Diamond and Plattner 1993). Entrepreneurs also promote the social development by resolving many social problems (e.g. Schumpeter 1942 [1950]), as witnessed in the recent growth of social ventures (Zahra et al. 2009). Further, entrepreneurs play a major role in making the public goods available and accessible to the common public (Drucker 2006).

## DYSFUNCTIONAL ENTREPRENEURSHIP

Shane and Venkataraman (2000) view entrepreneurship as a process that consists of: identifying entrepreneurial opportunities; identifying who, when and by whom opportunities are discovered; and determining how these opportunities are exploited. Zahra and Dess (2001) recognize an additional important dimension, entrepreneurial outcomes, which they argue could be positive or negative, immediate or long term, tangible or intangible. Other scholars have also viewed entrepreneurs as individuals who establish and manage businesses for the principal purpose of profit and growth (Gartner 1988). Using these different dimensions of entre-preneurship, we discuss various forms of entrepreneurship which have negative or intermediate outcomes rather than positive outcomes. We call such entrepreneurship 'dysfunctional entrepreneurship'. These kinds of activity cannot be excluded from the domain of entrepreneurship by naming them as illegal or criminal activities, as they all share the various dimensions of entrepreneurship just mentioned. These entrepreneurs create or identify entrepreneurial opportunity, take risks, allocate resources and exploit these opportunities to create wealth, mostly for themselves.

Dysfunctional entrepreneurship falls into two broad types, depending on their legal status in the society. The first set of dysfunctional entrepreneurship consists of activities that are illegal or severely restricted by law (Table 2.1). Criminal entrepreneurship, controversial entrepreneurship and corrupt entrepreneurship are three prototypical activities that fall under this category. The second type consists of those entrepreneurial activities that are less severely restricted by society (Table 2.2). They typically include corrosive entrepreneurship, control-ling entrepreneurship and careless entrepreneurship. Next, we discuss each of the sets in detail, highlighting their characteristics and potential impact.

*Table 2.1    Different types of dysfunctional entrepreneurship (illegal and high social cost)*

| Type of entrepreneur-ship | Definition | Prominent forms | Loss to society | Some common attributes |
|---|---|---|---|---|
| Criminal | Exploit opportunity and use creative ways to perform activities forbidden by law | Illegal trade of items such as:<br>1. Drugs<br>2. Illegal immigrants<br>3. Arms<br>4. Rare wildlife and plants | 1. Financial loss<br>2. Violence and death<br>3. Encourages and facilitates robbery, extortion and other criminal activity<br>4. Violation of human rights | 1. Intensity of social cost – high<br>2. Legal status – illegal<br>3. Ethical standing – highly unethical<br>4. Final product & service (output) – harmful<br>5. Timeline of effect – immediate |
| Controversial | Exploit opportunities that might not be illegal but have serious counter-productive influence on society | Providing services such as:<br>1. Alcohol & tobacco<br>2. Prostitution<br>3. Gambling | 1. Illness & death<br>2. Decrease in productivity<br>3. Decrease standard of living<br>4. Exploitation of women | 1. Intensity of social cost – high<br>2. Legal status – illegal or legal with restrictions<br>3. Ethical standing – highly unethical<br>4. Final output & service (output) – harmful<br>5. Timeline of effect – immediate |
| Corrupt | Use corrupt and unethical practices to exploit opportunities | Can be seen in all forms of businesses | 1. Depletion of national wealth<br>2. Hinder growth rate<br>3. Threat to legal and judiciary system<br>4. Hinders productive entrepreneurship<br>5. Threat to public welfare<br>6. Fragmen-tation of national identity<br>7. Unrest in society | 1. Intensity of social cost – high<br>2. Legal status – illegal<br>3. Ethical standing – highly unethical<br>4. Final product & service (output) – harmful or useful<br>5. Timeline of effect – immediate or long term |

*Table 2.2 Different types of dysfunctional entrepreneurship (legal and low social cost)*

| Type of entrepreneur-ship | Definition | Prominent forms | Loss to society | Attributes |
|---|---|---|---|---|
| Corrosive | Exploits opportunity and generate personal wealth by exploitation of environment and/or individuals in the society | Create wealth by: 1. Rent seeking – (a) monopoly, (b) tax evasion, (c) non-sustainable investing, (d) religious imposters 2. Environmental exploitation 3. Exploitation of poor and underprivileged | 1. Economic and social gap in society increases 2. Social development hindered 3. Financial losses and unemployment 4. Environmental degradation and health issues 5. Human right issues | 1. Intensity of social cost – low 2. Legal status – legal 3. Ethical standing – unethical 4. Final product & service (output) – useful 5. Timeline of effect – long term |
| Controlling | Exploit the opportunity by controlling the environment and suppressing the development | Can be seen in all form of businesses | 1. Hinders technological development 2. Discourages innovation | 1. Intensity of social cost – low 2. Legal status – legal 3. Ethical standing – ethical or unethical 4. Final product & service (output) – useful 5. Timeline of effect – long term |
| Careless | Exploits opportunity and creates wealth but careless to neglect small yet important issues | Can be seen in all form of businesses | 1. Increases conflicts and tension in society 2. Family disputes and sibling rivalry 3. Higher divorce rates | 1. Intensity of social cost – low 2. Legal status – legal 3. Ethical standing – ethical 4. Final product & service (output) – useful 5. Timeline of effect – long term |

# CRIMINAL, CONTROVERSIAL AND CORRUPT ENTREPRENEURSHIP

Entrepreneurship rests on a theory of society and economy (Drucker 2006). Innovation and entrepreneurship typically thrive in those societies and environments that have individuality, provide incentives for risk taking, and recognize the role of the entrepreneur in creating new goods, services and institutions. Complementing the environment, entrepreneurs have a strong affinity towards innovation, creativity and risk to increase their personal wealth and power. However, sometimes the quest for profit and power encourages the entrepreneurs to seek opportunities which are illegal. Such illegal entrepreneurship generally has immediate and high social costs. Their outputs in terms of products and services such as illicit drugs, prostitution and alcohol, are highly dangerous and harmful to society. Even though society considers it highly unethical and does not sanction these activities, entrepreneurs pursue them to improve their own wealth even at the expense of society. Below, we will discuss these different forms of illegal entrepreneurship.

## Criminal Entrepreneurship

Perhaps the worst form of dysfunctional entrepreneurship is criminal entrepreneurship, which causes the most harm to both the social and the political environment. As Table 2.1 indicates, criminal entrepreneurs use creative (deceptive) ways to perform activities in formal or informal enterprises that are forbidden by law (Wright and Zahra 2011). They deal with goods and services that are prohibited by law such as illicit drugs, illegal prostitution, human trafficking, trafficking in arms, and underground trafficking in rare and protected wildlife (Chell 1985; Fadahunsi and Rosa 2002). These entrepreneurs exploit moral and legal ambiguity, institutional voids and failures to amass wealth.

A growing body of literature indicates that illegal business activities and criminal entrepreneurship are widespread (Baucus 1994). They seem to thrive when political and judiciary systems are weak or there is no social stigma associated with such illegal practices, leading to the emergence of a lawless underground economy (Sardar 1996). These activities are most prevalent in many underdeveloped, developing or transitional economies where the rule of law is weak and difficult to enforce. However, some of these activities also take place in well-developed economies (e.g., trading in illicit drugs and the sex trade).

The costs borne by society from these criminal entrepreneurial activities are enormous. For example, according to the report of the United Nations Office for Drugs and Crime (UNODC) in 2009, the transactional organized crime is an US$870 billion industry, representing 1.5 per cent of the global gross domestic product (GDP) (UNODC 2012a). Drug trafficking is the most lucrative form of business for criminal entrepreneurs, with an estimated annual value of US$320 billion. Human trafficking brings in about US$32 billion annually and the annual global value of smuggling of migrants is about US$7 billion.

Illegal entrepreneurs also exploit the environment and disturb the natural habitat. The trafficking of timber generates revenues of US$3.5 billion a year in South-East Asia alone, while elephant ivory, rhino horn and tiger parts from Africa and Asia produce an annual turnover of US$75 million. Moreover, yearly turnover from counterfeiting is US$250 billion (UNODC 2012c). This is a huge loss to the society as profits from the natural resources that belong to a nation go directly into the pockets of these criminal entrepreneurs in the black market. Besides money-making, criminal entrepreneurship has a wide dysfunctional social impact. For example, about 2.4 million people are victims of human trafficking every year, which feeds into many social evils such as illegal adoption, child prostitution and pornography, the sex trade, bondage labour and forced terrorism (UNODC 2012b). The victims of the human trafficking lose their human and legal rights as they are abused and exploited (Gozdziak and Collett 2005). Even if some of the victims have the opportunity to escape exploitation, they still struggle with difficulties in their lives because of the physiological and psychological trauma they have experienced.

These criminal entrepreneurs also influence a country's social, political and economic institutions (MacGaffey 1988; Tomass 1998). They create an environment in which legitimate entrepreneurs find it difficult to work and compete using legitimate means. Because of the huge profits in criminal businesses, these entrepreneurs establish cartels and work together with local criminals, leading to an increase in related criminal activities such as murder, violence, extortion, racketeering and corruption, among others. Many law enforcement officials also lose their lives because of gang wars associated with these cartels. Criminal entrepreneurs also make a city a dangerous place to live.

Besides the lives lost in the gang wars, violence and murders are related indirectly to criminal entrepreneurship. Easy access to illegal weapons helps robbers, burglars and extortionists get possession of illegal arms to commit crimes. According to a report by the United States Department of Justice, about 5 per cent of the murders are drug related.

Similarly, reports across the world (e.g., Latin America, the United Kingdom, Europe, Asia and Russia) also indicate that violence and murders because of criminal entrepreneurship and organized crime have increased over the years (Dorsey et al. 2000). Large amounts of money from the illegal trade also provide these criminal entrepreneurs with wealth and power to control and challenge local and national governments, which undermines the peace and development of the entire region. Clearly, as noted in Table 2.1, these activities disturb social harmony and challenge legitimate entrepreneurs.

## Controversial Entrepreneurship

Controversial entrepreneurship means that entrepreneurs engage in certain activities by crossing a delicate legal line that leads to a high social cost (Table 2.1). 'Controversial' has two meanings: the first is being contrary to the law; the second is violating moral norms. Controversial entrepreneurs use innovative ways to exploit negative opportunities in the society and provide products or services such as alcohol, tobacco, prostitution and gambling, to make huge personal profits. Whether these entrepreneurs make a fortune or not, the cost of their businesses is usually borne by the society. For instance, the major cost of entrepreneurship related to alcohol and tobacco is not only the direct cost of production and distribution: it also includes the indirect cost such as death, illness, productivity loss, accidents, fights, murders and social tension which is borne by the society. Studies highlight the ill effects of alcohol and tobacco abuse on public health (e.g. Hasin et al. 2011; Redonnet et al. 2012). Across the globe, billions of dollars have been (and are being) spent on the healthcare of individuals who suffer from substance abuse, which decreases the productivity of these individuals (Fenoglio et al. 2003). It is estimated that the overall loss in productivity attributed to substance abuse runs in the billions per year (Single et al. 1998). Worse still, money cannot replace loss of health and life. Even though considerable effort and money are being spent on healthcare by individuals and the government, substance abuse accounts for a major death toll across the world. Substance abuse is also one of the major causes of road accidents, leading to injuries and the deaths of many people.

Another controversial industry is the prostitution and sex industry, where entrepreneurs use various strategies to make this industry attractive and look clean. Illegal prostitution is associated with sexual violence, which results in economic profit for the entrepreneurs involved (Ugarte et al. 2004). Many governments acknowledge the commercial sex business as harassment to human beings and consider it illegal. However, the industry is prevalent in most countries, either as a legal business or under some other name such as escort services, health clubs, strip clubs and massage parlours (Farley et al. 2004). Prostitution, sexual harassment and exploitation are often portrayed wrongly as jobs that are voluntarily accepted by the sex workers. Most sex workers are dragged into this profession or enter it as a last resort. Often the prostitutes are either assaulted or threatened with assault, which leads to post-traumatic stress disorder. A study on Indonesia's sex workers found that 96 per cent of those interviewed wanted to leave prostitution if they could (Lim 1998). Over the years, many researchers have also documented and analysed the sexual and physical violence which is the normative experience for women in prostitution (e.g. Barry 1996; Baldwin 1999; Farley et al. 2004). Moreover, stress and trauma affects sex workers as well as their families.

Gambling is another controversial industry which is a widespread cultural phenomenon and a prime leisure industry (Abt et al. 1985). Although it is legal in most countries, many illegal gambling clubs do exist. Gambling directly transfers the financial resources from the losers to the winners, but the ultimate winners are entrepreneurs who provide these gambling services. At first glance, gambling looks harmless, but many gamblers eventually turn into pathological gamblers and cannot resist their impulse to gamble (Ladouceur et al. 1994). The gambling addiction is similar to the addiction of alcohol and drugs (Volberg 1994) and creates enormous problems for the gamblers, their families, employers and society. Gamblers' lives are gradually destroyed as they acquire considerable debts indulging in illegal activities which finally endanger their physical and psychological health (Overman 1990). Empirical evidence also highlights that gambling dependency increases financial, professional, emotional, family and health-related problems (Lorenz and Yaffee 1988).

As our discussion shows (see Table 2.1), the entrepreneurial activities dealing with substance abuse (alcohol and tobacco), prostitution, and gambling, undertaken by individuals or groups, have severe and enduring negative consequences on the society and its institutions, even though they might be conducted in legal forms.

**Corrupt Entrepreneurship**

The third type we highlight in Table 2.1 is corrupt entrepreneurship, where the entrepreneurs use corrupt, unethical and even illegal practices to conduct business. Corruption is a social cancer (Sardar 1996) and has a close but complicated relationship with entrepreneurship. Taking many forms (such as bribery, fraud and exchange of favours), corruption is prevalent in transitional economies, underdeveloped economies and even in advanced societies. Some researchers argue that corruption is highly counterproductive to entrepreneurship and the economic development of a society (e.g., Anokhin and Schulze 2009). Ironically, some research shows that entrepreneurs encourage and favour corruption and bribery in the society (e.g., Sanchez 2010; Tonoyan 2005; Tonoyan et al. 2010). The prevalence of corruption makes it almost an accepted norm where people are willing to pay the price to get their companies created or protected from attacks by underground organizations.

The literature suggests that corrupt entrepreneurship distorts market functions, leading to low foreign direct investment (FDI), low growth rate, and depletion of a nation's wealth (Lambsdorff 2003; Rivera-Batiz 2002). Using strong networks with the bureaucrats, officials or other politicians in power, corrupt entrepreneurs encourage unethical practices and gain undue advantages (Morck and Yeung 2004). This contributes to an environment that hinders the efficient legal and judiciary system and encourages practices that erode the potential value of the opportunity by increasing the agency and transaction costs. Over time, these activities eventually force honest entrepreneurs to be involved in corruption and bribery or go out of business (Tonoyan et al. 2010).

The situation becomes even worse when corrupt entrepreneurs deal with essential public goods and services such as basic water, healthcare, education, electricity and transportation, and absolve the state from responsibility. They bribe government officials and bureaucrats to become the agents to provide such public goods. Once these entrepreneurs become agents, they not only transfer the cost of the bribe to the public but also try to gain maximum profits by increasing the cost of these essential public goods and services. This will limit the poor's access to these goods.

Collaborating with corrupt officials, these entrepreneurs even siphon off any public aid money in the name of serving public goods. At worst, corrupt officials may prioritize spending according to the bribes paid by corrupt entrepreneurs, sacrificing public welfare. This perpetuates poverty and increases inequality. It also induces instability which over time weakens trust and the stability of national governments, creates social and political discord and even violence, breeds class warfare and may even lead to the fragmentation of the national identity (Wright and Zahra 2011).

Corruption and bribery also undermine the trust of common people in the government and legal system. Corrupt police and judiciary ignore the rights of people, especially the poor and underprivileged, and leave them with no other option but to be exploited. This increases economic, political and social inequality in the society. This has led to violent confrontations in many cities in the United States (US) and several European countries, where the masses (the '99 per cent') feel that their rights are being ignored in favour of the rich and well-connected entrepreneurs (i.e., the '1 per cent'). In some countries such as Argentina, crowds of the poor attacked and destroyed stores, taking goods and products without paying for them. These people feel that the few have stolen the fruits of their labour, keeping them poor and unable to meet the rising cost of living.

## CORROSIVE, CONTROLLING AND CARELESS ENTREPRENEURSHIP

In the previous section we discussed three different types of entrepreneurship that are illegal, highly unethical and have immediate and severe ill effects on society. But even some legal forms of entrepreneurship that are lightly restricted by the government might also have a negative influence on society at large. Though their products and services (outputs) are not directly harmful, the way they conduct business might create tension and unrest in society. In fact, many members of a society may also accept such entrepreneurship and not find it highly unethical. As a result, the social cost of such entrepreneurship is not always immediate, but hinders the development of a society in the long term. In this section, we will discuss three legal but dysfunctional types of entrepreneurship. Table 2.2 presents and contrasts these three types; they are corrosive, controlling and careless entrepreneurship.

### Corrosive Entrepreneurship

As indicated in Table 2.2, here entrepreneurs accumulate economic wealth through rent-seeking by damaging the natural environment or the exploitation of the poor and underprivileged. The literature highlights three different forms of rents: Ricardian rent, monopoly rent and entrepreneurial rent (Mahoney and Pandian 2006). Ricardian rent is generated by owning valuable and scarce resources such as land, locational advantages, patents and copyrights (Ricardo 1891). Monopoly rent is captured as a result of government protection or by collusive arrangements raising high barriers that will limit the entry of competitors or drive existing ones out of business (Bain and Qualls 1968). The final type of economic rent is entrepreneurial in nature. It is generated when entrepreneurs create new wealth by using their entrepreneurial insight to take risks in a complex and uncertain environment (Cooper et al. 1991). This latter type is the productive form of entrepreneurship that can renew society, enrich inventors, create new technologies, and transform the means of production and economic exchange.

Entrepreneurs usually generate entrepreneurial rents and create value for themselves and the society (Schumpeter 1934). But when entrepreneurs attempt to capture monopoly rents rather than entrepreneurial rents, they end up redistributing wealth instead of creating value. Rent-seeking entrepreneurs often attempt to obtain economic rents by shaping the social, economic and political environment around them without adding value. They use their money, power and/or networks to influence or even control the government in order to hinder competition by introducing trade restrictions that require licences and permits that will raise barriers to entry. In the process of restricting competition, these efforts also hinder the technological development and overall growth in society. Rent-seeking entrepreneurs also lobby and bribe government officials and legal systems in order to gain special privileges such as preferential tax treatment and benefits from public spending, which offer private gain from a common pool of the state (Park et al. 2005). They are involved in illegal activities such as tax evasion, theft of public funds and committing fraud to get privileged treatment (Angelopoulos et al. 2009; Zahra et al. 2005).

The current global economic turmoil and the financial crisis of 2008 highlight another extreme form of rent-seeking entrepreneurship in the US. To increase personal profits, a few rent-seeking entrepreneurs working as agents of the banks used creative tricks such as non-sustainable financial instruments (e.g., mortgage-backed securities, collateral debt obligations and credit default swaps). These were paper transactions that did not translate into real productivity gains. When uncovered, these activities led to huge financial losses in the US and across the globe (Acharya and Richardson 2009). Many have lost their jobs, life savings, homes and other belongings, which have created social tensions as well as decreased the standard of living while increasing unemployment. The financial institutions that have engaged in these institutions were also at risk of failing and going out of business. Industries that relied on these institutions have also suffered huge losses, causing the US and other governments to intervene to save these strategic industries, for example automotive industries.

Corrosive entrepreneurs also create private wealth by exploiting or degrading the environment. For instance, some developing countries' entrepreneurs do not make an effort to dispose of industrial waste in an environmental friendly way (Begley and Tan 2001). Some of this waste is toxic and hazardous and has led to water, land and air pollution when not disposed properly. Similarly, it also has harmful effects on climate change, deforestation and ozone depletion, and worldwide destruction of ocean fisheries (World Resources Institute 2004). Thus, disposing of the industrial waste in a non-environmentally friendly way increases the costs borne by entrepreneurial ventures at the cost of a sustainable environment. Thus, the environment becomes highly degraded, threatening the health of the population and reducing opportunities for development and growth. In the long run, this degradation might prove to be fatal because the major portion of the world's economic output is dependent upon natural resources and the environment (Costanza et al. 1997). Environmental degradation may also lead to multifold increases in the costs of healthcare. While the profits belong to the entrepreneurs, the costs of such entrepreneurship are ultimately borne by society. Clearly, corrosive entrepreneurship maximizes private wealth at the expense of the sustainable development of the environment and the exploitation of the individuals in the society.

**Controlling Entrepreneurship**

Entrepreneurs always try to exert maximum control over their businesses, environment and the competitors. Sometimes this leads to hindering the social and technological development of the society (Table 2.2). Entrepreneurship is the process of creative destruction and is accompanied by technological change (Schumpeter 1942 [1950]). This change in direction of the technological wind can be fatal for the entrepreneurs, employees, families, businesses, communities, countries and the society. As new and innovative technologies and products come to the market, many existing technologies, products, enterprises, institutions and individuals' skills in the market become obsolete and outdated. Accordingly, many businesses and institutions have to change their strategies in responses to the flood of technological improvements. This might also cause mass unemployment, dislocation and displacement of people as their individual skills do not match with the upgraded technological change. In many instances, enterprises, regions and even countries have lost their standing because they failed to anticipate and adjust to the technological changes (Wright and Zahra 2011).

Worse still, with the fear that the innovative technologies would make their current technology and investment obsolete, some entrepreneurs may exploit their money, power and influence to kill such changes and suppress innovative rival projects and new ideas. By doing so, they can keep their monopolistic market status, holding back other promising businesses' access to opportunities and achievements (Wright and Zahra 2011). Similarly, these entrepreneurs using their power and influence also delay or suppress the social and political changes for their personal benefit. As a result, these unadvisable dysfunctional tactics enhance the monopoly, and in the long run hinder competition, suppress technological advancements, and delay or suppress the overall development of the society.

In addition, inside the organizations, entrepreneurs are eager to build an empire in which they can control resources, decision-making power and the future of the corporates. The employees bear a lot of unfairness, because there is no formal management team in start-ups and the entrepreneurs always make decisions by themselves and may abuse their power, ending up with ignorance of the employees' willingness, rights and value. The fact that the start-ups fail at a high rate has direct or indirect consequences for the employees, to whom the entrepreneurs have made so many commitments about the success of the business. The employees may feel that they have suffered heavy losses and wish they had worked in a large corporation. Also, some businesses achieve their success based on the exploitation of child labour or disadvantaged people. Control in this way may cause class strife and conflicts in the organizations.

**Careless Entrepreneurship**

Finally, as we suggest in Table 2.2, there is also careless entrepreneurship where entrepreneurs exploit an opportunity and create wealth for themselves and society but at the expense of their personal and social life. A career as an entrepreneur can be tough and demanding. It is filled with physical and psychological pressures because of the need to deal with countless stakeholders with competing goals and expectations. Harmonizing these relationships can be a challenging task. Some entrepreneurs have a natural distrust towards others, which can cause friction with stakeholders and complicate their task of acquiring resources.

Entrepreneurs also value achievement, risk-taking and being in control. Working in a highly uncertain and financially constrained environment may also increase the stress levels entrepreneurs might experience, leading to illness. Given their demanding careers, entrepreneurs often devote themselves to their work while neglecting their health and family life. As a result, their health might suffer and family members may experience stress and conflicts (Beaver and Jennings 2005). These tensions increase the incidence of divorce and separation among entre- preneurs, adding further strain on their lives (Kets de Vries 1985).

Many entrepreneurs rely on members of their families as a key source of labour when building their business. A rich body of literature exists on the dysfunctional effects of family dynamics and how they may influence members of the family and the firm. This literature suggests that conflicts among family members engaged in the business are commonplace, often placing the firm itself at risk. Rivalries, favouritism and jealousies fuel and perpetuate these conflicts, which often extend to personal animosities that destroy the family's cohesion. Another serious consequence of the family dynamics is limiting the growth of the firm, as the owner's attention is directed away from the business. Sometimes, owners and other family members fail to separate what is good for them versus the company.

Careless entrepreneurship reflects an inability to balance personal and professional roles, goals and expectations. This imbalance can undermine the ability of the entrepreneur to enjoy the fruits of their labour. It can also have wide-ranging effects on health, social ties and relationships. Over time, these variables aggregate into serious problems that affect communities and society.

## DISCUSSION AND DIRECTIONS FOR FUTURE RESEARCH

As we have stated earlier, entrepreneurship is highly regarded worldwide as a creative process that generates new wealth and fortune for entre- preneurs, their families and society. As Baumol (1996) rightly observes, entrepreneurial activities can be productive (i.e., add value), under- productive (i.e., outcomes do not compensate for resources and other inputs used) and counterproductive (i.e., outcomes can have negative or depressive effects on the social and economic welfare of a community, region or nation).

In this chapter, we have focused on counterproductive entre- preneurship. Our discussion highlights three key points. Firstly, the effect of counterproductive entrepreneurship could be pervasive, affecting mul- tiple groups, institutions and processes. This pervasive effect makes this form of entrepreneurship socially undesirable and dangerous. It is hard to pinpoint the root causes of the ill effects of counterproductive entre- preneurship. This is why changing institutions and passing laws do not always curb this form of entrepreneurship. For example, countless organizations and laws exist to rid society of the illicit drug and sex trades, but entrepreneurs continue to find ways to carry out their businesses and make a profit.

Secondly, formal institutions alone may not succeed in addressing the dysfunctional effects of counterproductive entrepreneurs. Informal institutions (such as trust or building closer relationships with multiple groups) are necessary to offset the excesses of this form of entrepreneurship. Clearly articulated and widely shared social norms regarding acceptable moral values and the meaning of right and wrong are also useful in this regard.

Thirdly, counterproductive entrepreneurship takes several forms as explained throughout this chapter (see Tables 2.1 and 2.2); each has its own distinct causes and manifestations. Individually they can affect society in different ways, all of which are negative. These ill effects vary in their duration. Yet, on the whole these activities create an environment where legitimate entrepreneurs find it costly to do business, leading them to exit. In turn, this creates voids that are quickly filled through illegitimate activities. This vicious cycle stifles the flow of legitimate venture capital and other resources essential for creating and growing a new business. Countries that fall prey to this vicious cycle find it hard to develop or grow their economies, attract foreign capital and encourage people to create new businesses.

## Implications for Policy Makers

Entrepreneurship is the mechanism through which economic growth takes place. Government policy together with institutions that are shaped by the policies are important for entrepreneurship. From the literature, there are four types of government policies stimulating productive entrepreneurship: enhancing funding opportunities, setting appropriate level of taxes, regulating the movement of international business, and intervening when serious violations occur (Minniti 2008). This leads to the question: What policies can governments use to curtail counterproductive entrepreneurship?

Firstly, it is critical to build a sound legal system to crack down on entrepreneurial crimes. Secondly, when it comes to the policies for controversial entrepreneurship, one size does not fit all; different countries may carry out different policies. However, every government can only provide an environment where the productive rather than unproductive or counterproductive entrepreneurship emerges. Thirdly, it is important to revise, improve and perfect extant policies because there are still some entrepreneurs taking advantage of loopholes in the policies. Fourthly, it is necessary for governments to switch from encouraging traditional entrepreneurship into supporting social entrepreneurship, environmental entrepreneurship, and any other forms of sustainable entrepreneurship. These types of entrepreneurial activities are more likely to offset counterproductive entrepreneurship.

**Implications for Research and Theory**

Our discussion underscores the dearth of empirical studies on the dysfunctions of entrepreneurship. With research focus being given to formal entrepreneurial activities, the field might have underestimated the extent and prevalence of counterproductive entrepreneurship. Many of these activities occur within the informal sectors, which makes them harder to track and analyse (Bruton et al. 2012). The boundaries of informal entrepreneurship are hard to define, raising a legitimate question about the scope and scale of counterproductive entrepreneurship.

Future research would benefit from exploring the forms, manifestations and effects of these dysfunctions – building on existing theory. In particular, institutional theory could provide much needed guidance in explaining the various reasons for institutional failures and how they may lead to counterproductive entrepreneurship. Institutions, both formal (e.g., legal frameworks) and informal (e.g., national norms and values) have a profound effect on how individuals behave and engage in illegal, corrupt or simply unproductive entrepreneurship.

Institutional theory could also explain why certain dysfunctional entrepreneurial activities are imitated and widely diffused (Kostova and Zaheer 1999). Bribery and corruption, for example, become widespread not only because of institutional failure but also because more and more people come to view them as the de facto way of doing business. Thus, informal institutions legitimize illegitimate actions associated with entrepreneurial activities. Future researchers can use institutional theory, therefore, to explain the timing and speed of the diffusion of these behaviours. Understanding these factors can help in revamping existing institutions or erecting new ones to address the negative effects of counterproductive entrepreneurship. Given that changes in institutions take years, if not decades, it is important that future research on these issues should adopt longitudinal designs.

A complement to institutional theory is the normalization of a 'deviance perspective' that explains how small 'rotten apples' develop new ways of corrosive and dysfunctional activities and then succeed in making this behaviour a widely shared practice (Ashforth and Anand 2003; Ashforth and Gibbs 1990). For example, managerial fraud usually starts with one or a few individuals who work at gaining the tacit support of and solidarity with selected others to engage in such activities. The same applies to other forms of counterproductive entrepreneurship. The 'institutionalization of deviance' perspective focuses on individual behaviour that becomes the foundation for collective, counterproductive entrepreneurship. Institutional theory takes a more macro view that shows how formal and informal institutions influence major groups and, by extension, individuals.

Research on institutional change and the normalization of deviance would benefit from the large body of literature on criminology. This literature provides rich insights into who commits illegal acts, their motivations, and the implications of these activities on a group or society. With insights from psychology and sociology, this literature can complement explanations of how corrupt activities become more diffused and persistent over time, despite institutional changes (e.g., increasing punitive damages imposed by society on offenders). Thus, there are clear limits to what societies can do to bring about reforms that curtail counterproductive entrepreneurship.

Using institutions to bring about desired changes in counterproductive entrepreneurship opens the door for additional research opportunities using learning theory. How can a group or society come to learn new norms and unlearn those practices that have fostered counterproductive entrepreneurship? How can we induce this learning? How long does it take? When is it most effective in achieving the desired results? Institutional theory would suggest that developed institutional environments with overly restrictive regulation can hamper entrepreneurship (De Soto 2000). Do these conditions have the opposite effect on dysfunctional entrepreneurship? Do these institutions create opportunities for dysfunctional entrepreneurship? If this is the case, then unlearning existing norms and values is likely to be slow, perpetuating opportunities for counterproductive entrepreneurship. There is also the possibility that what individuals and institutions already know might sabotage unlearning to acquire new values and knowledge (Tsang and Zahra 2008).

Overall, future research on entrepreneurship should pay close attention to the dark side of entrepreneurship in order to be more productive from an economic and sociology perspective. Promising research questions can be asked and explored on different levels. For instance, what are the formal and informal institutional factors that help or hinder the different forms of entrepreneurship as it is associated with the negative influence on the society? What institutional factors encourage sustainable entrepreneurship? Do government restrictions on various forms of entrepreneurship increase or decrease the social cost? What should be made legal? What is the role of government to suppress such entrepreneurship? Does teaching entrepreneurship in the academic institutes benefit society?

## CONCLUSION

Entrepreneurship is a powerful force of social, economic and technological change. Research has focused mainly on formal, productive entrepreneurial activities. We have argued that having a more accurate appreciation of the value of entrepreneurship for a society requires us to consider counterproductive entrepreneurship that occurs with the formal and informal parts of a nation's economy. We have identified different types of counterproductive entrepreneurship, their forms, origins and potential implications on society. We have also stated the limitations of institutional reforms in curbing counterproductive entrepreneurship, highlighting the importance of social and environmental entrepreneurship to alleviate the ill effects of dysfunctional entrepreneurship. Together, these changes make entrepreneurship an important engine for economic prosperity while promoting the quality of life of a nation, thereby enhancing entrepreneurs' contributions to their societies.

## REFERENCES

Abt, V., J.F. Smith and E.M. Christiansen (1985), *The Business of Risk: Commercial Gambling in Mainstream America*, Lawrence, KS: University Press of Kansas.

Acharya, V.V. and M. Richardson (2009), 'Causes of the financial crisis', *Critical Review*, **21** (2–3), 195–210.

Angelopoulos, K., A. Philippopoulos and V. Vassilatos (2009), 'The social cost of rent seeking in Europe', *European Journal of Political Economy*, **25** (3), 280–299.

Anokhin, S. and W.S. Schulze (2009), 'Entrepreneurship, innovation, and corruption', *Journal of Business Venturing*, **24** (5), 465–476.

Ashforth, B.E. and V. Anand (2003), 'The normalization of corruption in organizations', *Research in Organizational Behavior*, **25**, 1–52.

Ashforth, B.E. and B.W. Gibbs (1990), 'The double-edge of organizational legitimation', *Organization Science*, **1** (2), 177–194.

Bain, J.S. and P.D. Qualls (1968), *Industrial Organization*, New York: Wiley.

Baldwin, M.A. (1999), 'Million dollars and an apology: prostitution and public benefits claims', *Hastings Women's Law Journal*, **10** (1), 189.

Barry, K. (1996), *The Prostitution of Sexuality*, New York: NYU Press.

Baucus, M.S. (1994), 'Pressure, opportunity and predisposition: a multivariate model of corporate illegality', *Journal of Management*, **20** (4), 699–721.

Baumol, W.J. (1996), 'Entrepreneurship: productive, unproductive, and destructive', *Journal of Business Venturing*, **11** (1), 3–22.

Beaver, G. and P. Jennings (2005), 'Competitive advantage and entrepreneurial power: the dark side of entrepreneurship', *Journal of Small Business and Enterprise Development*, **12** (1), 9–23.

Begley, T.M. and W.L. Tan (2001), 'The socio-cultural environment for entrepreneurship: a comparison between East Asian and Anglo-Saxon countries', *Journal of International Business Studies*, **32** (3), 537–553.

Birley, S. (1987), 'New ventures and employment growth', *Journal of Business Venturing*, **2** (2), 155–165.

Bruton, G., D. Ireland and D. Ketchen (2012), 'Toward a research agenda on the informal economy', *Academy of Management Perspectives*, **26** (3), 1–11.

Chell, E. (1985), 'The entrepreneurial personality: a few ghosts laid to rest?', *International Small Business Journal*, **3** (3), 43–54.

Cooper, A.C., F.J. Gimeno-Gascon and C.Y. Woo (1991), 'A resource-based prediction of new venture survival and growth', Institute for Research in the Behavioral, Economic, and Management Sciences, Krannert Graduate School of Management, Purdue University, USA.

Costanza, R., J.H. Cumberland, H. Daly, R. Goodland and R.B. Norgaard (1997), *An Introduction to Ecological Economics*, Boca Raton, FL: St Lucie Press.

De Soto, H. (2000), *The Mystery of Capital: Why Capitalism Triumphs in the West and Fails Everywhere Else*, New York: Basic Books.

Diamond, L.J. and M.F. Plattner (1993), *Capitalism, Socialism, and Democracy Revisited*, Baltimore, MD: Johns Hopkins University Press.

Dorsey, T.L., M.W. Zawitz and P. Middleton (2000), *Drugs and Crime Facts*, Washington, DC: Bureau of Justice Statistics.

Drucker, P.F. (2006), *Innovation and Entrepreneurship*, New York: HarperBusiness.

Fadahunsi, A. and P. Rosa (2002), 'Entrepreneurship and illegality: insights from the Nigerian cross-border trade', *Journal of Business Venturing*, **17** (5), 397–429.

Farley, M., A. Cotton, J. Lynne, S. Zumbeck, F. Spiwak, M.E. Reyes, D. Alvarez and U. Sezgin (2004), 'Prostitution and trafficking in nine countries', *Journal of Trauma Practice*, **2** (3–4), 33–74.

Fenoglio, P., V. Parel and P. Kopp (2003), 'The social cost of alcohol, tobacco and illicit drugs in France, 1997', *European Addiction Research*, **9** (1), 18–28.

Gartner, W.B. (1988), '"Who is an entrepreneur?" is the wrong question', *American Journal of Small Business*, **12** (4), 11–32.

Gozdziak, E.M. and E.A. Collett (2005), 'Research on human trafficking in North America: a review of literature', *International Migration*, **43** (1–2), 99–128.

Hasin, D., M.C. Fenton, A. Skodol, R. Krueger, K. Keyes, T. Geier, E. Greenstein, C. Blanco and B. Grant (2011), 'Personality disorders and the 3-year course of alcohol, drug, and nicotine use disorders', *Archives of General Psychiatry*, **68** (11), 1158–1167.

Kapp, K. (1950), *Social Cost of Private Enterprise*, Cambridge, MA: Harvard University Press.

Kets de Vries, M.F.R. (1985), 'The dark side of entrepreneurship', *Harvard Business Review*, **85** (6), 160–167.

Kostova, T. and S. Zaheer (1999), 'Organizational legitimacy under conditions of complexity: the case of the multinational enterprise', *Academy of Management Review*, **24** (1), 64–81.

Ladouceur, R., J.M. Boisvert and J. Dumont (1994), 'Cognitive-behavioral treatment for adolescent pathological gamblers', *Behavior Modification*, **18** (2), 230–242.

Lambsdorff, J.G. (2003), 'How corruption affects productivity', *Kyklos*, **56** (4), 457–474.

Larson, A. (2011), *Sustainability, Innovation, and Entrepreneurship*, New York: Flat World Knowledge.

Lim, L.L. (1998), *The Sex Sector: The Economic and Social Bases of Prostitution in Southeast Asia*, Geneva: International Labour Organization.

Lorenz, V.C. and R.A. Yaffee (1988), 'Pathological gambling: psychosomatic, emotional and marital difficulties as reported by the spouse', *Journal of Gambling Studies*, **4** (1), 13–26.

Low, M. and I. MacMillan (1988), 'Entrepreneurship: past research and future challenges', *Journal of Management*, **35**, 139–161.

MacGaffey, J. (1988), *Entrepreneurs and Parasites: The Struggle for Indigenous Capitalism in Zaire*, Cambridge: Cambridge University Press.

Mahoney, J.T. and J.R. Pandian (2006), 'The resource-based view within the conversation of strategic management', *Strategic Management Journal*, **13** (5), 363–380.

Minniti, M. (2008), 'The role of government policy on entrepreneurial activity: productive, unproductive, or destructive?', *Entrepreneurship Theory and Practice*, **32** (5), 779–790.

Morck, R. and B. Yeung (2004), 'Family control and the rent-seeking society', *Entrepreneurship: Theory and Practice*, **28**, 391–409.

Overman, S. (1990), 'Addiction: odds are, gamblers cost companies', *HR Magazine*, April, 50–54.

Park, H., A. Philippopoulos and V. Vassilatos (2005), 'Choosing the size of the public sector under rent seeking from state coffers', *European Journal of Political Economy*, **21** (4), 830–850.

Redonnet, B., A. Chollet, E. Fombonne, L. Bowes and M. Melchior (2012), 'Tobacco, alcohol, cannabis and other illegal drug use among young adults: the socioeconomic context', *Drug and Alcohol Dependence*, **121** (3), 231–239.

Ricardo, D. (1891), *On the Principles of Political Economy and Taxation*, London: G. Bell & Sons.

Rivera-Batiz, F. (2002), 'Democracy, governance, and economic growth: theory and evidence', *Review of Development Economics*, **6** (2), 225–247.

Sanchez, A. (2010), 'Capitalism, violence and the state: crime, corruption and entrepreneurship in an Indian company town', *Journal of Legal Anthropology*, **2** (1), 165–188.

Sardar, Z. (1996), 'A very British sort of bribery', *New Statesman*, **127** (4404), 51.

Schumpeter, J.A. (1934), *The Theory of Economic Development*, Cambridge, MA: Harvard University Press.

Schumpeter, J.A. (1942 [1950]), *Capitalism, Socialism and Democracy*, 3rd edn 1950, New York: Harper.

Shane, S. and S. Venkataraman (2000), 'The promise of entrepreneurship as a field of research', *Academy of Management Review*, **25** (1), 217–226.

Single, E., L. Robson, X. Xie and J. Rehm (1998), 'The economic costs of alcohol, tobacco and illicit drugs in Canada, 1992', *Addiction*, **93** (7), 991–1006.

Tomass, M. (1998), 'Mafianomics: how did mob entrepreneurs infiltrate and dominate the Russian economy?', *Journal of Economic Issues*, **32** (2), 565–574.

Tonoyan, V. (2005), 'The dark side of trust: corruption and entrepreneurship – a cross-national comparison between emerging and mature market economies', in H.-H. Höhmann and F. Welter (eds), *Trust and Entrepreneurship: An West–East Perspective*, Cheltenham, UK and Northampton, MA, USA: Edward Elgar, pp. 39–58.

Tonoyan, V., R. Strohmeyer, M. Habib and M. Perlitz (2010), 'Corruption and entrepreneurship: how formal and informal institutions shape small firm behavior in transition and mature market economies', *Entrepreneurship Theory and Practice*, **34** (5), 803–831.

Tsang, E.W.K. and S.A. Zahra (2008), 'Organizational unlearning', *Human Relations*, **61** (10), 1435–1462.

Ugarte, M.B., L. Zarate and M. Farley (2004), 'Prostitution and trafficking of women and children from Mexico to the United States', *Journal of Trauma Practice*, **2** (3–4), 147–165.

UNODC (2012a), 'Transnational organized crime – the globalized illegal economy', http://www.unodc.org/documents/toc/factsheets/TOC12_fs_general _EN_HIRES.pdf.

UNODC (2012b), 'Human trafficking – people for sale', http://www.unodc.org/ documents/toc/factsheets/TOC12_fs_humantrafficking_EN_HIRES.pdf.

UNODC (2012c), 'Environmental crime – the trafficking of wildlife and timber', http://www.unodc.org/documents/toc/factsheets/TOC12_fs_environment_EN_ HIRES.pdf.

Volberg, R.A. (1994), 'The prevalence and demographics of pathological gamblers: implications for public health', *American Journal of Public Health*, **84** (2), 237–241.

World Resources Institute (2004), 'Ideas into action: working at the intersection of environment and human needs. Annual Report 2004', http://pdf.wri.org/ annual_report_2004_full.pdf.

Wright, M. and S.A. Zahra (2011), 'The other side of paradise: examining the dark side of entrepreneurship', *Entrepreneurship Research Journal*, **1** (3), 1–5.

Zahra, S.A. and G.G. Dess (2001), 'Entrepreneurship as a field of research: encouraging dialogue and debate', *Academy of Management Review*, **26** (1), 8–10.

Zahra, S.A., E. Gedajlovic, D. Neubaum and J. Shulman (2009), 'A typology of social entrepreneurs: motives, search processes and ethical challenges', *Journal of Business Venturing*, **24** (5), 519–532.

Zahra, S.A., A. Rasheed and R. Priem (2005), 'Management fraud: antecedents and consequences', *Journal of Management* (Annual Review Issue), **31**, 803–828.
Zahra, S.A. and M. Wright (2011), 'Entrepreneurship's next act', *Academy of Management Perspectives*, **25** (4), 67–83.

PART II

Promoting Entrepreneurial Business and Society

# 3. Entrepreneurship policy as discourse: appropriation of entrepreneurial agency

## Örsan Örge

## INTRODUCTION

This chapter provides an analysis of a particular entrepreneurship policy initiative in an emerging economy, Turkey. The policy initiative analysed in the chapter involves a support programme that was launched in 2009 with the goal of providing seed-financing to young entrepreneurs for technology-based venture ideas. The analysis offered in the chapter primarily adopts a discourse-based approach. That is, rather than examine the objective premises, structure and outcomes of this particular support programme by the Turkish government, the chapter traces the discursive field this policy initiative created and the effects that were performed within this field. With a specific focus on the power relations that are performed in and through this discursive field, the chapter shows and discusses how the policy discourse serves to frame entrepreneurship in a way that enables the government to adopt and appropriate entrepreneurial agency and to discursively leverage this position to entrench its political power.

With this empirical focus, the chapter develops the argument that in addition to viewing policies as instruments to foster entrepreneurial activity, they can also be taken as discursive performances that serve to frame and construct the social or economic 'problems' that they address; define and limit the ways in which these problems could be approached and talked about; constitute the identities of various actors that are involved in the policy space and determine how these actors are to be interrelated. In doing so, the chapter intends to contribute to an emerging body of work in policy studies at large (e.g. Bacchi 2000; Ball 1993; Fischer 1998; Shaw 2010; Shore and Wright 1997; Wedel et al. 2005) and in entrepreneurship policy studies in particular (e.g. Dannreuther

2007; Kenny and Scriver 2012; Perren and Dannreuther forthcoming; Perren and Jennings 2005; Xheneti and Kitching 2011) that argue for a discursive approach to expand the domain of discussion in extant literature that mainly remains within an objectivist and instrumentalist framework.

With these goals, the chapter is structured as follows. Firstly, a brief review of the entrepreneurship policy literature is provided. In the next section of the chapter, the discursive approach to policy analysis is introduced as the main interpretive framework. This section provides illustrations of how a discourse-based perspective is deployed in various fields of policy and reviews the emerging body of work in entrepreneurship policy studies that adopts a discursive approach. Next, the empirical approach of the chapter is detailed. Based on a brief historical discussion of the Turkish economic context, the policy initiative that establishes the empirical domain of the study is introduced and data collection and analysis methods are discussed. Then, findings are presented and the interpretation of the particular policy discourse is developed. The chapter concludes with a discussion of the relevance of discourse perspective for entrepreneurship policy studies, with particular emphasis on transition and emerging economy contexts.

## BACKGROUND: ENTREPRENEURSHIP POLICY STUDIES

Today, policy initiatives to cultivate and foster entrepreneurship are commonly used by governments all around the world. In parallel, policy studies has now become an established research track in the field of entrepreneurship with a growing body of work through which policy initiatives to support entrepreneurship and increase the level of entrepreneurial economic activity are explored and justified, and their manifold intervention mechanisms and outcomes are analysed (e.g. Audretsch et al. 2007; Gilbert et al. 2004; Hart 2003; Lerner 2010; Minniti 2008).

For the most part, this literature traces the origins of entrepreneurship policy initiatives to the major structural economic changes that took place in the markets due to globalization and technological developments (Gilbert et al. 2004; Kumar and Liu 2005). With knowledge emerging as a critical economic input starting in the 1980s and with the consequent transition into the so-called knowledge economy, innovativeness is argued to have become the most critical skill for economic growth, competitiveness and prosperity (Audretsch and Thurik 2001; Lerner

2010; Minniti 2008). While large, established firms contribute to innovative capacity of economies to a great extent, they are argued to do so in an incremental fashion, whereas the revolutionary breakthroughs are shown to be predominantly carried out by small firms and entrepreneurial ventures (Baumol 2004). Accordingly, traditional industries and large companies are said to lose their competitive edge, which led to their replacement with smaller players such as entrepreneurial ventures and small and medium-sized enterprises (SMEs) as the primary innovation engines for economies, as well as the main providers of employment and economic growth (Birch 1987; Gilbert et al. 2006; Lerner 2010; Michael and Pearce 2009).

It is in this context that entrepreneurship emerged as an important policy domain for governments. Entrepreneurship policies and support programmes are now viewed as crucial and taken-for-granted instruments that are ubiquitously included in government policy toolboxes to reduce constraints on and to serve as enablers for entrepreneurial activity (Baumol 2004; Gilbert et al. 2004; Lerner 2010; Minniti 2008).

Several research volumes are dedicated to establishing the foundations for government intervention on entrepreneurship and to outlining macro frameworks for the development and implementation of entrepreneurship policy (e.g., Audretsch et al. 2007; Hart 2003). Entrepreneurship policies are deemed to provide the necessary institutional framework for entrepreneurial activity and thus create a supporting market environment for entrepreneurs (North 1990), as well as to secure the flow of entrepreneurial activity in an economy toward productive avenues, rather than unproductive ones (Baumol 1990). Another group of studies focuses on establishing the positive impacts of increased entrepreneurial activity on macroeconomic variables such as employment, innovation and economic growth (e.g. Carree 2002; Wennekers and Thurik 1999). Extant research also provides a typology of policy tools and shows that the ideal policy mix to foster entrepreneurial activity will depend on contextual variables in different countries such as the level of economic development, institutional frameworks, competitive dynamics and barriers to entrepreneurship (e.g. Acs and Szerb 2007; Dennis 2011a, 2011b; Minniti 2008; Verheul et al. 2001).

While the existing literature on entrepreneurship policy provides invaluable insights into various contextual precedents of policy actions, different types of policy instruments and varying modes of measuring policy performance, this body of work also reflects a great deal of homogeneity with respect to its fundamental assumptions on how policies are conceptualized. Mostly driven by economics, policy studies hinge upon an instrumentalist framework that rests on an essentialist ontological standpoint. In this dominant mode of policy studies, entrepreneurship-related market conditions such as lack of and need for entrepreneurial activity are assumed to exist a priori and independently of the policy interventions that are formulated and implemented to address them (Bacchi 2000). Put differently, policies are considered to come after and stand as a reaction to these market conditions. Presumed to rest on a 'discovery' of these market conditions, then, policy formulation appears as a process that involves an objective representation of the essence and the underlying dynamics of these market conditions that already exist 'out there'. In fact, what underlies the prevailing instrumentalist view of policies is exactly this essentialist ontological stance and the temporal (re)ordering it enables. Accordingly, policies are viewed as legal-rational instruments to act on and to achieve desired change in the social and market conditions that they are designed to address. Such instrumentalist framework also privileges a particular operationalization of policy in research design. Accordingly, policies are deemed equivalent to time markers (or point occurrences) in research, and their rationality and worth are then judged only in reference to the extent to which they meaningfully precede desired outcomes, that is, the extent to which they manage to change the objectively measurable aspects of the future.

This chapter argues that this strong set of assumptions serves to eclipse alternative ways in which policies could be approached and analysed. To that end, in the next section a discourse-based approach to policies is introduced as one such alternative not only to relax the binding assumptions of the instrumentalist approach to policy analysis but also to enable an exploration of power relations that underlie policy-making and implementation.

## POLICY AS DISCOURSE

The instrumentalist conceptualization of government's role in the dominant mode of entrepreneurship policy studies particularly neglects the dynamics of power and politics that are involved in the formulation and implementation of policies, and how policies not only act on but also constitute the field of social and economic problems and frame the viable ways in which they could be addressed. In fact, this observation is increasingly being voiced in an emerging body of critical work in entrepreneurship (e.g. Gibb 2000; Ogbor 2000; Perren and Jennings 2005; Weiskopf and Steyaert 2009), policy studies (Bacchi 2000; Ball 1993; Fischer 1998; Shaw 2010) and anthropology (Shore and Wright 1997; Wedel et al. 2005). These studies collectively argue that the essentialist and instrumentalist assumptions in policy research serve to overshadow and mute alternative, complementary ways in which policy could be examined and discussed. In doing so, they aim to problematize 'policy' and argue for a discourse-based approach that renders policy, and not just its effects, as the central object of inquiry. From this policy-as-discourse perspective, policies are not seen as governments 'responding to "problems" that exist "out there" in the community … [rather], "problems" are "created" or given shape in the very policy proposals that are offered as "responses"' (Bacchi 2000: 48). Accordingly, policy-making comes to be viewed as a reality construction process, rather than a rational-political response to objective social problems. As such, instead of taking the rational-instrumental view of policy as a premise for research agendas, a discursive approach examines the performative nature of policies and analyses, for example, how policies constitute the very problem field on and through which they act, what kinds of power relations policies enact and work through, or how the use of language in policy-making and implementation make policies appear as rational, and almost natural, instruments of intervention.

Policy-as-discourse perspective is now in use as an alternative approach to the rationalist framework in various fields of policy analysis (e.g. Bacchi 2004, 2008; Newman and Vidler 2006; Schram 1993; Shaw 2007, 2010) to examine how policy discourses serve to (re)define social issues and problems, create and delimit identity and agency for various social actors, and perform power shifts and relations between these actors. In the domain of healthcare policy, for example, various studies (e.g. Malone 1999; Newman and Vidler 2006; Shaw 2007) examine reforms and transformations in healthcare in the United Kingdom (UK) and the United States (US) to point out how a discourse of 'consumer-ism' came to pervade healthcare policy. It is argued that these changes created new moral agencies for healthcare 'users' and 'providers', and performed a shift in the balance of power between healthcare users and providers, as well as between governments and health practitioners. Schram (1993) offers an analysis of the US welfare policy to argue that the policy discourse constructs various identities for its intended benefi-ciaries and shows how the US welfare policy discourse does so through 'feminization of poverty' and marginalization of single women with children. In a similar vein, Bacchi (2004) analyses affirmative action policy and shows how it constructs a hegemonic reality of preferential treatment.

Being a relatively more recent domain of public policy, entre-preneurship policy literature continues for the most part to operate within a rational-instrumental framework. Having said this, there is a growing literature in the field that approaches and analyses entrepreneurship policies through discursive lenses. Critical studies on entrepreneurial narratives and the ideological foundations of entrepreneurship studies and entrepreneurialism (e.g. Drakopoulou Dodd and Anderson 2007; Howorth et al. 2008; Ogbor 2000; Steyaert 1997, 2007; Steyaert and Katz 2004) serve as background. They openly scrutinize the unquestioningly positive and desirable conception of entrepreneurs and entrepreneurship and criticize its hegemonic discursive status as a cure for all economic and social ills. Reflections of this critical stance are also now becoming visible in entrepreneurship policy research (e.g. Dannreuther 2007; Kenny and Scriver 2012; Perren and Dannreuther forthcoming; Perren and Jennings 2005; Xheneti and Kitching 2011). Rather than taking a rationalist-instrumentalist approach to the analysis of entrepreneurship policies, this group of studies focuses on the discursive nature of policy and policy-making on entrepreneurship and reveals how such policies perform various forms of power relations.

In his insightful analysis of the European Union (EU) SME policy, for example, Dannreuther (2007) argues that the 'entrepreneurship zeal' that characterizes EU economic policies primarily springs from the definitional malleability of 'entrepreneurship' and 'SMEs'. He argues that this malleability offers policy makers a great deal of autonomy in setting policy frameworks and objectives based on their political priorities. Illustrating how this zeal reveals itself in policy transfer contexts, Xheneti and Kitching (2011) analyse enterprise policy development in Albania. In this post-communist context, they show how policy transfer takes place through coercive mechanisms such as hegemonic enterprise discourse, external pressure from powerful stakeholders and various micro control practices. The versatility of 'entrepreneurship' as a signifier is also picked up by Perren and Dannreuther (forthcoming) in their analysis of UK parliamentary debates and by Kenny and Scriver (2012) in their analysis of the government and public discourse in Ireland during times of crises. Both articles refer to the discursive quality of 'entrepreneurship' as a free-floating signifier and maintain that this plasticity enables political actors and policy makers to partially and temporarily fix the meaning of the term to serve their own purposes and agendas, such as supporting their communicative goals or entrenching their political hegemony. Another illustration of how entrepreneurship policy subtly serves hegemonic purposes is offered by Perren and Jennings (2005). Analysing discourses of governments in the websites of government agencies in seven developed economies including the USA, the UK and Japan, they convincingly show how the hegemonic discourse of the government is built on a subjugation of the entrepreneurs.

The current chapter is positioned to contribute to this literature in three ways. Firstly, it examines a particular entrepreneurship policy initiative – a support programme in Turkey – and performs a longitudinal critical analysis of the government discourse woven around this programme. With this, the chapter emphasizes power relations as a central feature of policy-making and implementation. Secondly, the chapter points out and foregrounds one particular way in which such power relations are played out in the case of entrepreneurship policies, that is, appropriation of entrepreneurial agency by policy makers. And thirdly, based on this analysis, the chapter offers insights for entrepreneurship policy-making and implementation in transition and emerging economy contexts.

## EMPIRICAL APPROACH

The context for the policy initiative analysed in the current chapter is an emerging economy, Turkey. In fact, popularization of entrepreneurship and development of extensive government support programmes to cultivate entrepreneurial activity in the country are relatively recent phenomena. To put this development in context, a brief account of the recent economic history of Turkey is in order.

Until the 1980s, the Turkish economy mostly operated under a strict import substitution industrialization regime with the heavy role of the state as an economic actor and restricted international trade and foreign direct investments. A liberal market approach was adopted during the 1980s. Indeed, this was not a smooth point occurrence but a bumpy transition that unfolded over a long period of time. While this era was characterized by intensive privatization efforts and gradual development of supportive legislation to vitalize liberal market mechanisms, it was also marked by a series of economic crises and political turmoil. As a result, up until the 2000s the economy looked entirely fragile with high inflation rates, heavy reliance on foreign direct investments and huge budget deficits. This era resulted in a significant economic breakdown in 2001 during which foreign exchange and interest rates soared, the stock market crashed and around 15 000 jobs were lost. Arguably, a turning point for the economy was the 2002 general elections in which the Justice and Development Party (JDP) emerged victorious with more than two-thirds of the parliamentary seats. This was a signal not only of an era of political stability after decades of coalition governments and political conflict, but also of the start of a structural reform in the economy. Strict monetary policies adopted by the JDP government, along with newly introduced legislation and regulations especially in banking and financial services, helped to end the hyperinflation period and stabilize the economy. These reforms paid off as the economy entered a period of steady growth in the second half of the last decade. Today, Turkey is one of the fastest growing economies despite the global financial crisis (9.2 per cent and 8.5 per cent GDP growth in 2010 and 2011, respectively) and is considered as a significant emerging market with a strengthened global competitive position.

It is in this growing economic context that 'entrepreneurship' started to become a buzzword, where the emergence of an 'entrepreneurship ecosystem' in the country is celebrated and the new 'entrepreneurial economy' is applauded. This entrepreneurship fervour revealed itself on multiple fronts. Especially since 2005, a number of technology development zones and incubation centres were established to host and help develop entrepreneurial companies. New entrepreneurship centres and curricula were launched one after another in universities. An increasing number of nationwide entrepreneurship competitions held by universities, financial service companies and civic organizations served to legitimize and encourage entrepreneurship. And with increased media coverage, the discourse of the new Turkish economy was put into wider circulation and 'entrepreneurship' was firmly entrenched in everyday public language.

These developments were not without significant policy support. In fact, the government launched various support programmes to cultivate entrepreneurial activity in the economy since 2008. Ranging from free entrepreneurship education and business advice to various tax subsidies, grants and no-interest loans, support programmes of the government are considered as the primary and most viable path to entrepreneurship. For many, government agency programmes such as those of the Ministry of Science, Industry and Technology[1] (name changed from the Ministry of Industry and Trade in June 2011), or the Small and Medium Enterprises Development Organization,[2] appear as the most natural route to fulfil entrepreneurial dreams, so much so that, in one Turkish venture capitalist's words, 'in this environment, it would be just plain stupid not to get state's money to launch an entrepreneurial venture'. In parallel to these support programmes, there was an observed increase in the government discourse on entrepreneurship and its entrepreneurship policies. Aiming to introduce and legitimize various entrepreneurship policy initiatives of the government, this discourse on entrepreneurship came to play an important part in the political statements and vernacular of the government. It is this particular observation that gave shape to the empirical approach of this chapter.

Accordingly, the empirical domain of the current chapter revolves around the government discourse on entrepreneurship, and in particular, on one of its most recent and popular policy initiatives, the Technology Entrepreneurship Support Programme (TESP). Launched by the Turkish Ministry of Science, Industry and Technology (then, the Ministry of Industry and Trade) in 2009 and legislated to continue until 2023, the centennial of the Turkish Republic, this support programme is designed to provide seed-financing to entrepreneurs with technology-based venture ideas. Eligible applicants for the programme range from fourth-year university students to graduates who completed their terminal university degree (Bachelors, Masters or PhD) within the previous five calendar years. Through an annually held competitive process, the programme provides 100 000 Turkish liras (€45 000 as of June 2012) seed-financing in the form of a grant to a maximum of 100 young entrepreneurs each year (increased to 300 from 2011 on). With four annual funding rounds already completed, to date the programme distributed around 75 million Turkish liras (€34 million) to a total of 741 newly established technology-based entrepreneurial ventures (see Table 3.1 for a yearly breakdown of supported ventures). Given the nature of the programme, these ventures are mostly in various fields of engineering and natural sciences (see Table 3.2 for sector breakdown of supported ventures).

To trace the government discourse on entrepreneurship and this particular policy initiative, multiple data sources were tapped. First of these sources was the actual policy text, in this case, Legislation # 5746 on 'The Support of Research and Development Activity' that was accepted by the Council of Ministries of the Republic of Turkey on 28 February 2008 and put into motion until 31 December 2023.

*Table 3.1    TESP statistics – year breakdown (adopted from the Ministry website)*

| Year | Number of applications | Number of supported ventures |
| --- | --- | --- |
| 2009 | 159 | 78 |
| 2010 | 724 | 102 |
| 2011 | 859 | 272 |
| 2012 | 1597 | 289 |
| Total | 3339 | 741 |

*Source:*    TESP 2009–2012 Analysis Report at http://sagm.sanayi.gov.tr/ServiceDetails.aspx?dataID=217.

*Table 3.2    TESP statistics – sector breakdown (adopted from the Ministry website)*

| Sectors | % of supported ventures |
| --- | --- |
| Information technology | 41 |
| Electronics and electro-mechanics | 21 |
| Mechanical | 15 |
| Bio/Agro technology | 11 |
| Materials | 6 |
| Chemistry | 5 |
| Other | 1 |

*Source:*   TESP 2009–2012 Analysis Report at http://sagm.sanayi.gov.tr/ServiceDetails. aspx?dataID=217.

The second data source included the various statements from the Ministry of Science, Industry and Technology with regards to its entrepreneurship support programmes. This was done with the assumption that policy is more than just a legislative document, and that the discursive qualities of policies could be better revealed by focusing not only on the legislative text but also on other linguistic devices that aim to circulate, promote and seek enlistment to the espoused goals of the policy. While some of these materials were collected through the Ministry's website, a big chunk of this data was collected through various public statements (interviews, keynote addresses and press conferences) of the Minister himself, who appears as the primary spokesperson for the entrepreneurship policies of the government. For this, a comprehensive press search was conducted between January 2009 (the year when the first round of funding was distributed) and March 2011. After eliminating the recurring items in different outlets, the search resulted in 65 unique news items which included Minister's statements on entrepreneurship and the support programmes of the government to foster entrepreneurial activity.

A third data collection opportunity presented itself in the form of a promotional meeting for the Technology Entrepreneurship Support Programme that was held in Istanbul on 25 June 2010. The meeting was attended by the researcher, and the speeches of the Minister, as well as of three entrepreneurs who were funded in the first round, were digitally recorded for purposes of later analysis.

Guided by principles of discourse analysis (e.g. Alvesson and Karre-man 2000), and especially of critical discourse analysis (Fairclough 1995; Meyer 2001), a textual analysis of the government discourse was undertaken with an explicit focus on how the government discursively frames entrepreneurship, how it constitutes and situates its support programmes, and what kind of subject positions and relations it enacts for the various actors involved in the policy. This analysis was conducted through multiple iterations of coding and categorizing discursive units to generate an in-depth interpretation of the performative nature of govern-ment policy discourse.

## ENTREPRENEURSHIP POLICY DISCOURSE: APPROPRIATING ENTREPRENEURIAL AGENCY

From a discourse-based approach, policies construct the very field on which they act. That is, rather than being instruments that react to already existing social problems and conditions, policies discursively frame and enact the nature of these problems and thus create a field of rationaliza-tion and legitimization for their very existence (Bacchi 2000; Shaw 2010).

As such, the first performative effect of policy discourse analysed in this chapter involves constructing entrepreneurship as a national impera-tive and creating a sense of urgency to foster entrepreneurial activity. Accordingly, entrepreneurship is portrayed as a domain of business activity that Turkcy has been late to adopt and one that is to be undertaken without any delay or reluctance if the country is to achieve its ambitions as an emerging economic power.

In the government's discourse, entrepreneurship is firmly situated with reference to Turkey's macroeconomic goals and ambitions in the context of the global economy that is argued to be driven by technology and knowledge-intensive industries. In this context, developing its own tech-nology and becoming a global technology producer is articulated as a main economic goal for the country and entrepreneurship as a 'vital means to steer the economy toward high value-added products and services'. This, in turn, is argued to better serve the new competitive ambitions of the country to carve out a more meaningful role for itself in the global economic environment, as well as to increase employment and enable economic growth. In fact, these ambitions are generally framed around the macro goal of 'becoming one of the top ten economies of the world by 2023', the centennial of the Turkish Republic, which also serves as a significant ideological time-marker as seen in the most recent election campaign of the ruling party. As such, entrepreneurship is framed as an important part of the country's march to 2023.

While entrepreneurship is situated as an integral part of this long-term objective, to enact a sense of urgency for entrepreneurship government discourse also provides a particularly bleak depiction of the current situation. This often takes the form of comparing Turkey with other (developed) countries. For example, it is frequently mentioned that Turkey is currently a technology importer, and thus, is 'dependent on the main technology producers of the globe'. While the current manufacturing capabilities of the country are generously praised, it is also mentioned that 'remaining as a low-cost manufacturer is no longer acceptable' for Turkey. In one repeated example, the Minister draws on a comparison with South Korea. In fact, this choice is not accidental and is justified by the fact that 'South Korea was in comparable economic situation with Turkey about 40 years ago'. Praising South Korea's investment in technology-based industries since then, the Minister continues to compare Hyundai and Samsung with two Turkish companies in electronics and automotive that had been established around the same time with their Korean counterparts. 'Today, the entire world knows about Hyundai and Samsung,' he argues, 'but now, even we cannot remember the name of our companies.' This comparative failure is then explained as an outcome of how the Turkish economy has been late to adopt the entrepreneurial mindset and thus has been sluggish in terms of entrepreneurial economic activity. The discursive mean to establish this frequently appears in the form of a set of statistics such as the percentage of adult population who own their businesses. 'Only 4.6 adults out of 100 create their own businesses in Turkey,' it is reported, but 'this number is 11.6 in the US, 15 in South Korea and almost 18 in Mexico.' 'It is clear,' the Minster urges, 'that we have a long distance to cover.' As such, pushing these numbers up is portrayed as a key priority to catch up with the rest of the developed world.

Government discourse also lists a number of factors that account for the relatively slow entrepreneurial activity in the economy. To that end, there are ongoing references to the historical instability of the Turkish economy. As the Minister argued, 'it is quite normal to see a suppressed appetite for entrepreneurship in an economic environment that is riddled with unstable growth and crises every few years'. The discourse also hints at the endemic corruption that plagued the country's economy for decades. The Minister stated, for example, that in the past (read: during the reigns of previous governments), 'we chose to protect individuals, rather than industries', which is argued to have led to an erosion of trust and motivation for business venturing. With these historical references, the government discourse frames these impediments as a 'thing of the past' and positions itself as the primary creator of an entrepreneurial environment. It is argued that the government has overcome these problems since 2002 (the first year of the government) to create 'an environment of trust and stability' that is conducive for entrepreneurial venturing.

Placed in this context of the national and global economy, the policy initiative in question appears as a timely and natural intervention to foster entrepreneurship. With these ripe conditions, entrepreneurship, and especially technology entrepreneurship, is framed as a matter of national urgency. The citizens, or the entrepreneurs, are obliged to participate in this activity if they are to live in a country that is on a par with the developed nations of the world. It is a mandate with no alternative.

With a particular framing of the problem to be addressed, policy discourse also defines and limits the possibilities of the means through which this problem will be addressed. In this particular policy case, the discourse overtly positions the young population as the most likely undertaker of the entrepreneurial imperative discussed above. In fact, with frequent reference to more than 10 million students in the primary education system alone, the government discourse portrays the youth of the country as a 'national wealth', that is argued to be 'more valuable than any natural resource'. Stating that 'the youngsters of this country are no less smart than their counterparts in other countries', the government expresses, albeit clumsily and in a patronizing tone, its confidence in the young population. This sense of confidence is strengthened through repeated references and comparisons to global entrepreneurial icons such as Bill Gates and Steve Jobs: 'Why wouldn't we find a Bill Gates among our youngsters?', the Minister pleads, 'Don't you think we need to have global technology brands like Microsoft, Apple, Dell or Oracle?'

Celebration of this abundant 'national wealth', however, is smoothly subdued with a portrayal of entrepreneurship among the youth as mere 'latent potential'. First and foremost, it is argued, they need to be encouraged and motivated to pursue entrepreneurship and they 'need to be persuaded that entrepreneurship is a viable career option'. This persuasion appears in the form of discursively constructing a future for the youth within which entrepreneurship can be meaningfully situated. For this, entrepreneurship in government discourse is often juxtaposed not with other career alternatives, but with unemployment. As such, entrepreneurial activity is dichotomously situated as the (only) alternative to unemployment to create a sense of a predictable and stable future. 'We don't want our university graduates to be *searching* for jobs,' the Minister states, 'we want them to be *creating* jobs.' These sentiments are echoed

by a grant recipient in his public address where he expresses his gratitude
to the Ministry for their financial support in his venture. 'Without this
support,' he argues, 'I would have been just another member of the army
of the unemployed.' It appears that the sense of entrepreneurship as a
national duty is now individualized through evoking and exploiting a
particular vulnerability of the youth: namely, uncertainty of the future.
That is, one has no alternative but to pursue entrepreneurship if one
desires to avoid searching for a job and to secure a predictable future
away from the possibility of remaining unemployed.

In addition to the unpredictable future, the government discourse also
calls forth and builds upon 'lack of resources' as an obstacle that could
prevent the youth from pursuing entrepreneurship. Arguing that 'the most
important wealth for the youth is their dreams', the Minister also
acknowledges, 'we know that the most unbearable experience for a
youngster is when her dreams are imprisoned in her mind only due to
lack of resources'. The support programme then is positioned as a means
for the young entrepreneurs 'to turn those dreams into reality'. The
condition for this benevolence, of course, is the alignment of these
dreams with the national economic goals and priorities of the government. 'In the past,' the Minister states, 'entrepreneurs said to the
government, "you give us the funds and we know how to put it to good
use"'. 'Things have changed,' he firmly adds, 'now you bring us your
project and let's see if we are going to get convinced.'

Thus, the discourse openly positions the government as a benevolent
ally and frames it as the ultimate enabler that 'clears the roadblocks'
standing between the dreams of the young population and entrepreneurial
success. At the same time, the government is also framed as an
all-knowing arbiter of entrepreneurial dreams. Its generosity is not
limitless; its benevolence is conditional. For young entrepreneurs, the
government stands as an obligatory point of passage to which they need
to unquestioningly submit themselves in order to turn their dreams into
reality. Discursively constituted through their various vulnerabilities and
lack of resources, young entrepreneurs are placed in an entirely dependent position, and their individual dreams and ambitions are completely
subjugated to the macroeconomic goals of the government.

Through this subjugation, the policy discourse excludes young entrepreneurs from any discursive possibility to claim entrepreneurial agency.
In fact, it actively displaces this potentiality and opens up space for the
government to appropriate entrepreneurial agency and present itself
positively in desirable entrepreneurial terms.

To that end, the policy discourse first establishes parallels and similar-
ities between the intended target audience of the policy initiative, the

young population of the country, and the government itself. More specifically, the particular policy initiative is discursively leveraged to constitute that the government also resembles the young population of the country, which it intends to support. To establish that the government is also 'young', policy discourse makes ongoing references to 2002, which witnessed the first of the three general election victories for the ruling party just after one year of its foundation. Just like the young entrepreneurs they address, 'we were also once accused of being dreamers'. But, 'what they accomplished in a short period of time' should attest to their vision and be a guiding model for the young entrepreneurs.

The government discourse then portrays the particular policy initiative as an entrepreneurial act that serves as evidence of the entrepreneurial qualities of the government. Accordingly, the support programme for young entrepreneurs is openly framed as a form of risk-taking by the government. 'They keep asking us,' the Minister states, '"Don't you think these youngsters are going to lose the money?"' Recognizing that this is a possibility, the Minister proudly continues that 'at least [they] will have sunk the money in smart folks, rather than in the thieves and the scumbags that used to drain the state'. This courageous attitude towards risk is further entrenched by a depiction of the government as a brave change agent. 'Our governments have never tried to preserve the status quo,' the Minister argues, 'but strived to break longstanding beliefs and memorizations.' As exemplified by the entrepreneurship support programmes that it introduced, government 'not only tackled problems that should have been solved 30–40 years ago, but also initiated projects that will secure our future'. Unlike the 'stale political atmosphere of the country' in the past, the reign of the current government is an era of breaking with the tradition and initiating courageous change to 'unshackle the feet of the country' from problems such as corruption and economic instability.

## DISCUSSION AND CONCLUSION

As mentioned at the outset, the current chapter aims to offer a discursive approach to entrepreneurship policy inquiry. As such, the analysis is based on the assumption that in addition to being taken as rational instruments of intervention, policies can also be viewed as discursive devices that perform various outcomes. To start with, policies create their own space. That is, they frame and constitute the very 'problem' to be addressed and thus, in a way, justify and legitimize their own existence to render the intervention they propose natural and inevitable. Furthermore, policies as discursive devices also constitute and limit the means and the ways in which these problems can be addressed. Unlike the instrumentalist view of policies that focus mainly on policy mechanisms and outcomes, a discursive approach deals primarily with this framing process (Bacchi 2000; Shaw 2010) and the particular power relations it performs.

As can be seen in the presentation of the findings, the particular policy discourse analysed in this chapter frames entrepreneurship within a set of macroeconomic goals and positions entrepreneurs as cogs and mere 'business soldiers' to serve these ambitions. The discourse further subjugates entrepreneurs, and especially young entrepreneurs, by framing them through their vulnerabilities and weaknesses, which they can offset only by enlisting themselves to the policy goals and mechanisms. In this way, then, the policy discourse performs a dependent and passive subject position for entrepreneurs and strips them of their entrepreneurial agency. The analysis further illustrates how another actor (i.e., the government) discursively adopts and appropriates entrepreneurial agency. Accordingly, through policy discourse, the government is reconstituted as entrepreneur *par excellence*, endowed with qualities of a 'heroic entrepreneur' such as being young, a dreamer, visionary, a courageous risk-taker and rule-breaker. Through this displacement, the government appears to possess, and in fact embody, the very conditions and qualities that are needed for successful entrepreneurship, and thus, to epitomize entrepreneurial spirit and action.

This discursive enactment of the 'heroic entrepreneur' myth suggests that policy-making and politics are inherently intermeshed (Shaw 2010) and that policy-making as a domain of governmental activity cannot be separated from political interests and struggles. While this observation applies to various other policy domains, 'entrepreneurship' appears to be special in its potential to offer an especially opportune discursive arena for governments to enact power relations, to undertake political struggles and reap political benefit.

This is partly due to the fact that in both academic and practical use 'entrepreneurship' discourse reflects a tendency to frequently and unquestioningly slip into a language of individualism and heroism (Drakopoulou Dodd and Anderson 2007; Ogbor 2000; Steyaert 2007). Arguably, then, it is this slippage that renders entrepreneurship a favourable policy domain for governments. As the findings suggest, entrepreneurship policy offers unique discursive possibilities for policy makers to displace and appropriate socially desirable and sought-after 'entrepreneurial agency', as well as the heroic qualities unquestioningly attached to it. Without doubt, this subject position serves a number of political interests as it not only endows policy makers with qualities such as courage, vision, risk-taking and benevolence, but also serves as a shield against criticism, scrutiny and accountability.

The findings also suggest that an additional way through which policy discourse serves political interests is due to the versatile nature of the term 'entrepreneurship'. This finding is in line with extant literature (e.g. Dannreuther 2007; Howorth et al. 2008; Kenny and Scriver 2012; Perren and Dannreuther forthcoming) that shows how the malleable nature of 'entrepreneurship' as a signifier allows it to be deployed to serve a diverse set of political agendas. To that end, the analysis shows that in the government discourse, 'entrepreneurship' is constructed as a national imperative for progress without an alternative. This language of progress is firmly tied to the performance of the government. That is, entrepreneurship and the progress it promises are used to reaffirm and emphasize the past performance of the ruling party, and thus, to secure their political power. Moreover, this mandate is situated within a time perspective marked by a desirable and romanticized end-goal ('to become one of the top ten economies of the world') and an ideologically and emotionally loaded due date (2023, the centennial of the Republic) to secure an entrenched political hegemony for the government.

Finally, as entrepreneurial practice and discourse take shape in a social, political and historical context (Welter 2011), the discursive approach to policy offered in this chapter would be incomplete without taking into consideration the context in which policy is shaped and embedded. To that end, the findings also carry relevance to understand entrepreneurship and policy development in emerging and transition economic contexts.

Given its particular economic history, Turkey represents a recently liberalized market economy. With its history of central planning and state-dependence, the development of the Turkish economy shows signs and trends that bear an uncanny resemblance to those experienced in transition economies (Tatoglu and Demirbag 2008). As discussed in the literature on transition economies (e.g. Puffer et al. 2010; Smallbone and Welter 2001a, 2001b; Xheneti and Kitching 2011), such contexts are characterized by many voids and deficiencies in institutional frameworks to enable, structure and regulate new firm formation and entrepreneurial activity. For many of the transition and emerging countries, including Turkey, various actors and mechanisms of a healthy entrepreneurial institutional framework such as the regulatory environment, a well-developed and refined investment community, incubation systems and alternative exit avenues for entrepreneurs are either non-existent or severely underdeveloped. Thus, as suggested by the existing literature on transition economies (Puffer et al. 2010; Smallbone and Welter 2001a,

2001b), governments play a key role in these contexts to set up the necessary conditions for the development of the private sector and entrepreneurial ventures.

At the same time, the discursive analysis also shows that the lack of a well-developed institutional framework may also create conditions for a few powerful actors (such as the state or the special interest and lobby groups) to frame what counts as entrepreneurship and unilaterally define the role of entrepreneurship for the society and the economy. Given the lack of other formal actors and institutional arrangements, these actors can exert a considerable power in the definition of the field. This arguably presents the risk of creating a monolithic and uncontested societal discourse on entrepreneurship. In this regard, one particularly pronounced risk is the emergence of government to play a central and powerful role in the entrepreneurial ecosystem. This would re-enact the role of the state as the primary source for commercial opportunity, wealth creation and maintenance, and thus, it would represent a reconstitution of state dependence in transition economies under the veil of entrepreneurship.

## NOTES

1. http://www.sanayi.gov.tr/Default.aspx?lng=en.
2. http://www.kosgeb.gov.tr/Pages/UI/Default.aspx.

## REFERENCES

Acs, Z. and L. Szerb (2007), 'Entrepreneurship: economic growth and public policy', *Small Business Economics*, **28** (2–3), 109–22.

Alvesson, M. and D. Karreman (2000), 'Varieties of discourse: on the study of organizations through discourse analysis', *Human Relations*, **53** (9), 1125–1149.

Audretsch, D.B., I. Grilo and A.R Thurik (2007), 'Explaining entrepreneurship and the role of policy: a framework', in D.B. Audretsch, I. Grilo and A.R Thurik (eds), *Handbook of Entrepreneurship Policy*, Cheltenham, UK and Northampton, MA, USA: Edward Elgar Publishing, pp. 1–17.

Audretsch, D. and R. Thurik (2001), 'What's new about the new economy? Sources of growth in the managed and entrepreneurial economies', *Industrial and Corporate Change*, **10** (1), 267–315.

Bacchi, C. (2000), 'Policy as discourse: What does it mean? Where does it get us?', *Discourse: Studies in the Cultural Politics of Education*, **21** (1), 45–57.

Bacchi, C. (2004), 'Policy and discourse: challenging the construction of affirmative action as preferential treatment', *Journal of European Public Policy*, **11** (1), 128–146.

Bacchi, C. (2008), 'The politics of research management: reflections on the gap between what we "know" and what we do', *Health Sociology Review*, **17** (2), 165–176.

Ball, S.J. (1993), 'What is policy? Texts, trajectories and toolboxes', *Discourse: Studies in the Cultural Politics of Education*, **13** (2), 9–17.

Baumol, W.J. (1990), 'Entrepreneurship: productive, unproductive, and destructive', *Journal of Political Economy*, **98** (5), 893–921.

Baumol, W.J. (2004), 'Entrepreneurial enterprises, large established firms and other components of the free-market growth machine', *Small Business Economics*, **23**, 9–21.

Birch, D.L. (1987), *Job creation in America: How Our Smallest Companies Put the Most People to Work*, London: Collier Macmillan.

Carree, M.A. (2002), 'Industrial restructuring and economic growth', *Small Business Economics*, **18**, 243–255.

Dannreuther, C. (2007), 'A zeal for a zeal? SME policy and the political economy of the EU', *Comparative European Politics*, **5**, 377–399.

Dennis, W.J. (2011a), 'Entrepreneurship, small business, and public policy levers (Part 1)', *Journal of Small Business Management*, **49** (1), 92–106.

Dennis, W.J. (2011b), 'Entrepreneurship, small business, and public policy levers (Part 2)', *Journal of Small Business Management*, **49** (2), 92–106.

Drakopoulou Dodd, S. and A.R. Anderson (2007), 'Mumpsimus and the mything of the individualistic entrepreneur', *International Small Business Journal*, **25** (4), 341–360.

Fairclough, N. (1995), *Critical Discourse Analysis: The Critical Study of Language*, Harlow: Longman.

Fischer, F. (1998), 'Beyond empiricism: policy inquiry in post positivistic perspective', *Policy Studies Journal*, **26** (1), 129–146.

Gibb, A.A. (2000), 'SME policy, academic research and the growth of ignorance, mythical concepts, myths, assumptions, rituals and confusions', *International Small Business Journal*, **18** (3), 13–35.

Gilbert, B.A., D.B. Audretsch and P. McDougall (2004), 'The emergence of entrepreneurship policy', *Small Business Economics*, **22**, 313–323.

Gilbert, B.A., P. McDougall and D.B. Audretsch (2006), 'New venture growth: a review and extension', *Journal of Management*, **32**, 926–950.

Hart, D.M. (2003), *Emergence of Entrepreneurship Policy*, Cambridge: Cambridge University Press.

Howorth, C.A., C.R. Parkinson and A. Southern (2008), 'Does enterprise discourse have the power to enable or disable deprived communities?', in D. Smallbone, H. Landström and D. Jones-Evans (eds), *Entrepreneurship and Growth in Local, Regional and National Economies: Frontiers in European Entrepreneurship Research*, Cheltenham, UK and Northampton, MA, USA: Edward Elgar, pp. 281–311.

Kenny, K. and S. Scriver (2012), 'Dangerously empty? Hegemony and the construction of the Irish entrepreneur', *Organization*, **19** (5), 615–633.

Kumar, S. and D. Liu (2005), 'Impact of globalization on entrepreneurial enterprises in the world markets', *International Journal of Management and Enterprise Development*, **2** (1), 46–64.

Lerner, J. (2010), 'The future of public efforts to boost entrepreneurship and venture capital', *Small Business Economics*, **35**, 255–264.

Malone, R.E. (1999), 'Policy as product: morality and metaphor in health policy discourse', *Hastings Center Report*, **29** (3), 16–22.

Meyer, M. (2001), 'Between theory, method and politics: positioning of approaches to CDA', in R. Wodak and M. Meyer (eds), *Methods of Critical Discourse Analysis*, London: Sage, pp. 14–31.

Michael, S.C. and J.A. Pearce (2009), 'The need for innovation as a rationale for government involvement in entrepreneurship', *Entrepreneurship and Regional Development*, **21** (3), 285–302.

Minniti, M. (2008), 'The role of government policy on entrepreneurial activity: productive, unproductive, or destructive?', *Entrepreneurship Theory and Practice*, **32**, 779–90.

Newman, J. and E. Vidler (2006), 'Discriminating customers, responsible patients, empowered users: consumerism and the modernisation of health care', *Journal of Social Policy*, **35** (2), 193–209.

North, D.C. (1990), *Institutions, Institutional Change and Economic Performance*, Cambridge, UK and New York, USA: Cambridge University Press.

Ogbor, J. (2000), 'Mythicizing and reification in entrepreneurial discourse: ideology-critique of entrepreneurial studies', *Journal of Management Studies*, **37** (5), 605–635.

Perren, L. and C. Dannreuther (forthcoming), 'Political signification of the entrepreneur: temporal analysis of constructs, agency and reification', *International Small Business Journal*, **30**.

Perren, L. and P.L. Jennings (2005), 'Government discourses on entrepreneurship: issues of legitimization, subjugation, and power', *Entrepreneurship Theory and Practice*, **29**, 173–184.

Puffer, S.M., D.J. McCarthy and M. Boisot (2010), 'Entrepreneurship in China and Russia: the impact of formal institutional voids', *Entrepreneurship Theory and Practice*, **34**, 441–467.

Schram, S.F. (1993), 'Postmodern policy analysis: discourse and identity in welfare policy', *Policy Sciences*, **26**, 249–270.

Shaw, S.E. (2007), 'Driving out alternative ways of seeing: the significance of neo-liberal policy mechanisms for UK primary care research', *Social Theory and Health*, **5** (4), 316–337.

Shaw, S.E. (2010), 'Researching the parts that other theories and methods can't reach: how and why a policy-as-discourse approach can inform health-related policy', *Health*, **14** (2), 196–212.

Shore, C. and S. Wright (eds) (1997), *Anthropology of Policy: Critical Perspectives on Governance and Power*, London: Routledge.

Smallbone, D. and F. Welter (2001a), 'The distinctiveness of entrepreneurship in transition economies', *Small Business Economics*, **16**, 249–262.

Smallbone, D. and F. Welter (2001b), 'The role of government in SME development in transition economies', *International Small Business Journal*, **19** (4), 63–77.

Steayert, C. (1997), 'A qualitative methodology for process studies of entrepreneurship', *International Studies of Management and Organization*, **27** (3), 13–33.

Steyaert, C. (2007), '"Entrepreneuring" as a conceptual attractor? A review of process theories in 20 years of entrepreneurship studies', *Entrepreneurship and Regional Development*, **19**, 453–477.

Steyaert, C. and J. Katz (2004), 'Reclaiming the space of entrepreneurship in society: geographical, discursive and social dimensions', *Entrepreneurship and Regional Development*, **16** (3), 179–196.

Tatoglu, E. and M. Demirbag (2008), 'Transition in the age of anxiety: the Turkish case', *Journal of Management Development*, **27** (7), 653–659.

Verheul, I., S. Wennekers and D. Audretsch (2001), *An Eclectic Theory of Entrepreneurship: Policies, Institutions, and Culture*, Zoetermeer: EIM Business and Policy Research.

Wedel, J.R., C. Shore and G. Feldman (2005), 'Toward an anthropology of public policy', *Annals of the American Academy of Political and Social Science*, **600** (1), 30–51.

Weiskopf, R. and C. Steyaert (2009), 'Metamorphoses in entrepreneurship studies: Towards and affirmative politics of entrepreneuring', in D. Hjorth and C. Steyaert (eds), *The Politics and Aesthetics of Entrepreneurship*, Cheltenham, UK and Northampton, MA, USA: Edward Elgar, pp. 183–201.

Welter, F. (2011), 'Contextualizing entrepreneurship: conceptual challenges and ways forward', *Entrepreneurship Theory and Practice*, **35**, 165–184.

Wennekers, S. and R. Thurik (1999), 'Linking entrepreneurship and economic growth', *Small Business Economics*, **13**, 27–55.

Xheneti, M. and J. Kitching (2011), 'From discourse to implementation: enterprise policy development in postcommunist Albania', *Environment and Planning C: Government and Policy*, **29**, 1018–1036.

# 4. The bearable lightness of the administrative burden: UK financial reporting regulation and small company performance

## John Kitching, Eva Kašperová and Jill Collis*

## INTRODUCTION AND AIMS

Successive United Kingdom (UK) governments have, over three decades, sought to reduce the 'administrative burden' of regulation on small enterprises (DTI 1985; HM Treasury 2005; HM Government 2012). One source, derived from the UK government's own impact assessments, recently suggested that new legislation generated an administrative burden for UK businesses of approximately £112 billion between 1998 and 2010 (IoD 2011). The UK government has implemented a number of initiatives intended to reduce the regulatory administrative burden on businesses, particularly for micro and small firms (e.g. Better Regulation Executive 2010), as part of a policy agenda to make the UK one of the best places in Europe to start, finance and grow a business (HM Treasury/BIS 2011). Other commentators, conversely, have insisted on the 'unbearable lightness' of regulatory costs (Ackerman 2006), suggesting that there is no significant trade-off between prosperity and regulation. Indeed, the UK regularly ranks highly in World Bank indices of the easiest countries in the world to do business: 7th of 185 countries in 2012 (World Bank 2012).

This study explores how regulation governing the public disclosure of financial information – allowing small companies to file abbreviated accounts in place of full accounts at Companies House, the UK public registry – influences business performance, in the context of the new Accounting Directive (2012/6/EU). The Directive permits member states to exempt 'micro-entities' from 'certain obligations that may impose on them an unnecessarily onerous administrative burden' (European Commission 2012: para. 5).

We begin by setting out the UK regulatory context of financial reporting for small companies. Next, we review the literature on small company financial reporting and its effects. Then, we outline our analytical framework and methodological approach before presenting findings drawn from a study investigating the value of small company abbreviated accounts to preparers and users (Kitching et al. 2011), highlighting changes arising since the global financial crisis of 2007–08. We then conclude before briefly considering the policy implications.

## UK FINANCIAL REPORTING REGULATION: CURRENT CONTEXT AND FUTURE PROSPECTS

Under the Companies Act 2006, limited companies in the UK are required to prepare an annual report and accounts for members and place a copy on the public record by registering them at Companies House. The financial and other disclosures allow accounts users to assess a company's financial performance and financial position. Publication of financial statements is widely regarded as the price companies must pay for the privilege of limited liability. European Union (EU) law permits member states to operate different reporting regimes for companies of different sizes. The UK, like other member states, operates different regimes.

Companies required to prepare full accounts must provide a profit and loss account (statement of comprehensive income) and a balance sheet (statement of financial position). The profit and loss account summarises the revenue and expenditure over the accounting period, and the balance sheet summarises the value of the entity's assets, liabilities and equity on the last day of the accounting period for which the profit and loss account has been prepared. Small companies are permitted to file abbreviated accounts comprising an abbreviated balance sheet and related notes. This is not compulsory – small companies may file full accounts if they wish. Companies must still prepare full accounts for members.

The EU Fourth Company Law Directive allows member states to permit qualifying small and medium-sized reporting entities to register less detailed abbreviated accounts[1] in place of the full statutory accounts that large companies are required to file.[2] Unless it is excluded for reasons of public interest,[3] a company in the UK will generally qualify as small if it does not exceed any two of the following three size thresholds: annual turnover £6.5 million, balance sheet total £3.26 million and average employment of 50. Apart from newly incorporated entities, these conditions must have been satisfied in two of the last three years. In

2011/12, approximately 3 per cent of the annual accounts registered in the UK were categorised as 'abbreviated – small' (Companies House 2012: Table F2). The 'audit exempt' category, comprising 71 per cent of accounts filed, includes many small companies filing abbreviated accounts, as these are also exempt from the statutory audit.

The new Accounting Directive (2012/6/EU) permits member states to exempt 'micro-entities' from a general publication requirement, provided that balance sheet information is duly filed, in accordance with national law, with at least one designated competent authority, and that the information is transmitted to the business register so that a copy is obtainable upon application (European Commission 2012). The purpose of the measure is to reduce the administrative burden of filing accounts on the public register and to align micro-entities' reporting requirements with the purported real needs of users and preparers of accounts. The published Directive has watered down the original draft which exempted micro-entities from *any* reporting requirement. The impact of the Directive on micro-entity reporting behaviour may, therefore, be more limited than envisaged initially. The draft Directive estimated cost savings of €5.9–6.9bn (European Union 2011), a figure which should perhaps now be reduced. The Directive defines micro-entities as companies not exceeding two of three criteria – total assets €350 000, net turnover €700 000 and average employment of ten. The UK government has welcomed the Directive and plans to implement changes following consultation (Department for Business, Innovation and Skills 2013). These plans should be seen in the context of a wider programme intended to modernise company law, with the aim of enabling companies to compete and grow effectively (Department for Business, Innovation and Skills 2012a, 2012b). Although we do not yet know what precise shape the UK government proposals will take, in conclusion, we briefly consider some likely options and their consequences.

## PRIOR RESEARCH ON THE IMPACT OF FINANCIAL REPORTING REGULATION ON SMALL BUSINESSES

Different literatures imply opposing positions on the impact of financial reporting regulations on small companies. Most studies of the impact of regulation on small businesses emphasise the administrative, substantive and psychological costs regulation imposes on them (e.g. Chittenden et al. 2002; Crain and Crain 2010), costs alleged to deter start-up, investment, innovation and growth. Such a view underpins the new Accounting Directive and the logic behind the UK government's initial response.

In contrast, the finance literature emphasises the crucial role of disclosure – and, by implication, of regulations requiring disclosure – in addressing the information and agency risks faced by investors and creditors contemplating financing particular companies (e.g. Beyer et al. 2010; Healy and Palepu 2001). Disclosure reduces information asymmetries. Creditors lack the information possessed by company insiders to judge whether companies report their financial position and performance accurately (the information problem) or, having invested, they lack the information to know whether company insiders are acting in creditors' best interests (the agency problem). These information asymmetries between financiers and company insiders render accurate credit assessments more difficult. While most studies focus on large, publicly listed companies, and their access to capital markets, similar arguments have been proffered in relation to small businesses accessing bank and trade credit. Indeed, small companies are argued to be more informationally opaque than larger ones because ownership is often held privately and they are subject to fewer disclosure requirements than public companies (Ang 1992).

Information disclosure reduces risk for financiers and encourages the supply of finance to companies. Financiers may seek public or private information and/or make financing conditional on the provision of collateral or personal guarantees (Ang 1992; Ang et al. 1995; Berger and Udell 2006; Berry et al. 1993; Binks et al. 1992; Marriott et al. 2006). Powerful stakeholders may be able to demand private information disclosure, in the form of detailed and timely management accounts (Berry et al. 2004), by making it a condition of trading, or providing credit (Marriot et al. 2006). Although several studies have questioned the value of mandatory financial disclosures, and the ratios that may be derived from them (e.g. Beaver et al. 2005), the key issue is not whether academic studies find such ratios to be good predictors of business failure but whether stakeholders believe such disclosures provide valuable insights. Stakeholders, of course, are fallible; their views may be incorrect, but false beliefs also motivate agents to act in particular ways. Other studies suggest that private disclosure founded on close ties with banks is a more important influence on decisions to provide credit to small companies (e.g. Berger and Udell 1995; Petersen and Rajan 1994).

Any costs alleged to be saved by not filing accounts on the public record might well be outweighed by the costs of disclosing information privately to individual stakeholders on request, particularly where this is a common occurrence or involves more than two parties to the transaction (Arruñada 2011). Alternatively, stakeholders might simply interpret the absence of statutory accounts information, where this is permitted, as evidence of poor financial management practice and avoid contact with such small companies. Allowing small companies not to publish accounts might generate negative externalities because stakeholders have less information upon which to develop their credit scoring models, with the consequence that they become less accurate and credit providers lose confidence in the credit risk assessments derived from them (Arruñada 2011).

## CONCEPTUALISING THE IMPACT OF REPORTING REGULATION ON SMALL COMPANIES

Most research examining the regulation–performance relationship in small enterprises suffers from a partial conceptualisation of regulation and its effects. Studies typically focus on the direct impacts of regulation, on small firms' responses to their obligations, including any purported 'administrative burden', and on their impact on profit-seeking activities and performance, but ignore the indirect impacts, on how important stakeholders with whom they interact – trade suppliers, customers, banks, credit reference agencies (CRAs), credit insurers and others – might respond to small company compliance in ways that benefit those small companies (Kitching 2006, 2007). By influencing small company agents' resources and reasoning (Pawson and Tilley 1997), financial reporting regulation influences small company activity which, in turn, generates responses from stakeholders that constrain or enable small companies to access resources and markets. Small companies often file full accounts, and undertake an audit, voluntarily because they perceive such possibilities arising from greater disclosure to accounts users (Collis 2012). It is notable that specific discussion of financial reporting regulation has been absent from the broader debate on small firms and regulation until recently – in the UK at least.

Stakeholders vary in their objectives, capacities and willingness to act in particular ways with regard to small companies, with implications for the latter's activity and performance. Where stakeholder interests in greater disclosure clash with small company directors seeking to retain information, this is likely to lead to stakeholders withholding important benefits from small companies, including valuable resources, particularly finance, or markets. Clearly, stakeholders with greater resources and a greater inclination to withhold them are likely to impact more seriously on small companies. Policy measures intended to reduce the administrative burden of financial reporting might inadvertently aggravate such adverse consequences for small companies – for example, by discouraging banks from providing overdraft and loan finance, suppliers from placing orders or providing trade credit, CRAs from providing high credit ratings, and credit insurers from providing adequate cover for those contemplating trading with small companies. Failure to obtain adequate finance and orders generates difficulties for small companies and, in extreme cases, might ultimately lead to market exit.

## METHODOLOGICAL APPROACH

To address the research objectives, data were collected from a wide range of sources (Table 4.1). Quantitative survey approaches to understanding financial reporting practices dominate the literature but arguably provide limited insight into the motivational and process issues surrounding filing and using abbreviated accounts. The study, therefore, incorporates a strong qualitative component in order to contribute fresh insights into small company directors' public filing choices, stakeholder perceptions of the value of publicly available small company financial data, problems of limited disclosure and their influence on decision-making and action. The primary focus is on diverse stakeholder responses to small companies taking up the option to file abbreviated accounts. We demonstrate the diversity of stakeholder interests in small company financial data, and their variable capacities to draw on a range of public and private information sources to pursue those interests. Although we rely principally on our qualitative material, we draw selectively on relevant quantitative data.

*Table 4.1    Respondent groups*

|  | Survey sample | Interview sample |
|---|---|---|
| Small company preparers/users of abbreviated accounts | 149 | 12 |
| Accounts users and intermediary bodies | – | 18 |
| Accountants in practice | 255 | 10 |
| Organisational accountants | 159 | 10 |

The small company preparers and users of abbreviated accounts interview sample was drawn from a broader sample of 149 respondents to a postal survey of small company preparers of abbreviated accounts, itself constructed from a stratified random sampling frame of 2750 companies from three broad regions (London, Scotland, and the rest of England and Wales) using the FAME database. Interviews were conducted with 12 small company respondents who were both preparers and users of abbreviated accounts; respondents from these companies were asked about their filing choices and their use of other small companies' abbreviated accounts and other information sources. The majority of companies in both the survey and interview samples were micro companies: more than 80 per cent of survey companies, and nine of the 12 interview companies, employed fewer than ten people. These companies are particularly relevant to the discussion of UK policy options surrounding the new Accounting Directive. Although current policy debates focus on micro companies, accounts user perceptions of small company filing choices are also relevant to understanding the problems of limited disclosure.

The accounts users and intermediary sample comprises a diverse group of senior managers or officials in 18 organisations, including banks, CRAs, credit insurance companies, professional bodies, trade associations, public sector organisations and a small business membership organisation. Respondents were asked questions regarding the value and limitations of abbreviated accounts information and its influence on their own decision-making and activities. As, at the outset of the study, we were unsure who used abbreviated accounts, we adopted a 'snowball' approach to sampling, asking respondents to identify potential sources. Survey and interview data were also obtained from two groups of accountants identified using the Institute of Chartered Accountants of Scotland (ICAS) database: 'accountants in practice' working in their own businesses, and 'organisational accountants' working as employees for private, public and voluntary sector organisations. The survey data from the two groups are drawn on very selectively in order to elaborate on particular processes. For space reasons we do not discuss the data from accountants in detail.

We now turn to the empirical findings to examine the impact of UK financial reporting regulation permitting small companies to file abbreviated accounts. We first examine small company directors' motivations for filing abbreviated accounts, before exploring stakeholder perceptions of abbreviated accounts information.

## THE BENEFITS OF FILING ABBREVIATED ACCOUNTS: REDUCING THE ADMINISTRATIVE BURDEN OR LIMITING DISCLOSURE?

Prior studies of small company financial reporting behaviour have identified restricting public disclosure of business information and following accountants' advice as the principal reasons for filing abbreviated accounts (Collis and Jarvis 2000; POBA 2006). The survey data from small company respondents strongly support the literature (Table 4.2). Moreover, survey data from accountants in practice indicated that, for most, filing abbreviated accounts is their 'default position' for small company clients: 71 per cent of accountants with small company clients reported all such clients filed abbreviated accounts.

*Table 4.2 Reasons for filing abbreviated accounts*

|  | % reporting as primary reason | % reporting as a reason |
|---|---|---|
| Following accountants' advice | 65 | 71 |
| To reduce public disclosure | 26 | 42 |
| Lower costs | 5 | 5 |
| Ease, simplicity, save time | 2 | 2 |
| Other reasons | 2 | 2 |
| All | 100 | n/a |
| Base: 149 | | |

*Note:* Respondents could rank up to three reasons as first, second or third most important.

Very few small company survey respondents reported reasons for filing abbreviated accounts consistent with the 'administrative burden' thesis, that their filing choice was motivated by administrative ease: only 2 per cent reported 'ease, simplicity, saving time' as reasons for their filing choice (Table 4.2). Given the widespread availability of accountancy software, researchers have questioned whether such costs are serious constraints (Arruñada 2011; Collis 2012). Indeed, several intermediary respondents reported that the administrative burden, and associated financial cost, of filing abbreviated accounts might be greater than for filing full accounts, as small companies must produce the full accounts in order to abbreviate them.

Our interview data reinforce the view that small company respondents prefer filing the legally prescribed minimum requirement in order to limit disclosure that might be used to their disadvantage rather than to avoid any purported administrative burden. No small company respondents reported administrative burdens in interview. Maintaining confidentiality – from competitors, customers, suppliers and employees – is believed to facilitate greater control over the terms of stakeholder relationships. Prospective competitors, for instance, might be attracted to the company's markets if they believe there are good profits to be made; high-margin items are often easier to identify in smaller companies where there are usually fewer product lines. Suppliers might raise prices, employees might seek higher salaries and customers might seek discounts in order to capture a greater share of the value created. Small company directors might also prefer to conceal company size in order to win business from clients cautious to award contracts to small firms.

Small company respondents value highly the option to file abbreviated accounts. But, importantly, in the context of the policy debate surrounding the new Accounting Directive, this is not because it reduces the administrative burden of filing full accounts but because it enables them to limit financial disclosure. Confidentiality, they believe, facilitates greater influence over the terms of relationships with competitors, suppliers, customers and employees, and enables small companies to capture a larger share of the value created.

## STAKEHOLDER INTERESTS IN SMALL COMPANY DISCLOSURE

When investigating the consequences of regulation for small companies, one must examine not only the burdens, costs and constraints regulation imposes upon them but also any benefits arising from stakeholder (accounts user) responses to compliance (e.g. Arruñada 2011). Stakeholders use statutory accounts information filed at Companies House, along with other sources, to assess the financial position and creditworthiness of existing and potential customers, suppliers, competitors and acquisition targets. The statutory accounts, whether abbreviated or full, are often a starting point for enquiry, influencing the decision to continue, or discontinue, information search, or as one element in a larger 'information jigsaw'. To explore stakeholder responses, we obtained data from a wide range of abbreviated accounts users whose actions are likely to impact upon small companies: small, medium-sized and large organisations in the private, public and voluntary sectors, as suppliers, customers, competitors and acquirers; banks; credit reference agencies, credit insurers and insurance brokers; professional bodies and trade associations. Our focus is on the users and uses of abbreviated accounts, however stakeholders acquire such information. Micro and small companies need not disclose such information directly to stakeholders; they may simply make it available at Companies House.

The impact on stakeholders of regulation permitting lower levels of public financial disclosure is contingent upon the availability and cost of alternative sources of information. Although stakeholders were uniformly critical of the restricted disclosure permitted by legislation, they differed considerably in their capacity to access alternative information sources and, consequently, in their perceptions of the value of abbreviated accounts. Large suppliers and customers, and banks, were perhaps in the strongest position to acquire more detailed and timely financial information from small companies on a private basis – and to avoid dependence on the statutory accounts. Small trading partners, CRAs and credit insurers were less able to obtain relevant and timely information on a private basis. Stakeholders with access to better information are in a stronger position to assess the creditworthiness of small companies in order to initiate, continue, renegotiate the terms of, or terminate, relations with them.

Large companies, with the power to demand detailed financial information from small companies, reported scrutiny of abbreviated accounts at Companies House as only the first stage of information search, when contemplating choosing a new supplier or customer, or considering an acquisition target.[4] Large companies are usually able to obtain information privately from small companies if considered necessary – or decline to place orders with, or offer credit to, them. Statutory accounts information often suffices to discourage further information search, but additional private data is usually required before deciding to enter a relationship with a small company:

> [Abbreviated accounts] would only give us enough information in a negative sense. Sometimes you look at the abbreviated accounts and realise that there is no point in getting any further information because we don't want to do any business with them. It's unlikely to give us enough information in a positive sense. We would always then have to go and get further information. (Organisational accountant #3: logistics, 1800 employees)

Banks are in a similarly powerful position to access information privately from small company applicants for finance. Where the applicant is an existing customer, banks have access to their account information; for non-customers, the bank can demand access to recent, comprehensive personal and business data. Statutory accounts information is of limited value in influencing bank lending decisions where more useful data sources are readily available. Filing choice was reported to be a 'soft' indicator of the seriousness of doing business rather than as a major source of information relevant to the company's capacity to repay debts, although companies filing abbreviated accounts were known to have a higher default rate than those filing full accounts. Banks also operate credit risk models to distinguish firms in terms of the likelihood of debt default, bankruptcy or other critical outcome; historical accounts usually play only a limited role in credit risk assessments:

> So we will actually decide whether we want to lend to someone principally using an analysis of their current account turnover, the money going through their accounts – money in, money out – compared to a sample of businesses like them. Do they have characteristics like people that have failed or not? (High street bank #1)

Conversely, some stakeholders, including many small companies themselves, possess limited power to demand more detailed, real-time financial information privately from prospective trading partners or to access data from other sources. Such companies, where they seek external information at all, may be heavily reliant on statutory accounts data at Companies House when choosing suppliers and customers, and deciding whether to offer credit:

> The only users are the ones who aren't powerful enough to get anything else. And they are going to be the small ones ... The key user of small company accounts is other small companies with whom they're doing business and there is an issue there. Because those small companies may not be in the position our members are in. Our members can say 'Look, if you want finance, you're going to provide your full set of accounts.' So if you're a small company seeking to sell to another small company, to use a bit of credit, you may not be in a position to insist on a full set of accounts. (Trade association)

In the survey of small company preparers, 42 per cent reported also being users of other small companies' abbreviated accounts, particularly those of potential customers. Despite greater reliance on public sources, small company respondents recognised the limited content of abbreviated accounts:

It's part of the jigsaw. It gives us context. Would I ever take someone on just based on them? No I wouldn't. It's one of the tools in the toolbox and we like to use as many tools in the toolbox as we can to make an informed decision. (Small company #5: mail service, 5 employees)

CRAs provide credit risk assessments to clients (including banks, finance houses, credit insurers and trade suppliers) to support their own decision-making relating to doing business with, or offering trade credit to, prospective suppliers and customers. Like the banks, CRAs operate proprietary credit scoring/ranking models, updated frequently to incorporate new information, in order to satisfy client requests for a credit score/ranking for large numbers of businesses. For small firms, credit scoring/ranking is largely an automated process whereby owner and business characteristics are identified, ratios calculated, weighted and combined to produce a score/rank. CRAs use information drawn from a range of sources, including Companies House, payment behaviour from businesses dealing with small companies, financial data direct from small companies, County Court judgments, directors' histories and business demographics (size, industry, trading history, location). Problems arise because the number of small companies is prohibitively large with regards to accessing financial information. Although CRAs contacted some small companies for additional information, they lacked sufficient time and money to address the information shortfall in this way. Hence their strong reliance on statutory accounts information, with its admittedly limited content:

Now when we say that it's very important, that's not to disguise the fact that there is a big difference between the full or medium-sized information filed at Companies House and when we just have the abbreviated accounts information. When you have the full information, you know what the company's turnover is, you know what the company's profitability is, you have some degree of breakdown of the items on the balance sheet. When you have the abbreviated accounts, it's still far better than not having the abbreviated information, obviously, but it's much more about having to make assumptions and make the best use of the available data. (Credit reference agency #1)

Trade credit insurance providers insure business policyholders' accounts receivable from loss due to debtor default. Policyholders typically apply a credit limit to particular buyers, and insurers approve and insure a proportion of losses up to these limits, with policyholders carrying the remainder of the risk. Beyond the credit limit, policyholders carry the risk for all losses. Credit insurance cover therefore encourages businesses to supply products and credit facilities to customers. Policyholders might also use credit insurance to access bank finance as it provides security for their creditors. Without credit insurance, businesses might simply refuse to trade with particular companies, demand cash up front or on delivery, or offer credit at their own risk.

Insurance premia reflect the value of cover provided and insurers' assessments of the credit risk of the insured buyer portfolio. Like banks and CRAs, insurers operate their own credit scoring/ranking models, drawing on statutory accounts information, whether abbreviated or full, and other information in order to assess the credit risk of particular companies. Credit risk assessments are automated up to a certain credit limit because resource constraints prohibit information acquisition from large numbers of, particularly, very small firms. Using abbreviated accounts information reduces the possibility of policyholders insuring higher levels of credit, or even obtaining cover at all:

> The problem with abbreviated accounts is that a lot of the information that we need to be able to calculate those [financial] ratios is just not available. So we're having to use a very much more limited model which is not nearly as accurate. Which means that … we have to be far more cautious in the level of cover that we are able to [provide]. I think where we do have abbreviated accounts, we would probably tend to reject a higher proportion of those buyers because of that. (Credit insurer #1)

CRAs and credit insurers were particularly critical of abbreviated accounts because of the limited information content, requiring supplementation from other sources – often more difficult and costly to access – in order to produce a well-informed credit rating or insurance decision. Limited disclosure encourages cautious approaches, with adverse consequences for small companies – as seekers and beneficiaries of credit ratings and credit insurance decisions. Other things being equal, companies with known turnover and profit data would likely obtain a superior credit rating than other companies – unless the figures reveal poor performance. The consequences for the wider economy were also likely to be adverse. More and better information facilitates trading, credit allocation and economic development:

> If abbreviated accounts were unavailable, I think there would be a serious deterioration in what we provide to our clients … It would inhibit risk-taking. It certainly wouldn't oil the wheels of commerce. It would have the reverse effect. (Credit reference agency #4)

To sum up, stakeholders varied in their dependence on abbreviated accounts information and their access to alternative information sources.

Some believed abbreviated accounts to be a useful data source to support credit risk assessments and credit decisions – but only up to a point. Some information is better than none, but most stakeholders were also critical. Others, able to access more comprehensive and timely small company information, felt more comfortable in making credit decisions. For accounts users, abbreviated accounts provide only limited financial transparency, with important consequences for users, small companies themselves and the wider economy.

## MANAGING CREDIT RISK IN TURBULENT TIMES

The recession and financial crisis of 2008–09 led CRAs to downgrade small firms' credit risk ratings substantially (Fraser 2009). Subsequently, this led businesses, financiers, and credit insurers to place even greater value on financial transparency (CBI/ACCA 2010). Credit risk ratings awarded by CRAs are inversely related to business size: the smaller the firm, the poorer the rating (BDRC 2012). Tighter lending criteria imposed by finance providers form part of the explanation for the decline in lending to small and medium-sized companies (Bank of England 2012a, 2012b); 'discouraged demand' also contributes to reduced borrowing (Freel et al. 2012). Banks reduced lending to small enterprises quickly following the onset of the recession in 2008 and subsequently restricted the range of lending criteria, principally by using business size as a proxy measure for credit risk, concentrating the supply of finance in larger small firms (Cowling et al. 2012).

Micro enterprises reported a lower, and declining, use of external finance during 2011; they were more likely to be 'permanent non-borrowers', that is, they had no external borrowing history and no plans to borrow in future (BDRC 2012), and had been less successful in loan applications due to cash flow and collateral considerations (CBI/ACCA 2010) than larger small and medium-sized enterprises (SMEs). Use of overdrafts, in particular, has fallen sharply among micro businesses. Marked declines in the use of external finance were evident among micro firms with an average or worse-than-average credit rating. Smaller operators have reportedly been squeezed by suppliers tightening payment terms and by customers seeking to extend them (Bank of England 2012b). There is considerable evidence, therefore, that banks and other lenders consider small, and especially micro, companies to be a growing credit risk in a difficult economic climate.

Credit management professionals reported that credit risk assessments had tightened considerably as a consequence of the financial crisis.

Accounts users increasingly considered filed accounts – both abbreviated and full – to be of only limited value in a volatile environment because they are several months out of date at the point they become available. The crisis has intensified demand for real-time management accounts or customer payment data (CBI/ACCA 2010). Companies filing abbreviated accounts were considered greater credit risks and likely to suffer as a consequence:

> I think things have moved on. So, even if they now filed full accounts – with cash flow, P&L [profit and loss account], balance sheet and notes to the accounts – as far as our market-place is concerned, it's not good enough anymore. Abbreviated accounts provide a snapshot of a particular scenario. Full accounts provide a bit more detail but a year to 18 months out of date. That's no use to anybody in this industry any more. What's important is real-time financial information that talks about what's going on currently – as opposed to what happened a year ago. (Trade credit insurance broker #1)

One credit insurer reported that the financial crisis had led to a 'credit limit cull' whereby insurers were simply refusing policyholder requests to obtain cover for their dealings with a small business unless detailed and timely management accounts information is provided by that small business. Insurers had, reportedly, been hit hard by a high volume of low-value claims, typically in relation to small firm defaults, and had adopted a more cautious approach to providing insurance cover. This, of course, aggravates problems for small firms seeking to survive in credit-starved times:

> Many of the leading insurers made significant losses through 2008–9. The majority of that was small claims on SME companies. That's an area where they need to improve ... Unless insurers have proper information on SME companies there's going to be a limit to how much they can support those companies. Certainly, in certain difficult sectors, there's going to be very little leeway given to providing credit unless full information is disclosed. (Credit insurer #1)

Summarising, accounts users made it clear that credit risk assessments were particularly sensitive to wider economic circumstances. Trade suppliers, CRAs and insurers reported a heightened sensitivity to credit risk. Small companies were required to disclose more detailed and timely information in order to access the financial resources and markets they need to survive. Without further information, suppliers have refused to grant credit, CRAs to award high credit ratings, and insurers to provide adequate cover to those trading with small companies. This has no doubt influenced micro company access to finance in recent years.

## THE INVISIBLE DISADVANTAGES OF LIMITED DISCLOSURE

Regulation produces benefits for small companies where it encourages disclosure that subsequently leads stakeholders to act in ways that enable small companies to achieve their business objectives. Stakeholder actions and their consequences might not be visible to small companies with whom they interact. Small companies might suffer constraints arising from the limited transparency associated with filing abbreviated accounts: for example, they might fail to win orders, obtain adequate credit ratings or access bank or trade credit. None of the 12 small company interview respondents, however, reported losing customers or being unable to access sufficient finance because they filed abbreviated accounts. They claimed to have access to sufficient internal or external finance to fund current operations and future plans. Most insisted that if major lenders, suppliers or customers requested more detailed and up-to-date accounts information, they were willing to provide it:

> I have no evidence to suggest that we've ever lost business, or we've ever failed to raise funding, as a result of filing limited accounts … I have no recollection in the 14 years of being in business of a time when we've lost a piece of business as a result of filing limited accounts … I *can* say that there have been occasions when I've probably won business because people have no idea how small we are. (Company #5: mail service, five employees)

It might be argued, however, that small company directors are simply unaware of the reasons for failing to win new business or to access finance, where these events occur. Some accounts users claimed that small companies are not fully aware of the risks associated with non-disclosure, or the benefits of greater disclosure, for example, concerning access to credit:

> A lot of companies say there's no negative impact. But they may not *know* they've had their credit limit reduced. They may not know that they could have opened up more credit with a particular supplier had they had that information available to them. (Credit reference agency #1)

Limited transparency, accounts users insisted, might generate unintended adverse consequences for small companies: orders not won, finance unaccessed, poorer credit ratings and lower credit insurance cover for those with whom they do business. None of the small company respondents interviewed reported any such problems, although it is highly likely that they are invisible to them. Small company access to key resources, such as credit, or to new markets is necessarily influenced by the actions of close and distant stakeholders, some of whom will be unknown to small company owners themselves.

## CONCLUSIONS AND POLICY IMPLICATIONS

Regulation, including financial reporting regulation, is a dynamic influence on small company activity and performance. The impact of regulation is contingent upon the activities of human agents, not only small company actors, but also a wide range of stakeholders, including trade suppliers, banks, CRAs, credit insurers and other organisations. In contrast to studies that focus on the burdens, costs and constraints imposed by regulation on small businesses, regulation might also enable small company directors to achieve their goals by encouraging important stakeholders to provide orders, finance, credit ratings and insurance cover. If suppliers decide not to trade with, or offer credit to, small company clients because of limited disclosure, this is as much an effect of the regulation permitting small companies to file abbreviated accounts as is any purported reduction in the administrative burden of financial reporting obligations.

There is a clear divergence of view between small company preparers and accounts users regarding the value of abbreviated accounts. For preparers, the option to file abbreviated accounts provides an important benefit – confidentiality – that they believe protects them from stakeholder action to appropriate more of the economic value created. For users, abbreviated accounts provide only limited financial transparency, with important consequences for users, small companies themselves and the wider economy.

The paradox for small companies is that both confidentiality and transparency potentially serve their interests. Confidentiality protects small companies from users whose actions might cause them economic harm while, at the same time, it limits the support that others – banks, trade suppliers, CRAs and credit insurers – might provide, possibly unbeknown to small companies themselves. Transparency potentially overcomes such consequences while at the same time making it easier for competitors and others to exploit information in a manner that might threaten small company performance. In the aftermath of the financial crisis, and the part played by poor credit risk assessment, greater transparency has become increasingly valued by accounts users as a means of assessing credit risk.

For policymakers, there is a trade-off between reducing the administrative burden of regulation on small companies in order to attempt to stimulate growth, and increasing financial transparency in order to reduce business uncertainty, improve credit allocation and facilitate economic development. The deregulatory thrust of the new Accounting Directive to relax micro entities' publication obligations, if taken up by the UK government, will likely benefit some companies more than others. Arguably, the very smallest companies with few tangible assets, funded by personal savings, with no intention to expand, which express a strong preference to avoid seeking external finance and which trade mainly with businesses whose decisions are not influenced by CRAs or credit insurers, may be the ones most likely to benefit. The question arises as to whether these are the kinds of companies that policy should support. These firms are not likely to be the innovative, high-growth enterprises which policymakers hope will spearhead the recovery. Micro companies tempted not to publish accounts might find themselves less able to win new business and/or secure favourable terms from banks and trade creditors, with obvious consequences for their performance and survival, as well as for the national economy. Deregulation might, therefore, produce the opposite consequences to those intended by policymakers – to make the UK one of the best places in Europe to start, finance and grow a business.

## NOTES

*   The authors are grateful to the Scottish Accountancy Trust for Education and Research for funding the research upon which the chapter is based, and to the Institute of Chartered Accountants of Scotland (ICAS) for supporting the research. The ICAS report, titled 'Small company abbreviated accounts: a regulatory burden or a vital disclosure?' can be downloaded at http:www.icas.org.uk/Kitching.
1.  The Fourth Company Law Directive refers to 'abridged' accounts. The UK Companies Act 1981 referred to 'modified' accounts, later changed to 'abbreviated' accounts in the Companies Act 1989 and retained in the Companies Act 2006.
2.  Entities qualifying as medium-sized are also permitted to file abbreviated accounts, but greater disclosure is required than for small companies.
3.  Under the Companies Act 2006, 'an entity is excluded from the small companies regime if it is a public company, a company that is an authorized insurance company, a banking company, an e-money issuer, an ISD investment firm or a UCITS management company, or carries on insurance market activity, or is a member of an ineligible group' (c. 46, Part 15, Chapter 1, p. 178).
4.  Some respondents were sceptical of unaudited accounts. Companies House is a public registry; it does not validate the accounts filed.

# REFERENCES

Ackerman, F. (2006), 'The unbearable lightness of regulatory costs', Global Development and Environment Institute, Working Paper No. 06-02, Tufts University, http://www.ase.tufts.edu/gdae/Pubs/wp/06-02UnbearableLightness Reg.pdf.

Ang, J.S. (1992), 'On the theory of finance for privately held firms', *Journal of Small Business Finance*, **1** (4), 185–203.

Ang, J.S., J. Wuh Lin and F. Tyler (1995), 'Evidence of the lack of separation between business and personal risk among small business', *Journal of Small Business Finance*, **4** (2–3), 197–210.

Arruñada, B. (2011), 'Mandatory accounting disclosure by small private companies', *European Journal of Law and Economics*, **32** (3), 377–413.

Bank of England (2012a), 'Trends in lending – January 2012', http://www.bankofengland.co.uk/publications/Pages/other/monetary/trendsinlending.aspx.

Bank of England (2012b), 'Agents' summaries of business conditions – April 2012', http://www.bankofengland.co.uk/publications/Pages/agentssummary/agsum12apr.aspx.

BDRC Continental (2012), 'SME Finance Monitor: Q4 2011, Assessing the appetite for finance during 2011', http://www.sme-finance-monitor.co.uk/.

Beaver, W.H., M.F. McNichols and J.-W. Rhie (2005), 'Have financial statements become less informative? Evidence from the ability of financial ratios to predict bankruptcy', *Review of Accounting Studies*, **10** (1), 93–122.

Berger, A.N. and G.F. Udell (1995), 'Relationship lending and the lines of credit in small firm finance', *Journal of Business*, **68** (3), 351–381.

Berger, A.N. and G.F. Udell (2006), 'A more complete conceptual framework for SME finance', *Journal of Banking and Finance*, **30** (11), 2945–2966.

Berry, A., D. Citron and R. Jarvis (1993), 'Financial information, the banker and the small business', *British Accounting Review*, **25** (2), 131–150.

Berry, A., P. Grant and R. Jarvis (2004), 'European bank lending to the UK SME sector: an investigation of approaches adopted', *International Small Business Journal*, **22** (2), 115–130.

Better Regulation Executive (2010), 'Lightening the load: the regulatory impact on UK's smallest businesses', http://www.bis.gov.uk/assets/biscore/better-regulation/docs/l/10-1251-lightening-the-load-regulatory-impact-smallest-busi nesses.

Beyer, A., D. Cohen, T. Lys and B. Walther (2010), 'The financial reporting environment: review of the recent literature', *Journal of Accounting and Economics*, **50** (2–3), 266–343.

Binks, M., C. Ennew and G. Reid (1992), 'Information asymmetries and the provision of finance to small firms', *International Small Business Journal*, **11** (1), 35–46.

CBI/ACCA (2010), 'Small business finance and the recovery: results of the 2010 SME Credit and Finance Surveys', http://www.accaglobal.com/content/dam/acca/global/PDF-technical/small-business/pol-af-sbf.pdf.

Chittenden, F., S. Kauser and P. Poutziouris (2002), 'Regulatory burdens of small business: a literature review', report for the Small Business Service, http://web archive.nationalarchives.gov.uk/+/http://www.berr.gov.uk/files/file38324.pdf.

Collis, J. (2012), 'Determinants of voluntary audit and voluntary full accounts in micro- and non-micro small companies in the UK', *Accounting and Business Research*, **42** (4), 1–28.

Collis, J. and R. Jarvis (2000), 'How owner-managers use accounts', ICAEW Research Report, London: Centre for Business Performance Research, http://www.icaew.com/index.cfm/route/157846/icaew_ga/en/pdf.

Companies House (2012), 'Statistical tables on companies registration activities 2011/12', http://www.companieshouse.gov.uk/about/pdf/companiesReg Activities2011_2012.pdf.

Cowling, M., W. Liu and A. Ledger (2012), 'Small business financing in the UK before and during the current financial crisis', *International Small Business Journal*, **30** (7), 778–800.

Crain, N. and M. Crain (2010), 'The impact of regulatory costs on small firms', online at: http://archive.sba.gov/advo/research/rs371tot.pdf.

Department for Business, Innovation and Skills (2012a), 'Audit exemptions and change of accounting framework: summary of responses to consultation', http://www.bis.gov.uk/assets/biscore/business-law/docs/a/12-609-audit-exemptions-accounting-framework-summary-responses.pdf.

Department for Business, Innovation and Skills (2012b), 'The future of narrative reporting: a new structure for narrative reporting in the UK', http://www.bis.gov.uk/assets/biscore/business-law/docs/f/12-979-future-of-narrative-reporting-new-structure.pdf.

Department for Business, Innovation and Skills (2013), 'Simpler financial reporting for micro-entities: the UK's proposal to implement the "Micros Directive"', https://www.gov.uk/government/uploads/system/uploads/attach ment_data/file/86259/13-626-simpler-financial-reporting-for-micro-entities-consultation.pdf.

Department of Trade and Industry (DTI) (1985), *Burdens on Business*, London: HMSO.

European Commission (2012), 'Directive 2012/6/EU of the European Parliament and of the Council of 14 March 2012 amending Council Directive 78/660/EEC on the annual accounts of certain types of companies as regards micro-entities', http://eur-lex.europa.eu/LexUriServ/LexUriServ.do?uri=OJ:L:2012:081:0003:0006:EN:PDF.

European Union (2011), 'Financial reporting: burden reduction for micro-entities – Frequently Asked Questions', Memo/11/911, Brussels, 14 December, http://europa.eu/rapid/pressReleasesAction.do?reference=MEMO/11/911&format=HTML.

Fraser, S. (2009), 'Small firms in the credit crisis: evidence from the UK Survey of SME Finances', http://www2.warwick.ac.uk/fac/soc/wbs/research/csme/research/latest/small_firms_in_the_credit_crisis_v3-oct09.pdf.

Freel, M., S. Carter, S. Tagg and C. Mason (2012), 'The latent demand for bank debt: characterising "discouraged borrowers"', *Small Business Economics*, **38** (4), 399–418.

Healy, P. and K. Palepu (2001), 'Information asymmetry, corporate disclosure, and the capital markets: a review of the empirical disclosure literature', *Journal of Accounting and Economics*, **31** (1–3), 405–440.

HM Government (2012), 'One-in, one-out: third statement of new regulation', http://www.bis.gov.uk/assets/biscore/better-regulation/docs/o/12-p96a-one-in-one-out-third-statement-new-regulation.

HM Treasury (2005), 'Chancellor launches better regulation action plan', http://webarchive.nationalarchives.gov.uk/+/http://www.hmtreasury.gov.uk/news room_and_speeches/press/2005/press_50_05.cfm.

HM Treasury/BIS (2011), 'The plan for growth', online at: http://cdn.hm-treasury.gov.uk/2011budget_growth.pdf.

Institute of Directors (IoD) (2011), 'The regulation reckoner: counting the real cost of regulation', http://www.iod.com/mainwebsite/resources/document/regulation_reckoner_2011.pdf.

Kitching, J. (2006), 'A burden on business? Reviewing the evidence base on regulation and small business performance', *Environment and Planning C: Government and Policy*, **24** (6), 799–814.

Kitching, J. (2007), 'Is less more? Better regulation and the small enterprise', in S. Weatherill (ed.), *Better Regulation*, Oxford: Hart, pp. 155–173.

Kitching, J., E. Kašperová, R. Blackburn and J. Collis (2011), 'Small company abbreviated accounts: a regulatory burden or a vital disclosure?', Institute of Chartered Accountants in Scotland, Edinburgh, http://www.icas.org.uk/site/cms/contentviewarticle.asp?article=7529.

Marriott, N., J. Collis and P. Marriott (2006), 'Qualitative review of the accounting and auditing needs of small and medium-sized companies and their stakeholders', London: Professional Oversight Board for Accountancy, http://frc.org.uk/FRC-Documents/POB/Qualitative-review-of-the-accounting-and-auditing.aspx.

Pawson, R. and N. Tilley (1997), *Realistic Evaluation*, London: Sage.

Petersen, M.A. and R.G. Rajan (1994), 'The benefits of lending relationships: evidence from small business data', *Journal of Finance*, **49** (1), 3–37.

Professional Oversight Board for Accountancy (POBA) (2006), 'Review of how accountants support the needs of small and medium-sized companies and their stakeholders', Professional Oversight Board for Accountancy, London, http://www.frc.org.uk/getattachment/ade68ea3-085b-45ad-9ecd-bbc8a3187cc6/Review-of-How-Accountants-Support-the-needs-of-Small-and-Medium-Sized-Companies-and-their-Stakeholders.aspx.

World Bank (2012), 'Doing business in 2013: smarter regulations for small and medium-size enterprises', World Bank, Washington, DC, http://www.doing business.org/~/media/GIAWB/Doing%20Business/Documents/Annual-Reports/English/DB13-full-report.pdf.

# 5. The effectiveness of public venture capital in supporting the investments of European young high-tech companies

## Fabio Bertoni, Annalisa Croce and Massimiliano Guerini

## INTRODUCTION

The creation of an active venture capital (VC) market is a long-standing issue on the agenda of European policymakers (Da Rin et al. 2006). The attempt to improve the framework conditions for the spontaneous growth of VC has been a significant, albeit unsystematic, policy effort (Bertoni and Croce 2011; Mason 2009). Often policymakers have accompanied this long-term endeavor with a direct intervention in capital markets: the creation of public VC (PVC) funds. The investment process of PVC funds is normally set to resemble that of independent VC (IVC) investors: PVC selects companies based on their business plan, invests in their equity (or in equity-like securities), may impose covenants and agree with other shareholders on a state-contingent allocation of cash flow and control rights, and eventually aims at exiting the investment. However the typical PVC funds invest public money, are controlled by a public agency and normally pursue political goals (e.g. job creation and local development) alongside financial ones. This engenders significant differences between PVC and IVC in terms, for instance, of their skills, investment horizon and compensation structure (Brander et al. 2010). This suggests that we should not take for granted that IVC and PVC have a similar impact on their portfolio companies.

It is then natural to wonder about the extent to which PVC is as effective as IVC in relaxing the financial constraints of their portfolio companies. This is what we aim to assess in this chapter. Our results may be summarized as follows. Firstly, we confirm that, on average, young high-tech companies in Europe are significantly financially constrained. Secondly, we substantiate the evidence suggesting that IVC is effective in alleviating firms' financial constraints, and that this effect is persistent over time. The positive effect of IVC on firms' investments seems to be both direct and indirect. The direct effect derives from the provision of a substantial amount of financial resources distributed over several rounds of investment. The indirect effect derives from the positive signal that IVC financing conveys to other investors about firms' quality.

Results on PVC are markedly different. The direct support of PVC investors is limited to the immediate aftermath of the financing round and no relaxation of financial constraints is found. On the one hand, this is due to the fact that PVC invests a smaller amount per round than IVC and is active in fewer investment rounds. On the other hand, we also find little evidence that PVC conveys a positive signal to other potential investors, thus generating an indirect effect.

The rest of the chapter is organized as follows. The next section reviews the literature on investment sensitivity to cash flows and the impact of VC. We then present the econometric methodology, sample and descriptive statistics. These are followed by the reporting of the results of the econometric models. Finally, we summarize the main results and draw some concluding remarks.

## RELATED LITERATURE

In their seminal paper, Fazzari et al. (1988) argue that whereas the marginal opportunity cost of internal capital is constant, the marginal cost of external capital follows an upward slope, whose steepness is higher the more capital markets are imperfect. Under these circumstances, one would expect that investments by firms that face a steep capital supply curve should be more sensitive to internal cash flows than those of firms whose cost of capital is shallow. According to Fazzari et al. (1988), this gives researchers a tool with which to gauge the severity of firms' financial constraints by estimating the sensitivity of their investments to internally available capital. Since their seminal contribution, a vast literature has developed discussing when the sensitivity of investments to cash flows can be considered a synonym of the presence of financial constraints and how it should be empirically estimated.

Kaplan and Zingales (1997, 2000) show that firms' investment sensitivity to cash flows does not necessarily decrease monotonically with the level of available internal capital when firms are close to distress. Using detailed qualitative and quantitative information contained in firms' annual reports and financial statements, they find that firms that were classified as the more financially constrained by Fazzari et al. (1988) exhibit lower investment–cash flow sensitivity than those classified as less financially constrained. Several more sophisticated empirical works proved that their critique was indeed well posed (e.g. Cleary 1999, 2006). Guariglia (2008) tries to conciliate these contradictory findings, by distinguishing between internal financial constraints (i.e., the lack of internally generated capital) and external financial constraints (i.e., the difficult access to external finance). She finds that, in line with Kaplan and Zingales (1997, 2000), when the sample is split on the basis of the level of firms' internal funds, the relationship between investment and cash flow is U-shaped. However, when the sample is split according to firm size the sensitivity of investment to cash flow tends to increase monotonically.

Young high-tech companies are extremely exposed to financial constraints due to asymmetries in information and the mismatch in the investment and revenue cycles (Carpenter and Petersen 2002). VC may have a twofold impact on firms' financial constraints. Firstly, VC may have a direct effect through the injection of capital. By expanding their stock of financial resources, VC allows financially constrained firms to adjust their investment level closer to the optimum. External capital is typically in part used to purchase collateralizable assets, and this allows access to additional capital (Carpenter and Petersen 2002). Secondly, VC may have an indirect effect linked to a reduction in information asymmetries. When VC invests in a company, it conveys a signal to other parties, certifying a firm's quality (Lee and Wahal 2004; Megginson and Weiss 1991). This reduces asymmetries in information between the company and other intermediaries and, as a consequence, relaxes financial constraints. Interestingly, while the direct impact is proportional to the amount invested by a VC, the indirect impact is proportional to its reputation (Hsu 2004).

VC investors constitute a very heterogeneous crowd, especially in Europe where non-traditional VC investors play an eminent role (Tykvová 2006). The general partners of IVC funds have a strong incentive in obtaining the maximum capital gain in the shortest period of time both because of their compensation structure and because of reputational concerns (Gompers and Lerner 1999). This suggests that, once an IVC investor has identified a promising investment opportunity, it has the incentive and the financial capacity to support it. There is sound empirical evidence for this view: most studies show that IVC-backed young high-tech companies increase their investments and are less dependent on current cash flows (Bertoni et al. 2010; Bertoni et al. 2013; Engel and Stiebale 2009).

The effect of PVC financing on a firm's investment rate and investment–cash flow sensitivity has received little empirical scrutiny. There are reasons to believe, however, that it could be different from the effect of IVCs. While there is, to the best of our knowledge, no study directly assessing this research question, the literature shows that other captive VC investors (notably corporate VC) are typically less effective than IVC in relaxing a firm's financial constraints (e.g. Bertoni et al. 2010). These results are normally explained by the differences between corporate and independent VC in terms of objectives, skills and governance structure. Notably, PVC also differs from IVC in all those respects. While the primary objective of IVC investors is to generate profits resulting from profitable investments, PVC often focuses on a broader (and less clear-cut) set of goals, including building links between universities and the private sector, supporting the development of the VC industry, and local employment levels (e.g. Cumming and MacIntosh 2004, 2006). Secondly, PVC is hardly as effective as IVC in coaching and monitoring portfolio companies (Leleux and Surlemont 2003; Luukkonen et al. 2013). This reduces its potential for overcoming asymmetries in information. Thirdly, in general, PVC managers have less performance-sensitive contracts than IVC managers (Jääskeläinen et al. 2007). As such, they have fewer incentives to provide their portfolio firms with the financial and non-financial resources they need to pursue investment opportunities. This is consistent with evidence showing that PVC injects less capital in portfolio company and participates in fewer follow-up investment rounds (Bottazzi et al. 2008; Nightingale et al. 2009). Using the terminology introduced in the previous section, this suggests that the direct impact of PVC could be less relevant than that of IVC. The indirect effect then becomes particularly important. Indeed, even though the direct support of PVC could be lower than that of IVC, if PVC could credibly certify that invested firms are of high quality, information problems could be overcome and other investors (e.g. other VCs and banks) could join the syndicate and confidently invest in these firms ('certification hypothesis', Lerner 2002). The signal provided by PVC is likely to be particularly valuable in high-tech industries, where traditional financial measures are of little use. The credibility of the signal also depends on the reputation that PVC investors have in screening the most promising ventures. Another important factor that determines the strength of the signal conveyed by PVC is its network of contacts within the financial community. Results on the SBIR Program in the United States

(US) (Lerner 1999) and public subsidies in Italy (Colombo et al. 2012) seem to support the certification hypothesis.

## METHODOLOGY

In this study, we adopt two different dynamic sales accelerator specifications that we present with the same structure and notation used by Engel and Stiebale (2009). These specifications relate the firm's investment rate to the current and lagged sales growth, the lagged investment rate and cash flows. Moreover, it includes lagged levels of intangible assets, as a proxy of high growth potential based on innovations. This should reduce the risk of a spurious correlation between VC and the investment of portfolio firms. Finally, we also control for the level of bank debt. Our first model shown, in equation (5.1), is built along the lines of Bertoni et al. (2010), and introduces in the baseline dynamic sales accelerator model two sets of additional parameters that capture the impact of IVC and PVC on the firm's investments and their sensitivity to cash flows:

$$\frac{I_{it}}{K_{it-1}} = \beta_1 \frac{I_{it-1}}{K_{it-2}} + \beta_2 \Delta y_{it} + \beta_2 \Delta y_{it-1} + \beta_4 \frac{ITA_{it-1}}{K_{it-1}} + \beta_5 \frac{B_{it}}{K_{it-1}} + \beta_6 \frac{C_{it}}{K_{it-1}} + \beta_6 age_{it} +$$
$$+ \sum_{xVC \in \Theta} \left( \varphi_{xVC} D_{it}^{xVC} + \delta_{xVC} D_{it}^{xVC} \frac{C_{it}}{K_{it-1}} \right) + D_i + Z_t + \varepsilon_{it} \qquad (5.1)$$

where $I_{it}$ denotes the increase in the end-of-period stock of tangible and intangible assets (net of depreciation) of firm $i$ between year $t$ and year $t - 1$, $K_{it}$ is the net value of the stock of tangible and intangible assets at the end of year $t$, $\Delta y_{it}$ is the change in the logarithm of firm's sales between year $t$ and year $t - 1$, $ITA_{it}$ denotes the end-of-period net value of intangible assets, $B_{it}$ denotes the value of total non-equity liabilities (i.e. total liabilities minus shareholders equity) at the end of year $t$, $C_{it}$ is firm's cash flow during year $t$, $age_{it}$ if the age of firm $i$ in year t, $D_i$ is a firm-fixed effect, $Z_i$ contains period fixed effects, $D_{it}^{xVC}$ is a dummy variable equal to one if VC type $xVC \in \Theta = \{IVC, PVC\}$ invested in company $i$ in year $t$ or before as lead investor and $\epsilon_{it}$ is an error term.

The first parameter of interest in equation (5.1) is $\beta_6$, which measures the firm's investment–cash flow sensitivity. In line with the literature, if the firm's financial constraints are substantial, we expect $\beta_6$ to be positive and statistically significant. The moderating role of IVC and PVC on the firm's investments is captured by $\varphi_{xVC}$ and $\delta_{xVC}$. These two sets of parameters capture two different dimensions of the impact of VC.

Parameter $\delta_{xVC}$ in equation (5.1) captures changes in the investment–cash flow sensitivity due to the presence of an $xVC$ investor. To the extent to which a VC investor reduces the firm's investment–cash flow sensitivity we should expect $\delta_{xVC} < 0$. Moreover, if the investment–cash flow sensitivity is not only reduced, but cancelled, we should expect that: $\beta_6 + \delta_{xVC} = 0$. Parameters $\varphi_{xVC}$ represent instead the long-term increase in investment rate observed after a firm becomes $xVC$-backed.

Our second model goes a step beyond and tries to identify the 'channel' through which investments of portfolio firms are affected by IVC and PVC. To do so, we introduce in the specification a control for the amount of financing received by the firm from each VC investor, as shown in equation (5.2):

$$
\frac{I_{it}}{K_{it-1}} = \beta_1 \frac{I_{it-1}}{K_{it-2}} + \beta_2 \Delta y_{it} + \beta_2 \Delta y_{it-1} + \beta_4 \frac{ITA_{it-1}}{K_{it-1}} + \beta_5 \frac{B_{it}}{K_{it-1}} + \beta_6 \frac{C_{it}}{K_{it-1}} + \beta_6 age_{it} +
$$
$$
+ \sum_{xVC \in \Theta} \left( \varphi_{xVC} D_{it}^{xVC} + \gamma_{1,xVC} \frac{A_{it}^{xVC}}{K_{it-1}} + \gamma_{1,xVC} \frac{A_{it-1}^{xVC}}{K_{it-2}} + \delta_{xVC} D_{it}^{xVC} \frac{C_{it}}{K_{it-1}} \right) + D_i + Z_t + \varepsilon_{it}
$$

(5.2)

where $A_{it}^{xVC}$ is amount of VC financing received by firm $i$ in year $t$ when $xVC$ is the lead investor. In order to take into account the fact that investments may require some time to be made after cash is injected, we also include the lag of the amount of VC financing. The extent to which the amount invested by $xVC$ translates in higher investment rate in the investment year is captured by $\gamma_{1,xVC}$. The increase in investments in the following year is captured by $\gamma_{2,xVC}$. Using the terminology introduced earlier, $\gamma_{1,xVC}$ and $\gamma_{2,xVC}$ capture the direct impact of $xVC$ on the firm's investment rate. In this specification, $\phi_{xVC}$ and $\delta_{xVC}$ represents the indirect effect of $xVC$ on the long-term investment rate and on the investment-cash flow sensitivity, respectively. In other words, equation (5.1) tells us whether the firm's investments change after receipt of $xVC$ financing, while equation (5.2) tells us the extent to which this is due to a direct or an indirect effect.

Equations (5.1) and (5.2), like all sales accelerator models, include the lagged dependent variable among the covariates. This results in pooled ordinary least squares and fixed-effects estimation to give biased estimates (Bond and Van Reenen 2007). To solve this problem it is customary to resort to generalized method of moments (GMM) estimation. In this work, in particular, we adopt a two-step system GMM estimation with finite-sample correction (Windmeijer 2005). The use of GMM estimation allows us to correct biases arising from endogeneity, by introducing moment conditions on the orthogonality of past levels (differences) of covariates to errors in first-differenced (level) equations. The actual set of conditions depends upon the assumptions about the nature of endogeneity which affects the variables in the model.

Following Engel and Stiebale (2009), we treat cash flow and current sales growth as endogenous and lagged intangible assets and bank debt as predetermined. More importantly, we consider that a firm with more investment opportunities could be more likely to look for external financing, thus leading to a correlation between investments and VC financing caused by reverse causation. We treat VC variables as endogenous, thus allowing the firm's investment to be correlated with unobservable shocks that also affect VC financing. To reduce the number of moment conditions of the model and avoid excessive over-identification, we limit the time span of instruments to $t - 4$. We test the validity of the overidentifying restrictions using Hansen tests and the null hypothesis of, respectively, no first- or second-order serial correlation with AR(1) and AR(2) tests.

Selection biases may arise when evaluating the impact of VC on the removal of the firm's financial constraints if we do not properly control for the fact that VC-backed firms are different from non-VC-backed firms before receiving the financing. Moreover, it is implausible that IVC and PVC select similar firms. Hence it is important to control for selection biases arising from the different selection criteria of VC investors. We control for this heterogeneity by adding a set of external instruments that measure the ratio between the net annual amount raised in every country by different types of VC investors (namely, IVC funds, governmental programmes and university funds) and gross domestic product (GDP). These exogenous variables should be useful in determining the likelihood, other things being equal, of a firm receiving IVC or PVC money and, accordingly, improve the set of instruments for VC variables. We extract this information from the Thomson Financial Venture Economics Database for the countries included in our sample. As a robustness check, we estimate our models also by using only internal instruments.

We implement a test on survivorship bias. Firms' survival rates can be influenced by access to VC financing either positively, because VC-backed firms might benefit from a larger endowment of financial and other resources (Puri and Zarutskie 2008), or negatively, because they might become more risk-taking (Manigart and Van Hyfte 1999). The presence of VC is also likely to influence the likelihood that companies are acquired, not least because trade sales are by far the most common way out for VC in Europe (Bertoni et al. 2012; Bottazzi et al. 2004). We implement a direct test to check the presence of survivorship bias in the spirit of Wooldridge (1995) and Semykina and Wooldridge (2010). The procedure, essentially, requires the estimation of a selection equation for exit. An inverse Mill's ratio is computed from this selection equation for each firm-year observation ($IMR_{it}$). This time-varying ratio is then inserted as an additional covariate in our models, which are then estimated via system GMM.

## SAMPLE AND DESCRIPTIVE STATISTICS

In this chapter we rely upon a sample of European high-tech companies extracted from the VICO database. This database has been developed by nine European universities and research centres through a project funded by the European Commission within the 7th Framework Programme. The database includes two strata of firms: the first is a sample of VC-backed firms and the second is a control group of non-VC-backed firms. The identification of control group companies was based on a matching procedure by country, with a relative ratio of VC-backed to control group companies kept at 1:10.

Overall, the VICO database includes detailed information about 8370 firms, 759 of which are VC-backed, operating in seven European countries: Belgium, Finland, France, Germany, Italy, Spain and the United Kingdom. Data were collected by local teams from each country (using a variety of commercial and proprietary sources) and checked for reliability and consistency by a centralized data collection unit. All firms included in the dataset are young (i.e. less than 20 years of age) and operate in high-tech industries. A detailed description of the sampling process and the sample distribution of the VICO database can be found in Bertoni and Pellón (2011).

In this work we focus on all manufacturing companies from the VICO dataset. The decision to limit the study to manufacturing companies and to exclude service companies is motivated by the attempt to build a sample with sufficient homogeneity in the modes of investment. While investments for high-tech manufacturing companies are significantly correlated with fixed assets (tangible and intangible), the same does not apply to service companies, such as software companies, whose investments are mostly expensed and do not appear on firms' balance sheets. We also exclude biotech companies from the sample since they follow an investment path that is substantially different from all other high-tech manufacturing companies. A further election with respect to the whole VICO sample is the exclusion of German companies which is motivated by the lack of accounting information necessary for this study (in

Germany only large companies are mandated to deposit detailed accounts at Chambers of Commerce). We also excluded companies backed by other types of VC investors, such as banks and corporations.

Restricting the VICO dataset according to these criteria and considering firms for which accounting data are available, we obtain a sample of 1312 companies, 74 of which are VC-backed. As previously discussed, in this work we consider as *xVC*-backed a firm that receives financing from an *xVC* or a syndicate of investors led by an *xVC*. An *xVC* type is defined as lead investor in a syndicate based on a hierarchical criterion. In the majority of cases secondary sources included in the VICO database indicate the identity of lead investor. When this information is not available, we assumed that among the investors involved in a particular round of financing, the lead investor is the one investing the highest amount. When the invested amount is not available we use equity interest. When neither amount nor equity interest are available we assume the lead investor to be the one located at the minimum distance to the company. According to these criteria, we identify 49 firms backed by an IVC and 32 firms backed by a PVC, with seven cases in which both investor types are involved at different stages. Table 5.1 reports the distribution of sample firms across industries, countries and foundation dates.

The largest industry in our sample is information and communication technology (ICT) manufacturing, with 874 companies (66.62 per cent of the sample). This is also the industry where most IVC and PVC investments are concentrated (77.55 per cent and 56.25 per cent). In relative terms, IVC seems to be more focused in ICT manufacturing than PVC, which is instead relatively more focused in aerospace and robotics. This difference in the relative presence of IVC and PVC in manufacturing sectors is broadly consistent with the study by Bertoni et al. (2012) on the patterns of VC investments in Europe. We also observe differences in the relative presence of IVC and PVC in different countries. In particular, the UK represents 22.45 per cent of IVC but only 9.38 per cent of PVC investments. To the other extreme, Spain represents 12.24 per cent of IVC and 34.38 per cent of PVC. These sectoral and country differences prove to be extremely useful in our analysis because they represent exogenous variations in the likelihood of firms to receive IVC and PVC that make the GMM approach of instrumenting VC variables much stronger. Finally, there is little difference between IVC and PVC in the foundation period of their portfolio companies (a $\chi^2$ test does not reject at conventional confidence levels the null hypothesis that the two underlying distributions are equal $\chi^2(3) = 2.28$).

*Entrepreneurial business and society*

*Table 5.1   Sample composition by industry, country, and foundation period*

|  | All sample | | IVC-backed | | PVC-backed | |
| --- | --- | --- | --- | --- | --- | --- |
|  | N | % | N | % | N | % |
| *Industry* | | | | | | |
| Aerospace and robotics | 318 | 24.24 | 5 | 10.20 | 10 | 31.25 |
| ICT manufacturing | 874 | 66.62 | 38 | 77.55 | 18 | 56.25 |
| Pharmaceutical | 120 | 9.15 | 6 | 12.24 | 4 | 12.50 |
| Total | 1312 | 100.00 | 49 | 100.00 | 32 | 100.00 |
| *Country* | | | | | | |
| Belgium | 90 | 6.86 | 7 | 14.29 | 1 | 3.13 |
| Finland | 205 | 15.63 | 12 | 24.49 | 7 | 21.88 |
| France | 139 | 10.59 | 7 | 14.29 | 4 | 12.50 |
| Italy | 341 | 25.99 | 6 | 12.24 | 6 | 18.75 |
| Spain | 337 | 25.69 | 6 | 12.24 | 11 | 34.38 |
| UK | 200 | 15.24 | 11 | 22.45 | 3 | 9.38 |
| Total | 1312 | 100.00 | 49 | 100.00 | 32 | 100.00 |
| *Foundation* | | | | | | |
| 1984–89 | 321 | 24.47 | 3 | 6.12 | 1 | 3.13 |
| 1990–94 | 350 | 26.68 | 13 | 26.53 | 10 | 31.25 |
| 1995–99 | 362 | 27.59 | 23 | 46.94 | 12 | 37.50 |
| 2000–2004 | 279 | 21.27 | 10 | 20.41 | 9 | 28.13 |
| Total | 1312 | 100.00 | 49 | 100.00 | 32 | 100.00 |

*Source:*   Authors' calculation on a sample extracted from the VICO dataset.

Some interesting insights on the characteristics of IVC and PVC invest-ments can be gained by looking at the descriptive statistics in Table 5.2, reporting mean values and standard deviations of the variables used in the regression models. In order to obtain some preliminary evidence, we also perform a t-test on the difference between non-VC-backed and IVC- or PVC-backed companies.

*Table 5.2    Description of key variables*

Panel A: Descriptive statistics of variables used in the econometric models

| | All sample | No VC | IVC-backed | | PVC-backed | |
|---|---|---|---|---|---|---|
| $I_{i,t}/K_{i,t-1}$ | 0.55 | 0.54 | 0.61 | | 0.62 | |
| | (1.11) | (1.10) | (1.02) | | (1.20) | |
| $\Delta y_{i,t}$ | 0.09 | 0.08 | 0.24 | *** | 0.24 | *** |
| | (0.46) | (0.41) | (0.62) | | (0.53) | |
| $ITA_{i,t}/K_{i,t-1}$ | 0.36 | 0.35 | 0.55 | *** | 0.56 | *** |
| | (0.50) | (0.49) | (0.53) | | (0.60) | |
| $B_{i,t}/K_{i,t-1}$ | 8.37 | 8.49 | 6.38 | ** | 5.71 | *** |
| | (13.86) | (13.98) | (11.79) | | (9.51) | |
| $C_{i,t}/K_{i,t-1}$ | 0.91 | 0.97 | −0.46 | *** | 0.20 | *** |
| | (2.41) | (2.41) | (2.03) | | (2.02) | |
| $age_{i,t}$ | 10.02 | 10.11 | 8.57 | *** | 7.54 | *** |
| | (5.29) | (5.31) | (4.26) | | (4.23) | |

Panel B: Investment rounds and average invested amount

| | IVC-backed firms | PVC-backed firms |
|---|---|---|
| Single investment round | 29 [59.18%] | 25 [78.13%] |
| Two investment rounds | 12 [24.49%] | 5 [15.63%] |
| Three or more investment rounds | 8 [16.33%] | 2 [6.24%] |
| Average amount invested per round (million €) | 3.26 | 1.62 |

*Notes:*
Mean values of variables included in equations (5.1)–(5.2). Standard deviations in round brackets. Percentage of column total in squared brackets.
Column 'No VC' in Panel A is computed on all firm-year observation corresponding on non-VC-backed companies. Figures in columns 'IVC-backed' and 'PVC-backed' in Panel A are computed on firm-year observations for which the condition is the firm is, respectively, IVC- or PVC-backed.
All ratios are winsorized at the 2% threshold. All monetary amounts are deflated using country-level Consumer Price Index (2005 used as reference year).
In Panel A mean values of IVC- and PVC-backed firms are compared to non-VC-backed firms through t-test whose significance level is: * p-value<10%; ** p-value<5%*** ; p-value<1%.

*Source:*    Authors' calculation on a sample extracted from the VICO dataset.

In our sample the mean investment rate $I_{it}$ is 0.55. This value is substantially higher than that reported by Engel and Stiebale (2009), consistent with the fact that our sample is composed only of young high-tech companies that invest significantly more than older companies in more mature sectors. The figure is instead similar to the median investment rate reported by Bertoni et al. (2010), who analyse a sample of companies more comparable to ours. The cash flow rate, whose average is 0.91, is higher than the investment rate. However, if we look at how investment and cash flow rates vary across different groups, we see that non-VC-backed companies invest, on average, substantially less than their cash flow (0.54 against 0.97), while the opposite occurs for VC-backed companies. An IVC-backed company invests slightly more than a non-VC-backed one (0.61) but on average it has negative cash flows (–0.46). The difference in the average investment rate between non-VC-backed and IVC-backed firms is not statistically significant, while the difference in cash flows is highly significant. Similarly, a PVC-backed company has an investment rate of 0.62 (again, the difference with respect to non-VC-backed companies is not significant), but its cash flow rate is significantly lower (and significant at a 99 per cent confidence level). In addition, no significant differences appear among IVC- and PVC-backed companies in either cash flow ratio or investment ratio.

Panel B in Table 5.2 reports some interesting statistics on the financial support provided by IVC and PVC investors. In absolute terms, at any round, the financial support provided by IVC is higher than that of PVC. On average, an IVC-backed firm receives €3.26 million per financing round, while the corresponding figure for PVC-backed firms is €1.62 million. Moreover, IVC investors participate in more follow-on rounds of financing. Among IVC-backed firms, 16.33 per cent receive three or more rounds of financing, while this occurs only for 6.24 per cent of PVC-backed firms. On the contrary, only 59.18 per cent of IVC-backed companies receive only one round of financing, while this occurs for 78.13 per cent of PVC-backed firms. This simple univariate comparison suggests that the direct financial support provided by IVC is higher than that of PVC.

## RESULTS

Table 5.3 reports the estimates of equations (5.1) and (5.2). Models (I), (II) and (III) in Table 5.3 are different estimates of equation (5.1), while models (IV), (V) and (VI) refer to equation (5.2). In models (I) and (IV) all instruments are included in the analysis, while in models (II) and (V) we exclude the additional instruments described earlier, so that estimates are based only on internal moment conditions. Finally, models (III) and (VI) include the control for survivorship bias.

Before moving to the parameters of interest, it is worth pointing out that, in all estimates, the validity of the overidentifying restrictions (Hansen test) is never rejected. The same holds for external instruments included in models (I) and (IV). Furthermore AR(1) and AR(2) tests of the null hypothesis of, respectively, no first-order or second-order serial correlation, always behave as required for the consistency of the estimates. Finally, the control for survivorship in model (III) and model (VI) is not statistically significant; this indicates that survivorship does not seem to significantly bias our results.

In all estimates we observe, as expected, that investments are positively correlated with sales growth, debt and, especially, cash flows. A non-VC-backed company exhibits, on average, a degree of correlation between investments and cash flow that is both statistically significant and economically relevant. An increase in the firm's current cash flows equal to 10 per cent of the firm's stock of tangible and intangible assets yields an increase in current investment rate of around 1.3 per cent. This amount is of the same order of magnitude as that found by Bertoni et al. (2010) (between 1.9 per cent and 2.3 per cent in Table 4) and by Engel and Stiebale (2009) (1.7 per cent to 2.2 per cent in Tables 7 and 8). Following the earlier discussion, we interpret this positive investment–cash flow sensitivity as confirmatory evidence that high-tech companies in Europe are financially constrained.

Let us first focus on the impact of IVC and PVC on a firm's investment rate. We begin the analysis of the role of IVC and PVC by the estimates of equation (5.1) in models (I)–(III). If we take a look at the impact of VC financing on a firm's investment rate, we note that the coefficient $\varphi_{IVC}$ is positive and significant in the three estimates (at a 95 per cent confidence level). On average, the presence of IVC generates a stable increase in a firm's investments between 0.27 and 0.31. The size of this increase is economically significant if compared to the average investment rate of an IVC-backed firm: that is, 0.66, from Table 5.2. Conversely, our estimates of the impact of PVC on the firm's investment rate is very close to zero in absolute terms and not statistically different from zero at customary confidence levels. PVC seems not to be able to increase the long-term level of investments of its portfolio companies.

Table 5.3  Estimates of dynamic sales accelerator models

| | Model I | Model II | Model III | Model IV | Model V | Model VI |
|---|---|---|---|---|---|---|
| $I_{i,t-1}/K_{i,t-2}$ | -0.0294 | -0.0306 | -0.0277 | -0.0226 | -0.0234 | -0.0221 |
| | (0.026) | (0.025) | (0.022) | (0.024) | (0.024) | (0.024) |
| $\Delta y_{i,t}$ | 0.1155 | 0.1046 | 0.1085 | 0.1726 * | 0.1628 | 0.1714 * |
| | (0.107) | (0.109) | (0.102) | (0.098) | (0.100) | (0.099) |
| $\Delta y_{i,t-1}$ | 0.1418 ** | 0.1419 ** | 0.1256 ** | 0.1373 *** | 0.1383 *** | 0.1397 *** |
| | (0.061) | (0.057) | (0.061) | (0.052) | (0.052) | (0.053) |
| $ITA_{i,t-1}/K_{i,t-2}$ | 0.0471 | 0.0501 | 0.0482 | 0.0077 | 0.0098 | 0.0090 |
| | (0.064) | (0.064) | (0.060) | (0.061) | (0.061) | (0.060) |
| $B_{i,t-1}/K_{i,t-2}$ | 0.0090 *** | 0.0091 *** | 0.0091 *** | 0.0087 ** | 0.0088 ** | 0.0087 ** |
| | (0.004) | (0.004) | (0.003) | (0.004) | (0.004) | (0.004) |
| $C_{i,t-1}/K_{i,t-2}$ | 0.1292 *** | 0.1283 *** | 0.1299 *** | 0.1333 *** | 0.1312 *** | 0.1317 *** |
| | (0.028) | (0.028) | (0.030) | (0.030) | (0.030) | (0.031) |
| $D_{i,t}^{IVC}$ | 0.2803 ** | 0.2730 ** | 0.3144 ** | 0.1288 | 0.1225 | 0.1607 |
| | (0.142) | (0.139) | (0.134) | (0.118) | (0.123) | (0.132) |
| $D_{i,t}^{PVC}$ | -0.0234 | -0.0294 | 0.0008 | 0.0567 | 0.0578 | 0.0613 |
| | (0.123) | (0.121) | (0.128) | (0.129) | (0.128) | (0.130) |
| $D_{i,t}^{IVC} C_{i,t}/K_{i,t-1}$ | -0.0841 | -0.0838 | -0.0815 | -0.0705 | -0.0684 | -0.0705 |
| | (0.054) | (0.054) | (0.050) | (0.055) | (0.055) | (0.054) |
| $D_{i,t}^{PVC} C_{i,t}/K_{i,t-1}$ | 0.0613 | 0.0632 | 0.0635 | 0.0811 | 0.0833 | 0.0739 |
| | (0.115) | (0.115) | (0.105) | (0.116) | (0.114) | (0.117) |
| $age_{i,t}$ | -0.0216 *** | -0.0220 *** | -0.0200 *** | -0.0207 *** | -0.0209 *** | -0.0163 *** |
| | (0.003) | (0.003) | (0.005) | (0.003) | (0.003) | (0.005) |

| | (I) | (II) | (III) | (IV) | (V) | (VI) |
|---|---|---|---|---|---|---|
| $A^{IVC}_{i,t-1}/K_{i,t-1}$ | -0.0362 | -0.0422 | -0.0422 | | | |
| | (0.029) | (0.038) | (0.039) | | | |
| $A^{IVC}_{i,t-2}/K_{i,t-2}$ | 0.0481*** | 0.0487*** | 0.0482*** | | | |
| | (0.017) | (0.016) | (0.016) | | | |
| $A^{PVC}_{i,t-1}/K_{i,t-1}$ | 0.0912*** | 0.0882*** | 0.0895*** | | | |
| | (0.005) | (0.006) | (0.005) | | | |
| $A^{PVC}_{i,t-2}/K_{i,t-2}$ | -0.0018 | -0.0020 | -0.0020 | | | |
| | (0.002) | (0.003) | (0.003) | | | |
| $IMR_{it}$ | -0.4789 | | | -0.2437 | | |
| | (0.545) | | | (0.611) | | |
| Constant | 0.4150*** | 0.4096*** | 0.4008*** | 0.3795*** | 0.3816*** | 0.3746*** |
| | (0.068) | (0.064) | (0.064) | (0.065) | (0.062) | (0.062) |
| N. Obs. | 8031 | 8036 | 8036 | 8031 | 8036 | 8036 |
| N. firms | 1312 | 1312 | 1312 | 1312 | 1312 | 1312 |
| Hansen test | 330.025 [499] | 322.657 [496] | 329.778 [500] | 339.785 [436] | 332.839 [433] | 339.833 [437] |
| AR(1) | -11.293*** | -11.370*** | -11.331*** | -11.505*** | -11.200*** | -11.095*** |
| AR(2) | -0.353 | -0.372 | -0.367 | -0.209 | -0.281 | -0.2707 |

*Notes:*

Estimates of sales accelerator model reported in equations (5.1) and (5.2). Country, industry and time dummies are also included in the estimates (coefficients omitted for clarity).

All ratios are winsorized at the 2% threshold. Estimates are derived from two-step system GMM with finite sample correction (Windmeijer 2005). AR(1) and AR(2) are tests of the null hypothesis of, respectively, no first- or second-order serial correlation. Hansen is a test of the validity of the overidentifying restrictions based on the efficient two-step GMM estimator.

In columns (I) and (IV) fundraising of IVC and PVC in the relevant country is added to the moment conditions as exogenous instrument. Standard errors in round brackets; degrees of freedom in square brackets. ***, ** and * indicate, respectively, significance levels of <1%, <5% and <10%.

*Source:* Authors' calculation on a sample extracted from the VICO dataset.

It is useful to compare these results with those obtained from the estimation of equation (5.2), in models (IV)–(VI). First, we observe that the coefficient $\phi_{IVC}$ is no longer significant. Since the difference between equations (5.1) and (5.2) is that the latter includes a control for the amount invested, this evidence suggest that the impact of IVC on the firm's investment rate can be explained by the direct effect of IVC: capital injections by IVC boost the firm's investments, as indicated by the coefficient $\gamma_{2,IVC}$, which is positive and significant at a 99 per cent level. Quite interestingly, we observe a similar (and even stronger) impact of $\gamma_{1,PVC}$ on the investment rate. In other words, one euro of VC investment coming from IVC generates an increase in the firm's investment of around 0.05, while this increase is around 0.09 if the money comes from a PVC investor. Despite this evidence, as previously mentioned, the coefficient $\varphi_{PVC}$ reported in columns (I)–(III) is never significant. This can be explained by going back to Panel B in Table 5.2: PVC provides portfolio companies with a lower amount of capital and, more importantly, participates in fewer follow-on rounds than IVC. Therefore, the increase in the firm's investment rate following capital infusions from PVC (i.e. a direct effect) occurs less often than happens with IVC. The result is that PVC-backed firms receive too little direct financial support to increase their equilibrium investment rate.

We also observe a difference in the time lag between the capital injection and the actual increase in the firm's investments in IVC- and PVC-backed companies. The impact of PVC seems to be immediate, while that of IVC is not significant until the year after the round occurs. A rationale can be found in the work of Bottazzi et al. (2008), who show how IVC is more active than PVC in terms of hiring new key personnel and interacting with entrepreneurs. These activities typically take time to become effective, and this may delay the actual investment pattern of an invested firm. On the contrary, PVC is more of a silent investor, so that when a firm receives a cash injection it may use it immediately to finance its investment opportunities.

A second, and possibly more interesting, aspect about the influence of VC on the firm's investment decisions is whether it is effective in relaxing its sensitivity to cash flows. This effect is captured by the $\delta_{xVC}$ coefficients in equations (5.1) and (5.2). We find, again, significant differences between IVC and PVC. To evaluate this effect we look at the total sensitivity of investments to cash flows for companies that have been financed by different investors, obtained by linear combinations of parameters in Table 5.3. Columns (I)–(VI) in Table 5.4 report the estimate for the linear combination $\beta_6 + \delta_{xVC}$ for each type of investor.

*Table 5.4   Investment cash-flow sensitivity for firms backed by different VC investors and non-VC-backed firms*

|  | Model I | Model II | Model III | Model IV | Model V | Model VI |
|---|---|---|---|---|---|---|
| No VC | 0.1292*** | 0.1283*** | 0.1299 *** | 0.1333 *** | 0.1312 *** | 0.1317*** |
|  | (0.028) | (0.028) | (0.030) | (0.030) | (0.030) | (0.031) |
| IVC-backed | 0.0451 | 0.0445 | 0.0485 | 0.0628 | 0.0628 | 0.0645 |
|  | (0.0463) | (0.0458) | (0.0419) | (0.0448) | (0.0449) | (0.0458) |
| PVC-backed | 0.1905 * | 0.1915 * | 0.1935  * | 0.2144  * | 0.2145  * | 0.2056  * |
|  | (0.1153) | (0.1159) | (0.1077) | (0.1182) | (0.1164) | (0.1208) |

*Notes:*
Estimates of cash flow sensitivity obtained from linear combination of parameters in Table 5.3.
Standard errors in round brackets. ***, ** and * indicate, respectively, significance levels of <1%, <5% and <10%.

*Source:*   Authors' calculation on a sample extracted from the VICO dataset.

We observe that the investment–cash flow sensitivity of IVC-backed companies is no longer statistically different from zero. This result is expected and confirms that obtained by other studies (e.g. Bertoni et al. 2010). The investment–cash flow sensitivity is also not statistically significant in models (IV)–(VI), where we control for cash injections in different financing rounds. This suggests that the firm's financial constraints are not relaxed merely as a result of the direct effect of IVC financing, but they are, at least in part, significantly reduced because of an indirect signalling effect. The investment–cash flow sensitivity of PVC-backed firms remains significant, even if only at a 90 per cent confidence level. Again, results on investment–cash flow sensitivity of PVC-backed firms are consistent between models. In other words, we do not find support for any beneficial direct or indirect effect of PVC financing on the firm's dependence on internal capital.

## CONCLUSIONS

Young high-tech companies suffer from capital market imperfections that VC might overcome. Our work shows that this is indeed the case when the investor is an IVC: IVC-backed firms are able to invest more in the long term and their investment policy is unaffected by shocks in their current cash flows.

The picture is substantially different when we consider PVC. The equilibrium investment rate of invested companies is unaffected by the presence of PVC. Investment–cash flow sensitivity of PVC-backed companies is of the same order of magnitude as that found in non-VC-backed companies. When controlling for the direct impact of PVC, we observe that financing translates into an immediate surge in investments, but we also observe that cash injections are too small and too rare to really make a difference in the investment path of PVC-backed companies. Finally, we find no indication that other investors rely on signals from PVC, creating an indirect positive effect on the portfolio firm's investments. VC investors may not have the credibility or the network of contacts that are needed to attract other VCs in the syndicate or to provide follow-on investment.

Our results may be interpreted in light of the work by Nightingale et al. (2009). The authors find that hybrid VC schemes have a limited impact on the performance of invested firms and argue that this may be explained by the 'thinness' of VC markets. The thinness of the VC market could be an important factor in explaining why PVC is not as effective as IVC, since PVC funds are more likely to be created exactly when the VC market is thin.

Our study adds to two streams of academic literature: the study of financial constraints and their determinants, and the effectiveness of (various types of) VC in affecting firm performance. Our work contributes to the growing literature on VC heterogeneity by studying the difference between IVC and PVC. While IVC has been thoughtfully studied, the impact of PVC on firms' investments is still largely unexplored. Controlling for the amount invested by VC in different rounds we are able to differentiate between the direct and the indirect effect of VC.

Our work also has some limitations that suggest possible directions of future research. We implicitly consider PVC as a homogenous category, ignoring its multiplicity in terms of governance structure, objectives and investment horizon. Understanding which types of PVC are most effective in relaxing the financial constraints of portfolio companies would be an interesting research question for a future study. Another issue that we do not study, but that is potentially very important, is the extent to which syndication between PVC and other VC investors may be effective, as suggested for instance by Bertoni and Tykvová (2012). The relevance of 'informal investors' (such as business angels) is another area of research that, due to limitations of our data, we could not address in this work, but that we believe is an extremely promising field of research.

Finally, it is important to highlight that our findings should by no means be taken as an indiscriminate criticism of PVC programmes. Our study focuses on portfolio companies, but PVC may actually have broader objectives including building links between universities and the private sector, supporting local development, creating high-skilled employment and supporting the development of the VC industry. An overall judgement of the impact of PVC should not be made before its effectiveness along all these dimensions is assessed. For instance, the presence of PVC could generate a higher number of high-tech start-ups in a region or country that may, in turn, attract IVC or other private sector investors, thus making the VC market less thin.

## ACKNOWLEDGEMENTS

We would like to thank two anonymous reviewers, Massimo G. Colombo, David Devigne, Frédéric Delmar, Gary Dushnitsky, Luca Grilli, Hans Landström, Sophie Manigart, Miguel Meuleman, Frédéric Perdreau, Tereza Tykvová, Thomas Åstebro, and all the participants in the conference on 'Entrepreneurial Finance' organized by the VICO project in Stresa (Italy) and the RENT XXV conference in Bodø (Norway). Support from the 7th European Framework Programme (Grant Agreement no. 217485) is gratefully acknowledged.

## REFERENCES

Bertoni, F., M.G. Colombo and A. Croce (2010), 'The effect of venture capital financing on the sensitivity to cash flow of firm's investments', *European Financial Management*, **16** (4), 528–551.
Bertoni, F., M. Colombo and A. Quas (2012), 'Patterns of venture capital investments in Europe', SSRN Working Paper Series (1920351).
Bertoni, F. and A. Croce (2011), 'Policy reforms for venture capital in Europe', in M. Colombo, L. Grilli, L. Piscitello and C.R. Lamastra (eds), *Science and Innovation Policy for the New Knowledge Economy*, Cheltenham, UK and Northampton, MA, USA: Edward Elgar, pp. 137–161.
Bertoni, F., J. Martí Pellón and M. Ferrer (2013), 'The different role played by venture capital and private equity investors on the investment activity of their portfolio firms', *Journal of Small Business Economics*, **40** (3), 607–633.
Bertoni, F. and M. Pellón (2011), 'Financing entrepreneurial ventures in Europe: the VICO dataset', SSRN Working Paper Series (1904297).

Bertoni, F. and T. Tykvová (2012), 'Which form of venture capital is most supportive of innovation?', ZEW Discussion Paper No. 12-018, Mannheim: ZEW.

Bond, S. and J. Van Reenen (2007), 'Microeconometric models of investment and employment', in J. Heckman and E. Leamer (eds), *Handbook of Econometrics*, Vol. 6, Amsterdam: Elsevier, pp. 4417–4498.

Bottazzi, L., M. Da Rin and T. Hellmann (2004), 'The changing face of the European venture capital industry facts and analysis', *Journal of Private Equity*, **7** (2), 26–53.

Bottazzi, L., M. Da Rin and T. Hellmann (2008), 'Who are the active investors? Evidence from venture capital', *Journal of Financial Economics*, **89** (3), 488–512.

Brander, J.A., E. Egan and T.F. Hellmann (2010), 'Government sponsored versus private venture capital: Canadian evidence', in J. Lerner and A. Schoar (eds), *International Differences in Entrepreneurship*, Chicago, IL: University of Chicago, pp. 275–320.

Carpenter, R.E. and B.C. Petersen (2002), 'Is the growth of small firms constrained by internal finance?', *Review of Economics and Statistics*, **84** (2), 298–309.

Cleary, S. (1999), 'The relationship between firm investment and financial status', *Journal of Finance*, **54** (2), 673–692.

Cleary, S. (2006), 'International corporate investment and the relationships between financial constraint measures', *Journal of Banking and Finance*, **30** (5), 1559–1580.

Colombo, M.G., A. Croce and M. Guerini (2012), 'Is the Italian government effective in relaxing the financial constraints of high-tech firms? An analysis by firm's size, age and geographical area', *Prometheus*, **30** (1), 73–96.

Cumming, D. and J. MacIntosh (2004), 'Canadian labour sponsored venture capital corporations: bane or boon?', in A. Ginsberg and I. Hasan (eds), *New Venture Investment: Choices and Consequences*, Amsterdam: Elsevier, pp. 169–200.

Cumming, D. and J. MacIntosh (2006), 'Crowding out private equity: Canadian evidence', *Journal of Business Venturing*, **21**, 569–609.

Da Rin, M., G. Nicodano and A. Sembenelli (2006), 'Public policy and the creation of active venture capital markets', *Journal of Public Economics*, **90** (8–9), 1699–1723.

Engel, D. and J. Stiebale (2009), 'Private equity, investment and financial constraints: firm-level evidence for France and the United Kingdom', Ruhr Economic Papers 126, Berlin, Germany.

Fazzari, S., R.G. Hubbard and B. Petersen (1988), 'Financing constraints and corporate investment', NBER Working Paper 2387, Cambridge, MA: National Bureau of Economic Research.

Gompers, P. and J. Lerner (1999), 'An analysis of compensation in the US venture capital partnership', *Journal of Financial Economics*, **51**, 3–44.

Guariglia, A. (2008), 'Internal financial constraints, external financial constraints, and investment choice: evidence from a panel of UK firms', *Journal of Banking and Finance*, **32** (9), 1795–1809.

Hsu, D.H. (2004), 'What do entrepreneurs pay for venture capital affiliation?', *Journal of Finance*, **59** (4), 1805–1844.

Jääskeläinen, M., M. Maula and G. Murray (2007), 'Profit distribution and compensation structures in publicly and privately funded hybrid venture capital funds', *Research Policy*, **36** (7), 913–929.

Kaplan, S.N. and L. Zingales (1997), 'Do investment–cash flow sensitivities provide useful measures of financing constraints', *Quarterly Journal of Economics*, **112** (1), 169–215.

Kaplan, S.N. and L. Zingales (2000), 'Investment–cash flow sensitivities are not valid measures of financing constraints', *Quarterly Journal of Economics*, **115** (2), 707–712.

Lee, P.M. and S. Wahal (2004), 'Grandstanding, certification and the underpricing of venture capital backed IPOs', *Journal of Financial Economics*, **73** (2), 375–407.

Leleux, B. and B. Surlemont (2003), 'Public versus private venture capital: seeding or crowding out? A pan-European analysis', *Journal of Business Venturing*, **18** (1), 81–104.

Lerner, J. (1999), 'The government as venture capitalist: the long-run impact of the SBIR program', *Journal of Business*, **72** (3), 285–318.

Lerner, J. (2002), 'When bureaucrats meet entrepreneurs: the design of effective public venture capital programmes', *Economic Journal*, **112** (477), F73–F84.

Luukkonen, T., M. Deschryvere and F. Bertoni (2013), 'The value added by government venture capital funds compared with independent venture capital funds', *Technovation*, **33** (4–5), 154–62.

Manigart, S. and W. Van Hyfte (1999), 'Post-investment evolution of Belgian venture capital backed companies: an empirical study', *Frontiers of Entrepreneurship Research*, Babson Center for Entrepreneurial Studies, http://digitalknowledge.babson.edu/fer/.

Mason, C.M. (2009), 'Public policy support for the informal venture capital market in Europe: a critical review', *International Small Business Journal*, **27** (5), 536–556.

Megginson, W.L. and K.A. Weiss (1991), 'Venture capitalist certification in initial public offerings', *Journal of Finance*, **46** (3), 879–903.

Nightingale, P., G. Murray, M. Cowling, C. Baden-Fuller, C. Mason, J. Siepel, M. Hopkins and C. Dannreuther (2009), 'From funding gaps to thin markets: UK government support for early stage venture capital', NESTA Research Report, University of Essex, UK.

Puri, M. and R. Zarutskie (2008), 'On the lifecycle dynamics of venture-capital- and non-venture-capital-financed firms', NBER Working Paper 14250, Cambridge, MA: National Bureau of Economic Research.

Semykina, A. and J. Wooldridge (2010), 'Estimating panel data models in the presence of endogeneity and selection: theory and application', *Journal of Econometrics*, **157** (2), 375–380.

Tykvová, T. (2006), 'How do investment patterns of independent and captive private equity funds differ? Evidence from Germany', *Financial Markets and Portfolio Management*, **20** (4), 399–418.

Windmeijer, F. (2005), 'A finite sample correction for the variance of linear efficient two-step GMM estimators', *Journal of Econometrics*, **126**, 26–51.

Wooldridge, J. (1995), 'Selection corrections for panel data models under conditional mean independence assumptions', *Journal of Econometrics*, **68**, 115–132.

Wright, M. and K. Robbie (1998), 'Venture capital and private equity: a review and synthesis', *Journal of Business Finance and Accounting*, **25**, 521–570.

# 6. A dynamic capability view on the determinants of superior performance in university technology transfer offices

**Mattia Bianchi, Davide Chiaroni, Federico Frattini and Tommaso Minola**

## INTRODUCTION

In addition to the more traditional mandates of teaching and research, universities have recently amplified their missions to become increasingly entrepreneurial (Siegel 2006). Academic entrepreneurship encompasses all the activities through which universities fulfil their 'third mission' (economic development): patenting, licensing, creating spin-offs, investing equity in start-ups, creating technology transfer offices (TTOs), incubators and science parks (Rothaermel et al. 2007). Within the broad field of university entrepreneurship, the analysis of the commercialization processes by technology transfer offices, usually the formal gateway between university and industry, focuses on the different mechanisms through which academic research and intellectual property (IP) is capitalized and commercially exploited. The topic of TTO productivity has been quite largely studied (Rothaermel et al. 2007). Prior research, in the attempt to identify the key determinants of technology transfer (TT) success, has mainly focused on the characteristics of inventions, such as patent protection and scope (e.g., Nerkar and Shane 2007; Shane 2002). Studies such as Hsu and Bernstein (1997), Chapple et al. (2005) and Thursby and Thursby (2002), however, have shown that the value of technologies is a not sufficient driver of TT success, as many worthy IP rights remain unlicensed. Indeed, due to high transaction costs characterizing the markets for technologies (Gambardella et al. 2007), only a minority of university inventions are transferred to the industry (Di Gregorio and Shane 2003).

There is indeed a need to expand the search for performance determinants to other classes of factors (Rothaermel et al. 2007). Specifically, this chapter focuses on the management and organization of TT activities as key levers to overcome market failure and increase the productivity of TTOs. The study of these aspects is particularly critical because of the complexity of the technology commercialization process, which occurs in conditions of high uncertainty. The embryonic and idiosyncratic nature of academic research makes it difficult to assess its commercialization potential (Ziedonis 2007). Also, the diversity of tasks involved in the TT process requires a broad range of competencies (Geuna and Muscio 2009), that is, technical, marketing, legal and proper organizational mechanisms to integrate such knowledge. The complexity of TT activities is reflected in the substantial heterogeneity of performance among the various universities (e.g., Chapple et al. 2005; Markman et al. 2005).

By tackling the following research question, 'How do different managerial and organizational approaches to technology transfer relate to different levels of performance?', this chapter examines TT management and organization from a comprehensive standpoint. Adopting the dynamic capabilities perspective (Teece 2007) as theoretical lens, the chapter develops an interpretative framework, which aims to identify the managerial antecedents underlying superior capabilities in commercializing academic research. The model is then illustrated through the case of two Italian universities' TTOs, which have been active in TT for many years with very different degrees of success.

This work contributes to the literature on university TT in several ways. Firstly, the use of qualitative research is quite original – quantitative empirical research based on survey and patent data tend to dominate this literature – and allows an in-depth illustration of the technology transfer process as a whole. Secondly, the comprehensive description of technology transfer microfoundations is particularly relevant both theoretically, to grasp the underlying mechanisms and process dynamics of TT, and practically, to ascertain implications for the commercialization of academic knowledge. The literature on university TT is gaining in importance in entrepreneurship and management research; a growing community of scholars is collecting extensive evidence, especially on transfer performance and efficiency, but most research has an anecdotal and practice-oriented nature. Few papers adopt well-defined theoretical frameworks to explain transfer dynamics, thus robustly contributing to the debate. Following recent calls for an investigation of capabilities and skills as organizational dimensions of TTOs (e.g., Chapple et al. 2005), this chapter is, to our best knowledge, among the first research work that adopts the dynamic capabilities approach to interpret the phenomenon of

TT and to analyze its dynamics. Lastly, being our work based on a European Union (EU)-funded project, we follow Conti and Gaule (2011), who call for more investigation on the specificities of practices and performance of TTOs at the European level.

The chapter is structured as follows. The next sections develop the theoretical framework, review the existing literature and describe the methodology employed. This is followed by a section reporting and discussing the findings from the case studies. Finally, conclusions are drawn and some avenues for future research are outlined.

## THEORETICAL FRAMEWORK

The term 'technology transfer' refers to the process whereby an invention, technology and/or unstructured know-how deriving from academic research is transferred to another entity which is then responsible for its subsequent development and commercialization (Friedman and Silberman 2003). Several models have been proposed for the technology transfer process (Bercovitz et al. 2001; Rogers et al. 2000). Sorensen and Chambers (2008), for instance, mapped the major stages in a successful technology transfer transaction, breaking the process down into: receiving and handling new invention disclosures; evaluating the technology and, if worthy, patenting it; marketing the technology by identifying and contacting potential partners; negotiating the terms of the agreement; and finally, implementing the contract and actually transferring the technological knowledge to the recipient.

Responsibility over the execution of these activities typically lies within TTOs, intermediary offices in charge of commercializing research outcomes from their parent universities (Rothaermel et al. 2007). Although scholars disagree on the relevance of the role of TTOs in facilitating the relationship between university scientists and industry (Debackere and Veugelers 2005; Hülsbeck et al. forthcoming; Siegel et al. 2003), TTOs are widely acknowledged as the formal vehicles of university knowledge commercialization and the key players to determine the university's success in the TT process (Anderson et al. 2007; Caldera and Debande 2010). This view is supported by the strong attention of academic research to the topics of TTOs' operations and productivity (Rothaermel et al. 2007; Siegel et al. 2003).

This chapter aims to contribute to this stream of research by comprehensively exploring the drivers of performance in technology transfer by TTOs. Interestingly, anecdotal and empirical evidence reports a substantial heterogeneity of performance, with a few champions reaping the gains from commercialization of technologies (e.g. MIT, Stanford and the University of California) and the majority lagging behind. Indeed, despite a growing number of these structures being established, most TTOs have so far achieved disappointing results (Bianchi and Piccaluga 2012).

Notwithstanding the importance of social, non-monetary objectives for TTOs, performance in technology transfer has been typically conceptualized as the extent to which a TTO is capable of appropriating economic returns from investments in research by the parent university, that is, the share of economic value that accrues to the academic technology holder from the exploitation of its technologies (Bercovitz et al. 2001; Sorensen and Chambers 2008). Performance measurements depend on the contractual forms chosen for TT and thus include, for example, the number of licensing agreements and related revenues, earnings from the sale of patents, the amount of sponsored research and the value of equity positions in spin-offs (Rothaermel et al. 2007). Other more qualitative measures such as management satisfaction with TT activities and the degree of achievement of TT objectives also constitute TT performance. Given the exploratory nature of this chapter, we define TT performance *lato sensu* and hereby include all the above outputs.

Using the literature as a guideline to unearth and define the set of concepts and relationships that are important for investigation (Wacker 1998), a theoretical framework (Figure 6.1) is developed combining a number of factors that explain different levels of TT performance, that is, the dependent construct in our framework. These factors are grouped into three building blocks: TT resources, TT microfoundations and TT dynamic capabilities.

A first set of determinants, TT resources, refers to the pool of resources available to the TTO for the pursuit of TT activities. These can be thought of as the underlying assets, the 'raw materials' that serve as inputs to the TT 'production'. Among these, the quantity and quality of technologies made available for transfer clearly affect TT performance. At the level of the single asset, prior research has identified different attributes of technology that increase its likelihood to be transferred: for example, the degree of novelty and quality of invention (Nerkar and Shane 2007), stronger and broader patent defensibility (Shane 2002), and the stage of development (Jensen and Thursby 2001). At the organizational level, the extant literature has shown that universities generating more and higher-quality disclosed discoveries, employing eminent faculty from an intellectual point of view, attracting a larger amount of research funding and having higher institutional prestige, are more likely to achieve superior TT performance (Chapple et al. 2005; Di Gregorio and Shane 2003; Jensen et al. 2003; Rogers et al. 2000; Sine et al. 2003).

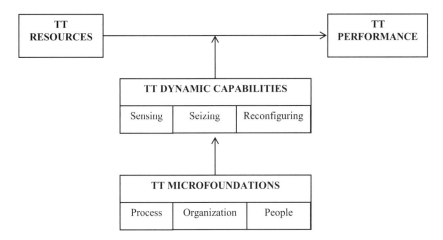

*Figure 6.1   Theoretical framework*

Consistent with the resource-based theory (Barney 1991), these findings show that TTO performance differences may arise from firms' resources that are valuable, rare, inimitable and non-substitutable (VRIN).

The framework developed in this chapter thus posits that greater resource endowments in TTOs are conducive to higher performance in TT. However, it also argues that TT resources by themselves do not fully explain performance. This claim is supported by recent empirical studies. Thursby and Thursby (2002) find that, in a context of increasing patent applications by US universities, the number of licenses executed has declined, meaning that having a patent does not necessarily imply licensing it. Chapple et al. (2005) offer evidence of persistent inefficiencies by universities in the passage from TT inputs (disclosures, patents) to outputs (licenses signed). A qualitative study on 14 TT deals carried out by Hsu and Bernstein (1997) shows that many intellectual property rights (IPRs) remain unlicensed, even though they have a strong potential, and that the managerial effort from the inventor and the appropriate design of licenses' remuneration structure are equally critical components to the successful outcome of a TT transaction. These contributions suggest that simple explanations related to resource endowments do not sufficiently explain the variation in technology transfer efficiencies. Additional characteristics must be examined, such as the impact of TT managerial practices and of organizational systems (Anderson et al. 2007). Indeed, Caldera and Debande (2010) show that universities with established policies and procedures for the management of technology transfer perform better.

Therefore we advance that the management and organization of TT activities are critical sources of performance. The inherent complexities in trading technologies represent managerial challenges, which call the TTOs to adopt adequate organizational solutions and to develop management systems in order to overcome the severe transaction costs characterizing the markets for technologies (Gambardella et al. 2007). Prior studies have explored the managerial and organizational mechanisms that TTOs have in place to improve their productivity. First, a set of critical levers that distinguish successful TTOs from unsuccessful refers to the way the TT process is designed and implemented. Clear planning of TT activities, systematic evaluation of TT opportunities, networking with captive current licensees and involving faculty-inventors in the TT process are key activities for TT performance (Di Gregorio and Shane 2003; Debackere and Veugelers 2005; Hsu and Bernstein 1997). Caldera and Debande (2010) suggest that well-defined rules regulating the participation of researchers in TT and the potential conflicts of interest improve performance. Markman et al. (2005) find that the faster the TT process from input factors to commercialization output, the more productive the TTO. Secondly, scholars have found that the choice of organizational structures and systems influences TT performance through the shaping of reporting relationships, degree of autonomy and incentives (Rothaermel et al. 2007). Organizational factors such as high-powered reward systems for faculty involvement, compensation practices in the TTO, decentralized organizational structures, and efforts to reduce cultural barriers between universities and firms have been found beneficial to TT performance (Bercovitz et al. 2001; Lach and Schankerman 2004). Thirdly, some contributions show that the odds of success in TT depend on the characteristics and skills of the human resources involved in TT tasks. Siegel et al. (2003) report that a complementary pool of professionals with scientific and business backgrounds is beneficial to TTO productivity. Given the TT multidisciplinary nature, a broad range of skills is needed to cope with both technical and market uncertainty (Chesbrough 2003).

In our theoretical framework, we include the organizational and managerial practices of a TTO in the building block 'TT microfoundations'. Microfoundations are defined by Teece (2007: 1319) as 'the distinct skills, processes, procedures, organizational structures, decision rules and disciplines' associated with a particular business. In order to bring structure to the fragmented evidence of extant literature, we distinguish the microfoundations block in three categories: process, organization and people. The process category is intended to assess the following key aspects in the way TTOs manage the flow of TT activities:

the critical tasks performed to accomplish a technology deal, for example, the identification of potential licensees, the pricing of technological knowledge and negotiation; the structure of the process, in terms of, for example, the degree of systematization, its parallel or sequential design and the events that trigger its activation; and the managerial tools that support the execution of TT activities such as IP pricing methodologies, marketing channels and network management practices. Within the organization category, three main dimensions are analyzed: the micro-organizational characteristics of the TT organization, in terms of, for example, horizontal and vertical specialization and coordination mechanisms; the structural characteristics, for example, the degree of centralization, the level of formalization and hierarchy, and the establishment of special roles such as gatekeepers; and the design of hybrid organizational forms, such as the TT project team composition and the weight of leadership. Finally, the people category encompasses the educational background, expertise, attitudinal and behavioral traits of TT professionals.

By including these aspects in the microfoundations block, we aim to capture what it is in the management and organization of the TTO that influences TT outcomes. However, what influences an outcome is different from why the outcome occurs. Following Argote et al. (2003), we add to our theoretical framework a construct acting as the causal mechanism that explains why management affects TT performance. This construct is 'TT dynamic capabilities'. Differently put, we posit that the influence of managerial and organizational microfoundations on performance occurs through the development and strengthening of dynamic capabilities in transferring technologies to external entities.

The dynamic capabilities (DC) framework (Teece 2007) is an emerging paradigm in strategic management arguing that competitive advantage does not necessarily stem from scarce difficult-to-imitate firm-specific assets, but from how they are configured by managers. Eisenhardt and Martin (2000) conceptualize dynamic capabilities as a set of specific and identifiable strategic and organizational processes 'that create value for organizations within dynamic markets by manipulating resources into value-creating strategies'. Consistent with this definition, we advance that technology transfer can be regarded as a dynamic capability, that is, a high-level routine that converts technological potential into economic value (Caldera and Debande 2010). This interpretation is supported by the fact that the dynamic capability perspective has been adopted in the literature for looking into a number of phenomena similar to technology transfer, for example new product development (Deeds et al. 2000) and alliance formation (Kale et al. 2002). Amesse and Cohendet (2001) argue that success in managing outward technology transfer depends on the organization's emitting capacity, that is, the capability of emission of knowledge outside its frontier.

Based on Teece's (2007) taxonomy, we disaggregate the concept of TT dynamic capabilities into three critical functions: sensing promising TT opportunities; seizing the highest-potential TT opportunities; and reconfiguring assets and management systems associated with TT to maintain competitiveness. This latter function highlights the dynamic character of the TT capability, which is geared toward flexibility in order to best respond to the specific contextual conditions in which TT occurs and toward organizational renewal to match the requirements of a changing environment.

Superior sensing, seizing and reconfiguring may be achieved through specific organizational and managerial solutions adopted by the TTO. For instance, initiatives that mobilize the networks of key people within the university can facilitate the identification of TT opportunities through the scanning of external technology and marketing environment, which is at the heart of the sensing function (Rasmussen and Borch 2010). On the other hand, the seizing component refers to the prompt and efficient implementation of TT transactions, which can be fostered by well-defined university policies that clearly regulate the allocation of resources and investments to TT projects (Caldera and Debande 2010). Finally, the reconfiguring function emphasizes the need for improving the management of TT over time, which calls for TT professionals who possess an entrepreneurial attitude and are stimulated by high-powered incentives (Siegel et al. 2003).

In our theoretical framework TT dynamic capabilities are suggested to play a moderating role. This accounts for the fact that a firm may have assets potentially able to drive superior TT performance, yet lack the dynamic capabilities to fully realize their potential. Conversely, a high level of dynamic capabilities reinforces the positive relationship between TT resources and TT performance. The rationale is that, while the underlying sources of value to the TTO are the technologies made available for commercialization, it is the effective use of dynamic capabilities, developed through appropriate managerial and organizational choices, that enables it to extract higher share of returns from TT.

To conclude, with this study we move away from resource-based explanations and, following recent calls (Chapple et al. 2005; Lockett and Wright 2005), we adopt a dynamic capability perspective to provide a comprehensive analysis of the managerial and organizational drivers of TT performance in technology transfer. A capability-based approach appears to be suitable for the aim of this chapter, for different reasons. Firstly, it enables a focus on processes rather than on strategies and resources (Rasmussen and Borch 2010). Secondly, it offers a framework to study the complex set of tasks and actors involved in TT at multiple levels. Thirdly, it is supported by preliminary studies that find a positive impact of TTO experience on performance (Markman et al. 2005; Rogers et al. 2000). The existence of learning-by-doing effects is consistent with the path-dependent nature of capabilities, which are built over time through experience.

## METHODOLOGY

This research has been performed within the context of an EU-funded project, specifically in the Tempus framework. The goal of the project was to generate new knowledge and tools and to support institutional reforms to foster entrepreneurial university systems in former communist countries. Following Rasmussen (2008), the project has tackled both structural reforms in the university sector and support to specific commercialization projects, based on EU members' advanced experience. The present research has been performed by the authors as a means to illustrate and analyze commercialization practices, and is part of a larger data collection from EU universities. Results from this activity have been processed with the aim of supporting proper strategy-making in newly established university TTOs (or equivalent organizations), and have also been presented in seminars and methodological workshops during the project development.

The empirical research employed a multiple case study analysis (Yin 2003). In particular, the chapter reports and discusses a rich empirical basis drawn from two leading Italian university TTOs, TTO.A and TTO.B (the real names of the firms have been changed for confidentiality reasons) engaged in commercializing academic research with very different degrees of success over a nine-year period of analysis (2000–2008). Our aim is to employ the case studies in order to illustrate the constructs and the logical relationships encompassed by the theoretical framework. As suggested by Siggelkow (2007: 22), the illustrative use of case studies is particularly powerful because 'by seeing a concrete example of every construct that is employed in a conceptual argument, the reader has a much easier time imagining how the conceptual argument might actually be applied to one or more empirical settings'. In order to pursue this illustrative objective, the selected TTOs need to be 'very special in the sense of allowing one to gain certain insights that other organizations would not be able to provide' (Siggelkow 2007: 20). This is why we choose to discuss and compare two 'extreme' cases of TTOs with very different levels of performance with the aim to identify contrasting patterns and relationships between the research constructs. This is particularly appropriate, as suggested by Swamidass and Vulasa (2009), in the case of university knowledge commercialization, in order to start gaining a deeper understanding of the reasons behind TTOs' superior performance.

For each TTO, we have undertaken two semi-structured interviews with key informants (managing director of the TTO and technology transfer senior manager for TTO.A; managing director of TTO and associate dean for technology transfer for TTO.B) with the aim to: (1) understand the extent to which their offices have developed over time a capability to effectively and efficiently manage technology transfer; (2) identify the managerial dimensions that have played a key role in nurturing this capability. Each interview lasted about two hours and was tape-recorded and transcribed; secondary sources of information (mainly internal reports, technology evaluation schemes and TT project documentation) were integrated, in a triangulation process, with the data drawn from the interviews, in order to avoid post hoc rationalization and retrospective interpretation (Yin 2003). In analyzing the information gathered through the case studies, we applied the following data manipulation techniques (Miles and Huberman 1984): (1) data categorization, which requires the decomposition and aggregation of data in order to highlight some characteristics (e.g., characteristics of the technologies available for transfer, design and structure of the TT process) and to facilitate comparisons; (2) data contextualization, which implies the analysis of contextual factors, not included in the conceptual model, that may reveal unforeseen relationships between events and circumstances; (3) preliminary within-case analysis, the purpose of which was to consider each case study as a separate one and to systematically document the variables of interest defined in the theoretical model. For each case study the manipulated information was aggregated in order to obtain a systematic description of the TT resources available to the TTO; the process, organizational and people-related solutions adopted by the TTO; the extent to which the TTO is able to sense TT opportunities, to seize them and to reconfigure its TT management systems; and finally, the level of TT performance achieved. Then, explanation-building procedures, which were grounded in the theoretical arguments that we put forth in the theoretical framework section, were applied so that the relationships between the critical research constructs could be spotted. Finally, (4) a cross-case analysis was undertaken for comparing the patterns that emerged in each case study in order to reach a general explanation of the observed phenomenon.

## FINDINGS AND DISCUSSION

The analysis of the experience of TTO.A and TTO.B with technology transfer allows us to discuss the theoretical framework presented above. The two TTOs under scrutiny show a very different TT performance, as presented in Table 6.1. Interestingly, however, the empirical evidence reveals that the stock of resources available for technology transfer (TT resources also reported in Table 6.1) does not explain by itself the aforementioned differences in TT performance. This is clear when comparing TTO.A and TTO.B, with the latter having a comparable portfolio of patents and higher number of researchers but earning revenues from TT at the end of the time period analyzed that were eight times lower than those of TTO.A.

*Table 6.1    TT performance and resources of the two case studies*

|  | TTO.A | TTO.B |
| --- | --- | --- |
| TT performance | • 26 licenses signed and 250 sponsored R&D contracts since 2000<br>• About €500 000 of yearly revenues in the period 2000–2004, up to €4.4 million in 2008 | • 3 licenses signed and 120 sponsored R&D contracts since 2000<br>• About €500 000 of yearly revenues since 2000 |
| TT resources | • 42 patents<br>• 550 researchers<br>• €44 million of research funding from public grants | • 41 patents<br>• 850 researchers<br>• €22 million of research funding from public grants |

Indeed, the mere possession of technologies and know-how does not automatically convert into higher TT performance. Consistent with our proposed theoretical framework, this result shows that an evaluation of outcomes grounded only on the resource-based theory does not hold, and points to the appropriateness of a dynamic capabilities perspective for studying antecedents of TT performance. The empirical evidence suggests that specific process and organizational mechanisms together with individual characteristics of the professionals engaged in TT are critical for the development within TTO.A of a dynamic capability in transferring technologies to the industry and play a clear moderating role between TT resources and TT performance in the studied cases. According to our framework, it is possible to investigate how the key microfoundations affect the dynamic capabilities of sensing, seizing and reconfiguring.

New opportunities for technology transfer come from both disclosures of inventions by the faculty (technology push trigger) or from expressions of interest (EOIs) in the university's research by firms (demand pull trigger). The importance of actively sensing for TT opportunities both inside and outside the university is clear when contrasting the two TTOs. The yearly average number of disclosures and EOI for TTO.A are respectively 40 and 100, whereas the same values for TTO.B are 10 and 20. Indeed, managers at TTO.A report having reached a satisfactory level of receptiveness to the different events triggering the TT process that allows them to catch weak signals; managers at TTO.B lament that they are able to make emerge only a minimum part of their parent institution's potential for TT. Table 6.2 shows the key microfoundations analyzed in the two TTOs, which explain differences in the TT dynamic capability of sensing new opportunities.

As opportunity creation requires both access to information and the ability to recognize opportunities (Teece 2007), antecedents to superior sensing can be recognized in the constant and systematic practices for networking (participation to conferences and forums to promote research and development – R&D – programs and know-how and develop contacts) and for scouting (programs to sensitize researchers toward TT, scan and foster disclosure of interesting R&D results) that TTO.A has in place. The definition by TTO.A of special roles within the organization acting as gatekeepers towards both university and external firms further strengthen the results from these practices, which TTO.B lacks or executes on an unsystematic basis. These practices emerge as critical for catching the attention of companies and researchers, guaranteeing broad exposure and enhancing the visibility of a TTO both inside and outside the university (Hsu and Bernstein 1997). Indeed, Shane (2002) finds that enriching the networks leads to richer opportunity recognition. In addition, a superior ability to recognize opportunities derives from the wealth of skills and knowledge owned by its professionals (Markman et al. 2005). Compared to people in TTO.B, who include a retired scientist and two administrative staff, the strong scientific background coupled with the extensive business experience of TTO.A's people represent a powerful mix with which to filter information and interpret new technological and market developments. Also, as argued by a TTO.A manager, 'TTO professionals need to speak the same language of researchers if they want to build trust and stimulate them'.

*Table 6.2    Microfoundations of the TT dynamic capability of sensing new TT opportunities*

|  | TTO.A | TTO.B |
|---|---|---|
| Process | TTO.A has in place an active scouting program for technologies within the faculty and also promotes sensitization campaigns to researchers by promoting R&D programs and scientific know-how currently under development in the university. Representatives of TTO.A participate frequently in events and national and international conferences in its scientific areas of interest. This contributed to creating a database of contacts with about 1700 firms and professionals. | In TTO.B there is no official procedure for disclosures of new discoveries from researchers who are reached through seminars periodically held by TTO.B staff members on intellectual property and new firm creation. Representatives of TTO.B participate occasionally in local conferences in the field of intellectual property. For establishing contacts with firms and potential partners for inventions TTO.B relays mostly on external entities (intermediaries and regional agencies): 'We try to act as a coordinator … we cannot do that alone.' |
| Organization | TTO.A is a for-profit dedicated business unit within a larger organization (offering other services to tenants and start-ups, and is also active as a conference center). TTO.A is organized in a functional structure, with 1 FTE (full-time equivalent staff member) dedicated to business development (i.e. to find opportunities among research conducted by the faculty) and 1 FTE dedicated to marketing and identification of partners (i.e. to increase the number of EOI – expressions of interest). Under the supervision of a Head who is in charge of planning, negotiation, monitoring, 1 FTE dedicated to negotiation and 1 FTE focused on prior art search and filing of patents, complete the picture of the organization of TTO.A. | TTO.B is a typical Industrial Liaison Office, composed by 3 FTE and is part of the Office of the Provost for Research, a not-for-profit organization within the University. In TTO.B two analysts (FTE) execute all activities within a TT project, under the direct supervision of the head of the Industrial Liaison Office (part time and focused on legal affairs related to TT activities) and of the Provost for Research (part time and focused on scientific evaluation of inventions). |

*Table 6.2*   (continued)

| People | Professionals working in TTO.A have a strong educational background in science (3 PhDs, 1 MSc) and engineering (1 MSc) disciplines; additional training in business administration: 2 staff persons has taken a MBA, one staff person has taken a Master in intellectual property management; 3 out of 5 people working in TTO.A have relevant industrial experience with an average of 10 years in R&D positions at pharmaceutical companies. | Provost of Research has a scientific background (Master of Science), served as R&D Director of an Italian firm for more than 10 years and is now retired. The Head of the Industrial Liaison Office is an experienced lawyer, whereas the 2 analysts are at the level of administrative staff and they took a refreshing course in technology transfer practices before joining TTO.B. |
| --- | --- | --- |

The relevance of seizing opportunities in technology transfer – that is, the capacity of addressing opportunities by promptly bringing forward disclosures and contacts – is clear when comparing the two TTOs. The average time to conclude a license by TTO.A is seven months, while licenses signed by TTO.B took more than one year. Also, over the period of analysis, TTO.A was able to license 25 per cent of its IP portfolio (some patents were also licensed to more than one firm), whereas the same indicator for TTO.B is below 10 per cent. Potential antecedents to the TT dynamic capability of seizing opportunities are listed in Table 6.3.

Among the antecedents to superior seizing of opportunities by TTO.A, the stage-gate design of its TT process with parallel phases of set duration allows the early disposal of poor opportunities and the timely investment of resources only in the most promising opportunities (Cooper and Kleinschmidt 1995). This is consistent with Hsu and Bernstein (1997), according to whom pursuing too many technologies might cause promising technologies to remain unlicensed as they compete with a greater number of unworthy technologies for scarce marketing resources. Also, the high level of delegation and empowerment of TT professionals allows quick and effective decision-making (Geanakoplos and Milgrom 1991), as decisions are made by the most informed specialists, who in this context of high technical and market uncertainty are the TTO professionals. Conversely, the multi-step procedure in TTO.B (where the decision of whether to invest in the commercialization of a technology is made first by a special committee, then by departments and finally by the board of directors of the university) represents a dysfunctional organizational mechanism that reduces seizing capacity from TTO.B. The

*Table 6.3    Microfoundations of the TT dynamic capability of seizing new TT opportunities*

|  | TTO.A | TTO.B |
|---|---|---|
| Process | TTO.A has introduced a structured stage-gate process for assessing the potential of innovations under scrutiny. The process, even if formally defined, is rather flexible: with different phases (e.g. prior art search and identification of potential partners) executed in parallel by dedicated professionals; and with a duration of each phase which is defined case by case accordingly to the characteristics of the ideas entering the process. | In TTO.B there is no a clear and predefined process for assessing the potential of new ideas. Once a new TT project is active the staff member who is in charge of it defines an ad hoc evaluation process, whose terms and timeline have to be formally approved by the Head of ILO and finally by the Provost of Research. |
| Organization | A low level of hierarchy characterizes the organization within TTO.A. Each professional is responsible for their own specific functional tasks and is in charge of setting the go/kill evaluation for each TT project. A high level of social support and informal sharing of ideas and procedures among members of TTO.A characterizes the working environment. A multidisciplinary steering committee exists with key faculty members at the university for defining long-term strategic goals of TTO.A. | TTO.B operates under a high level of hierarchy. Staff members prepare a summary of evaluation results for the scouted innovations; then there is a first check of strategic compliance made by a committee of faculty members, then the final decision on go/kill of the TT project is made by the board of directors of the university. Due to the absence of a formalized process and shared timeline for such approvals, decisions about TT projects require a significant amount of time. The same process is in place regardless the characteristics of the innovation under scrutiny. |

importance of timeliness and prompt commitment of resources for seizing opportunities is confirmed by Markman et al. (2005), who find that the faster a TTO can commercialize technologies, the greater its organizational outcomes.

Reconfiguring capacity delivers superior performance in technology transfer by allowing a TTO to maintain competitiveness as the business grows and external environment changes (Teece 2007). The importance of reconfiguring emerges to be critical when comparing the cases of TTO.A and TTO.B (see Table 6.4).

*Table 6.4    Microfoundations of the TT dynamic capability of reconfiguring for TT opportunities*

|  | TTO.A | TTO.B |
|---|---|---|
| Process | TTO.A undertook a major reconfiguring during 2004, in correspondence with the increase in performance. As far as processes are concerned, TTO.A worked on defining clear and structured routines. Standardized term sheets and option contracts are defined for different typologies of TT projects, leveraging relationships with a strong network of IP professionals in the UK and US. Separate standard contracts are made available for additional R&D services. Finally, during the negotiation phase an automatic software has been implemented for monitoring advances in contracts, exerting a strict control over exception to standard procedures and forcing termination clauses. | In TTO.B processes remained about the same during the period of analysis. Moreover, due to the fact that each staff member runs TT projects on their own, no standards have been developed and shared at TTO.B level. Severe difficulties are reported in the negotiation phase because contracting procedures from firms are often considered too strict and detailed. |
| Organization | TTO.A adopts informal coordination mechanisms, by setting weekly meetings for information sharing, and by coordinating the tasks of each professional by objectives related to their specialization. A performance-based reward system has consequently been introduced based on personal achievements (e.g. number of EOI – expressions of interest – collected) and execution of activities (e.g. performance in the stage-gate evaluation). | TTO.B adopts informal coordination mechanisms based on mutual adaption, which is particularly of help when defining who is in charge of a certain TT project. No incentives or reward systems are in place as TTO.B is considered like a central administrative office. Problems in setting such incentive systems are also envisioned due to the fact that TTO.B is part of a non-profit-making public university. |

Following the radical redesign of routines and organization of TT (e.g. functional specialization of professionals, introduction of option contracts, etc.) implemented in 2004, TTO.A has been able to double its performance in TT. On the contrary, the minor organizational changes operated by TTO.B in 2006 have not yet produced any significant improvement in performance. A key antecedent to superior reconfiguring may be the performance-based incentive system that TTO.A has in place (and TTO.B lacks) to reward its professionals according to the results achieved. This rewarding system encourages TTO.A professionals to continuously seek for more efficient and effective ways to execute TT so as to achieve higher performance. In doing so, it fosters an entrepreneurial attitude by professionals who are pushed to put increased effort and commitment in the achievement of objectives. The words of the TTO.A head confirm our interpretation: 'we are never satisfied … if we were, we would be rigid and static and this would mean missing many opportunities'. Finally, different levels of reconfiguring capacity may derive from different legal status of TTO.A and B parent institutions. In fact, according to Friedman and Silberman (2003), private universities are more likely than public universities to respond to changing environments surrounding technology transfer.

## DISCUSSION AND CONCLUSIONS

In light of the significant complexity of technology transfer and of the large discrepancies of performances between TTOs, this chapter focuses on the role of management and organization of technology transfer in driving organizational outcomes. Adopting the dynamic capabilities perspective as a theoretical lens to interpret empirical evidence from two case studies, the analysis unravels a number of managerial, organizational and individual aspects that appear to be associated with a superior capability in commercializing academic research. Table 6.5 provides a summary of the main findings.

The chapter is believed to be useful first of all to researchers in entrepreneurship, technology transfer and strategic management. Whereas the dynamic capabilities framework has been largely adopted in other management streams such as alliances and new product development (e.g., Deeds et al. 2000), this study is among the first to apply it to the context of university technology transfer. We therefore contribute to the literature in the direction suggested by Geuna and Muscio (2009), who highlight the importance and the need to analyze capabilities and skills in TTOs, as a means to bridge the cultural gap between the corporate and

*Table 6.5    Microfoundations of TT dynamic capabilities explaining
             superior performance in commercializing academic research*

| | |
|---|---|
| Process | • Constant and systematic networking practices (participation in events, conferences and creation of database of contacts)<br>• Constant and systematic scouting practices among researchers in university<br>• Formalized and structured evaluation process (stage-gate) for quick screening of ideas<br>• Standardized but flexible routines and documents |
| Organization | • High level of delegation and empowerment of TT professional<br>• High level of functional specialization<br>• Informal coordination mechanism based on shared objectives<br>• Performance-based incentive systems |
| People | • Strong scientific background coupled with an extensive business experience<br>• Entrepreneurial attitude and commitment to achieve objectives |

the academic contexts, to foster entrepreneurial behavior, and to enhance TTO performance.

We add to the literature on technology transfer by providing empirical evidence to the argument that proper approaches to TTO management and organization have a positive effect on university TT productivity (which has been recently questioned by works such as Hülsbeck et al. forthcoming). A holistic and comprehensive view of TT management and organization can only be gathered through qualitative evidence. Our qualitative in-depth research provides rich data on the TT phenomenon that significantly contribute to the extant literature, which is mostly based on quantitative analysis; in particular we have collected evidence on the relationship between dynamic capabilities, microfoundations and performance. To do so, we adopted a retrospective longitudinal perspective, which is particularly useful to analyze process dynamics and to overcome the limitations of existing cross-sectional studies.

Furthermore, this research speaks directly to three research works; with respect to Chapple et al. (2005) we move one step ahead in the quest for the determinants of TTO performance, addressing the need raised by the authors to advance our general understanding of the role of business skills and capabilities in TTOs. Our work is in the same direction of Lockett and Wright (2005), who suggest joint investigation of resource and capabilities for the analysis of spin-out creation process; we add to their work by enriching the description and understanding of what capabilities are and why are they important in the TTO context. We finally speak to Rasmussen and Borch (2010) by adopting the university TTO as a level of analysis and by encompassing the dynamic dimension, through a longitudinal analysis and an explicit focus on change in the TTO governance by university (George 2005).

This chapter represents a promising starting point for future confirmatory empirical research that statistically tests relationships between the constructs identified by our framework. As suggested by Markman et al. (2008), further research should delve into the heterogeneity of TTO outcomes. One of the limitations of this study is the measurement of the dependent variable, which focuses on economic outcomes. Further research should instead disentangle the different types of performance, including social and non-monetary aspects, for example, knowledge access and relationship with external stakeholders. Another major direction for future research on TTO process and performance is one that extends the domain of analysis: from a merely internal perspective, which is adopted in this chapter, research on TTO could look outwards (Bruneel et al. 2010) and consider TTO as an embedded organization. We also encourage scholars to include in future analysis the influence of social capital as well as of different types of stakeholders (Anderson et al. 2007), or the role of university structures such as incubators (Markman et al. 2008) in creating and deploying dynamic capabilities to generate returns to the commercialization process.

As far as managerial implications are concerned, the model developed in the chapter, and especially the rich empirical basis that it discusses, provides TT managers with a number of suggestions for organizing and managing TT that are likely to improve TTO performance. The chapter provides example of practices, tools and lessons that proved useful in the development of the project and guided the development of knowledge transfer centers at the universities from partner countries (Russia, Moldova and Kazakhstan). In particular, the description of the TTO process and the adoption of the dynamic capabilities perspective have been valuable for two main reasons: firstly, they allow the traditional tension between business and academia to be overcome (Ambos et al. 2008), which is particularly pronounced in the early stage of the creation of an entrepreneurial university; secondly, they drive the effort of TTO managers toward the development of properly educated and skilled staff, to bridge the cultural gaps between university dynamics and external environment as invoked by Siegel et al. (2003). This has set the background for an approach to the project that encompasses a top-down governance reform with an explicit university commitment toward the TTO, before the mere implementation of practices and structure (Rasmussen 2008). Although the capability-based perspective adopted here has a high level of generalizability, it is worth stressing that it has been of particular value in universities from emerging economies; indeed our research suggests that an acceleration in filling the gap in innovation and competitiveness of those regions may occur through a joint organizational effort on improving TT resources (inputs) based on excellent research, and consequently, TT performance (output) by means of an investment on the management, the organization and the capabilities of university TTOs.

## ACKNOWLEDGEMENT

The authors acknowledge financial support from the European Community through the TEMPUS framework (Project Agreement No. JPHES-144950-2008).

## REFERENCES

Ambos, T.C., K. Mäkelä, J. Birkinshaw and P. D'Este (2008), 'When does university research get commercialized? Creating ambidexterity in research institutions', *Journal of Management Studies*, **45** (8), 1424–1447.

Amesse, F. and P. Cohendet (2001), 'Technology transfer revisited from the perspective of the knowledge-based economy', *Research Policy*, **30** (9), 1459–1478.

Anderson, T.R., T.U. Daim and F.F. Lavoie (2007), 'Measuring the efficiency of university technology transfer', *Technovation*, **27** (5), 306–318.

Argote, L., B. McEvily and R. Reagans (2003), 'Managing knowledge in organizations: an integrative framework and review of emerging themes', *Management Science*, **49** (4), 571–582.

Barney, J. (1991), 'Firm resources and sustained competitive advantage', *Journal of Management*, **17**, 99–120.

Bercovitz, J., M. Feldman, I. Feller and R. Burton (2001), 'Organizational structure as a determinant of academic patent and licensing behavior: an exploratory study of Duke, Johns Hopkins, and Pennsylvania state universities', *Journal of Technology Transfer*, **26** (1–2), 21–35.

Bianchi, M. and A. Piccaluga (eds) (2012), *La Sfida del Trasferimento Tecnologico: Le Università Italiane si Raccontano*, Springer: Milan.

Bruneel, J., P. D'Este and A. Salter (2010), 'Investigating the factors that diminish the barriers to university–industry collaboration', *Research Policy*, **39** (7), 858–868.

Caldera, A. and O. Debande (2010), 'Performance of Spanish universities in technology transfer: an empirical analysis', *Research Policy*, **39** (9), 1160–1173.

Chapple, W., A. Lockett, D. Siegel and M. Wright (2005), 'Assessing the relative performance of UK university technology transfer offices: parametric and non-parametric evidence', *Research Policy*, **34** (3), 369–384.

Chesbrough, H. (2003), *Open Innovation: The New Imperative for Creating and Profiting from Technology*, Cambridge, MA: Harvard Business School Press.

Conti, A. and P. Gaule (2011), 'Is the US outperforming Europe in university technology licensing? A new perspective on the European Paradox', *Research Policy*, **40** (1), 123–135.

Cooper, R.G. and E.J. Kleinschmidt (1995), 'Benchmarking the firm's critical success factors in new product development', *Journal of Product Innovation Management*, **12**, 374–391.

Debackere, K. and R. Veugelers (2005), 'The role of academic technology transfer organizations in improving industry science links', *Research Policy*, **34** (3), 321–342.

Deeds, D., D. De Carolis and J. Coombs (2000), 'Dynamic capabilities and new product development in high technology ventures: an empirical analysis of new biotechnology firms', *Journal of Business Venturing*, **15** (3), 211 229.

Di Gregorio, D. and S. Shane (2003), 'Why do some universities generate more start-ups than others?', *Research Policy*, **32** (2), 209–227.

Eisenhardt, K.M. and J.A. Martin (2000), 'Dynamic capabilities: what are they?', *Strategic Management Journal*, **21**, 1105–1121.

Friedman, J. and J. Silberman (2003), 'University technology transfer: do incentives, management, and location matter?', *Journal of Technology Transfer*, **28** (1), 17–30.

Gambardella, A., P. Giuri and A. Luzzi (2007), 'The market for patents in Europe', *Research Policy*, **36** (8), 1163–1183.

Geanakoplos, J. and P. Milgrom (1991), 'A theory of hierarchies based on limited managerial attention', *Journal of the Japanese and International Economies*, **5**, 205–225.

George, G. (2005), 'Learning to be capable: patenting and licensing at the Wisconsin Alumni Research Foundation 1925–2002,' *Industrial and Corporate Change*, **14** (1), 119–151.

Geuna, A. and A. Muscio (2009), 'The governance of university knowledge transfer: a critical review of the literature', *Minerva*, **47** (1), 93–114.

Hsu, D. and D. Bernstein (1997), 'Managing the university technology licensing process: findings from case studies', *Journal of Association of University Technology Managers*, **9**, 1–33.

Hülsbeck, M., E.E. Lehmann and A. Starnecker (forthcoming), 'Performance of technology transfer offices in Germany', *Journal of Technology Transfer*.

Jensen, R.A. and M.C. Thursby (2001), 'Proofs and prototypes for sale: the licensing of university inventions', *American Economic Review*, **91** (1), 240–259.

Jensen, R.A., J.G. Thursby and M.C. Thursby (2003), 'Disclosure and licensing of university inventions: the best we can do with the s**t we get to work with?', *International Journal of Industrial Organization*, **21** (9), 1271–1300.

Kale, P., J.H. Dyer and H. Singh (2002), 'Alliance capability, stock market response, and long term alliance success: the role of the alliance function', *Strategic Management Journal*, **23** (8), 747–767.

Lach, S. and M. Schankerman (2004), 'Royalty sharing and technology licensing in universities', *Journal of the European Economic Association*, **2** (2–3), 252–264.

Lockett, A. and M. Wright (2005), 'Resources, capabilities, risk capital and the creation of university spin-out companies', *Research Policy*, **34** (7), 1043–1057.

Markman, G.D., P.T. Gianiodis, P.H. Phan and D.B. Balkin (2005), 'Innovation speed: transferring university technology to market', *Research Policy*, **34**, 1058–1075.

Markman, G.D., D.S. Siegel and M. Wright (2008), 'Research and technology commercialization', *Journal of Management Studies*, **45** (8), 1401–1423.

Miles, M. and M. Huberman (1984), *Qualitative Data Analysis: A Source Book for New Methods*, Thousand Oaks, CA: Sage Publications.

Nerkar, A. and S. Shane (2007), 'Determinants of invention commercialization: an empirical examination of academically sourced inventions', *Strategic Management Journal*, **28** (11), 1155–1166.

Rasmussen, E. (2008), 'Government instruments to support the commercialization of university research: Lessons from Canada', *Technovation*, **28** (8), 506–517.

Rasmussen, E. and O.J. Borch (2010), 'University capabilities in facilitating entrepreneurship: a longitudinal study of spin-off ventures at mid-range universities', *Research Policy*, **39** (5), 602–612.

Rogers, E.M., Y. Yin and J. Hoffmann (2000), 'Assessing the effectiveness of technology transfer offices at US research universities', *Journal of Association of University Technology Managers*, **12**, 47–80.

Rothaermel, F.T., S.D.A. Agung and L. Jiang (2007), 'University entrepreneurship: a taxonomy of the literature', *Industrial and Corporate Change*, **16** (4), 691–791.

Shane, S. (2002), 'Selling university technology: patterns from MIT', *Management Science*, **48** (1), 122–137.

Siegel, D.S. (2006), *Technology Entrepreneurship: Institutions and Agents Involved in University Technology Transfer*, Vol. 1, Cheltenham, UK and Northampton, MA, USA: Edward Elgar.

Siegel, D.S., D.A. Waldman and A.N. Link (2003), 'Assessing the impact of organizational practices on the productivity of university technology transfer offices: an exploratory study', *Research Policy*, **32** (1), 27–48.

Siggelkow, N. (2007), 'Persuasion with case studies', *Academy of Management Journal*, **50** (1), 20–24.

Sine, W.D., S. Shane and D. Di Gregorio (2003), 'The halo effect and technology licensing: the influence of institutional prestige on the licensing of university inventions', *Management Science*, **49** (4), 478–496.

Sorensen, J. and D. Chambers (2008), 'Evaluating academic technology transfer performance by how well access to knowledge is facilitated – defining an access metric', *Journal of Technology Transfer*, **33** (5), 534–547.

Swamidass, P.M. and V. Vulasa (2009), 'Why university inventions rarely produce income? Bottlenecks in university technology transfer', *Journal of Technology Transfer*, **34** (4), 343–363.

Teece, D.J. (2007), 'Explicating dynamic capabilities: the nature and micro-foundations of (sustainable) enterprise performance', *Strategic Management Journal*, **28**, 1319–1350.

Thursby, J.G. and M.C. Thursby (2002), 'Who is selling the ivory tower? Sources of growth in university licensing', *Management Science*, **48** (1), 90–104.

Wacker, J.C. (1998), 'A definition of theory: research guidelines for different theory-building research methods in operations management', *Journal of Operations Management*, **16**, 361–385.

Yin, R.K. (2003), *Case Study Research: Design and Methods*, Thousand Oaks, CA: Sage.

Ziedonis, A.A. (2007), 'Real options in technology licensing', *Management Science*, **53** (10), 1618–1633.

# PART III

# Entrepreneurial People, Entrepreneurial Sectors

# 7. Adding missing parts to the intention puzzle in entrepreneurship education: entrepreneurial self-efficacy, its antecedents and their direct and mediated effects

**René Mauer, Philipp Eckerle and Malte Brettel**

## INTRODUCTION

Universities all over the world invest enormous resources into fostering entrepreneurship (Katz 2003; Klandt 2004; Kuratko 2005). Researchers commonly agree that one aim of entrepreneurship education should be to enforce people's beliefs in their capacity to start a venture – that is, strengthening their entrepreneurial self-efficacy (ESE) (e.g. Krueger and Brazeal 1994; Lucas and Cooper 2004; Peterman and Kennedy 2003). Strengthening ESE may ultimately lead to higher entrepreneurial intentions and more start-ups. However, increasing or retaining a high level of entrepreneurial intentions should not be the sole aim of entrepreneurship programmes. Recent studies also indicate that cognitive factors such as overconfidence may lead to business failures (Hayward et al. 2006; Koellinger et al. 2007). Therefore, Townsend et al. (2010: 200) corroborate that educational experiences may or should lead potential entrepreneurs to assess their real skills and abilities and therefore also 'improve the quality of associated entrepreneurial entry'. Thus, any knowledge on an increasing or decreasing impact of entrepreneurship programme modules on ESE and entrepreneurial intentions is beneficial for entrepreneurial education research, as we can find conceptual reasoning for both directions. To make way for these kinds of studies relating entrepreneurship education and ESE, it is important to have an advanced understanding about the influencing factors that play a role in the formation of ESE and entrepreneurial intentions of students.

Until now empirical results on the impact of entrepreneurship education on ESE[1] and entrepreneurial intentions are controversial. Fayolle and Gailly (2009) find an increasing effect of entrepreneurship education on perceived behavioural control and intention. Von Graevenitz et al. (2010) find a significant increase in some feasibility- or confidence-related items, no significant change in an averaged ESE scale but a significant decrease in intention. Oosterbeek et al. (2010) find no impact on self-assessed entrepreneurial skills but a significant decrease in intentions in their group of students completing an entrepreneurship education. Peterman and Kennedy (2003) report a significant increase of feasibility while Souitaris et al. (2007) did not find a significant effect on perceived behavioural control but a significant increase in intentions. Such differences in the effect of entrepreneurship education on ESE and intention are multifaceted. Sample characteristics, entrepreneurship education content and forms of teaching may indeed account for a big part of these differences, as does the higher methodological complexity of pre- and post-test studies with regard to measuring differences. Thus, comparability in general is very limited.

The fundamental issue with most of these studies is that they are only able to tell us whether a difference in ESE occurred, but mostly are not able to tell us a lot about why the difference occurred. Hence, we argue that entrepreneurship education researchers should focus on the development of ESE, as this will improve our understanding of the effects of entrepreneurship education modules and methods on students' ESE and entrepreneurial intentions. Entrepreneurship education research still lacks detailed knowledge on the drivers of ESE. However, such knowledge is inevitable to explain the impact of entrepreneurship education on ESE and subsequent intention.

Social cognitive theory (SCT) (Bandura 1986; Wood and Bandura 1989) offers a comprehensive framework to study the underlying mechanisms of ESE. Bandura revealed four ways to influence self-efficacy: (1) mastery experience; (2) vicarious experience or role-modelling; (3) social and verbal persuasion; and (4) judgements of one's own physiological states. Yet, entrepreneurship researchers have not put much focus on the underlying mechanisms of ESE, and we find calls for further research on its antecedents (e.g. Carr and Sequeira 2007; Krueger 2007; Mauer et al. 2009; Scherer et al. 1989; Wilson et al. 2007; Zellweger et al. 2010; Zhao et al. 2005). Research within the entrepreneurship environment especially lacks empirical findings on two of the antecedents: verbal persuasion and judgements of one's own physiological states. Further, previous empirical studies miss deploying all antecedents in one study to shed light on the relative importance of single antecedents while controlling for all others.

Verbal persuasion or judgements of one's own physiological state are in general hypothesized to have a weaker effect on self-efficacy than, for example, mastery experience (Bandura 1977a). Yet if a task is new to individuals they cannot refer to the same extent to previous performance levels as a determinant for self-efficacy, but use more information derived from other sources (Gist and Mitchell 1992). Most students in entrepreneurship have not started their own venture yet. Hence, information on the impact of other sources of self-efficacy is especially important with regard to ESE. In addition, we do know that theoretically the antecedents influence each other and that the relative importance varies across domains (Bandura 1977a, 1986). However, knowledge on the combined influence of all sources on ESE is missing (Zhao et al. 2005).

This chapter aims at further investigating antecedents of ESE and their direct and mediated effects on the formation of entrepreneurial intentions. With the results we will be able to inform future studies on the link between entrepreneurship education and ESE. To our knowledge, we deploy for the first time measures for all main antecedents derived from SCT (mastery experiences, vicarious experiences, social and verbal persuasion, and judgements on one's own physiological states) simultaneously within one study. This contributes to the research stream in two ways. Firstly, we add empirical findings on two possible antecedents of ESE that have been left out of the discussion so far (verbal persuasion and judgement of one's own physiological state). Secondly, previous studies focused only on single or a few antecedents. Thus, we add findings on the significance of single antecedents while controlling for the others.

## THEORETICAL FRAMEWORK AND HYPOTHESIS DEVELOPMENT

Self-efficacy is the central part of Bandura's (1986) SCT, a theory describing a triadic reciprocal causation model where behaviour, cognition and environment influence each other (Bandura 1977b). Bandura (1986: 391) defined self-efficacy as 'people's judgments of their capabilities to organize and execute courses of action required to attain designated types of performances'. The concept reflects people's beliefs as to whether or not they can achieve a desired outcome dependent on their perceptions about their abilities with regard to a certain task. It is important to note that 'people's level of motivation, affective states, and actions are based more on what they believe than on what is objectively true' (Bandura 1997: 2). 'Unless people believe they can produce desired results and forestall detrimental ones by their actions they have little incentive to act or to persevere in the face of difficulties' (Bandura 2001: 10). Thus, perceived self-efficacy is an important predictor of human action and also indicates whether people may persist in a certain task (Bandura 1997). To understand the concept it is important to know that self-efficacy is task- or domain-specific (Bandura 1997). Hence, a person's self-efficacy can vary from one field of activity to another. In addition, self-efficacy can change over time (Bandura 1997; Gist and Mitchell 1992; Wood and Bandura 1989).

Adapted from SCT, ESE is a 'construct that measures a person's belief in their ability to successfully launch an entrepreneurial venture' (McGee et al. 2009: 965). The construct integrates environmental as well as personal influences and is a key antecedent of entrepreneurial intentions and also ultimately a strong predictor of action (Boyd and Vozikis 1994; Chen et al. 1998; Krueger and Brazeal 1994). According to SCT, self-efficacy can be influenced through four ways: mastery experience; vicarious experience or role-modelling; social and verbal persuasion; and judgements of one's own physiological states (e.g. emotional arousal) (Bandura 1997). The following paragraphs will describe the antecedents in more detail, refer to previous empirical research, and include hypothesis development for our research model.

**Mastery Experiences**

Practical experiences and repeated performance accomplishments are regarded to be the most influential source of self-efficacy (Wood and Bandura 1989). Performance successes strengthen beliefs about one's own skills, and failures weaken them (Bandura 1977a; Wood and Bandura 1989). Yet, to develop strong efficacy expectations people have to overcome obstacles and difficult situations; that is, easy successes only will not be beneficial: they rather create high expectations and lead to frustration in the case of failures (Wood and Bandura 1989).

With regard to students within entrepreneurship education, it is not easy to define, measure and interpret possible mastery experiences. Previous studies (e.g. Erikson 1999; Kolvereid 1996b; Krueger 1993; Peterman and Kennedy 2003; Thun and Kelloway 2006) often ask whether the students have already started a venture. However, on average we expect the entrepreneurship students at universities not to have done so. In addition, the results of such studies are controversial: Erikson (1999) and Peterman and Kennedy (2003) did not find a significant relation to ESE, while Kolvereid (1996b), Krueger (1993) and Thun and Kelloway (2006) did. Hence, we have to decompose the whole process of starting or running a venture into steps and ask whether students have experienced similar steps in the past. Zhao et al. (2005) used a similar approach and found a significant positive effect on ESE. Yet, the authors call for further research as they acknowledge that the measure they used could also cover vicarious experience. Some studies measuring the breadth of experience (e.g. Krueger 1993; Peterman and Kennedy 2003) also found a positive influence of prior entrepreneurial experience. With regard to SCT this may as well be difficult to interpret. An experience may have been very stressful and tough, but overcoming it may have led to an increase in self-efficacy. Bandura (2000) mentions other factors that may affect the influence of enactive efficacy information, such as interpretive bias, perceived task difficulty, effort expenditure, amount of external aid received, temporal pattern of successes and failures, and selective biases. Given that complex underlying mechanism and the controversial results of previous studies, we think a simpler measurement may result in findings that can be better generalized. Hence, we hypothesize that on average having any experiences in entrepreneurship-related activities is positively related to ESE, irrelevant of the amount and the perceived positive influence of the respective experience:

*Hypothesis 1:*   Students with some kind of mastery experiences related to venturing will have a stronger entrepreneurial self-efficacy than those without.

## Vicarious Experiences

People do not solely rely on their mastery experiences when judging their level of self-efficacy. Much information is also derived from observing others (Bandura 1977a). A person 'observes the model engaging in various social behaviors and notes the reinforcements received by the model. The observer values the reinforcements or recognizes the positive outcomes of such behavior, and may attempt to replicate the model's behavior and obtain similar types of reinforcements' (Scherer et al. 1989: 55). Within career theory this plays an important role in the formation of beliefs about a career and affects self-efficacy with regard to tasks needed for entering the career path (Krumboltz et al. 1976; Mitchell and Krumboltz 1984; Scherer et al. 1989). An observer can evaluate whether he possesses or is capable of developing the competencies that the role models use effectively. Qualified models can convey strategies that observers can use for managing similar situations and offer role-model experience and performance standards (Bandura 1977b; Wood and Bandura 1989). In addition, seeing different models with varying characteristics succeeding in relevant tasks has a stronger influence than the observation of only one role model. Furthermore, the outcome of the modelled behaviour should be clear to the observer (Bandura 1977a).

With regard to ESE, the interpretation and measurement of vicarious experience is complex. Some studies have used the mode of occupation of parents as a proxy for vicarious experience (e.g. Carr and Sequeira 2007; Kolvereid 1996b; Krueger 1993; Peterman and Kennedy 2003; Scherer et al. 1989). Obviously, this reflects the possibility to observe entrepreneurs in action and judge if associated tasks performed by the parents are perceived to be feasible or not. The majority of previous studies show that the existence of entrepreneurial role models in the family background has a positive influence on ESE. Kolvereid (1996b) found a significant positive relation of parental employment status on perceived behavioural control. Scherer et al. (1989) also found a significant positive relationship of the presence of a parental entrepreneurial role model on ESE, and in addition found that high performers have a more positive effect than low-performing role models. Carr and Sequeira (2007) found a significant positive effect of the presence of prior family business exposure on ESE. In contrast, Peterman and Kennedy (2003) did not find a significant relationship between breadth of experience and feasibility. Although we may conclude that role models within the family may have a positive effect on ESE, some open questions remain with regard to the definition and measurement of vicarious experiences: (1) What kind of performances may serve as a vicarious experience for ESE? (2) Is it only possible to observe such performances with persons who are self-employed? (3) Is the observed performance and outcome conveying a positive or negative influence with regard to venturing? (4) What kind of persons may serve as role models and how strong is their influence?

With regard to (1) and (2) we want to question that only those people who are or have been self-employed may be able to convey strategies on dealing with situations that are related to venturing. In addition, we suggest adding new sources of vicarious experiences, as we do not see a reason to exclude sources such as friends or acquaintances. Furthermore, as described by Bandura (1977a), observing different sources increases the effect of vicarious experiences. We therefore include the idea of 'inverse role models', that is, a negative influence of entrepreneurial role models and positive influence of non-entrepreneurial role models on ESE. While our hypothesis with regard to vicarious experience is similar to hypotheses in previous studies, we want to note that we measure vicarious experiences in a broader way, covering more potential models and their perceived influence with regard to venturing. Formally stated:

*Hypothesis 2:* The more favourable the students' vicarious experiences with regard to venturing, the stronger their ESE will be.

## Social and Verbal Persuasion

A third way of influencing self-efficacy beliefs is verbal persuasion and other types of social influences (Bandura 1977a). Bandura (1977a: 198) describes the instrument as 'widely used because of its ease and ready availability'. Through verbal persuasion people can be influenced to think that they can cope successfully with a certain task. Used in a realistic manner, it may lead to an increase in effort and persistence, while a rise to an unrealistic level may result in rapid depression when facing failures (Bandura 2000; Wood and Bandura 1989). Persuasion without accompanying help through guided mastery experiences is therefore a tool that may lead to short-term increases, but decreases self-efficacy in the long term. Factors that play an important role in the formation of efficacy beliefs through social and verbal persuasion are, for example, credibility states, expertness, consensus, degree of appraisal disparity and familiarity with task demands (Bandura 2000). When considered alone, social and verbal persuasion is generally thought to have less effect on self-efficacy than mastery and vicarious experiences (Bandura 1982).

With regard to entrepreneurship education and its aim to raise ESE and entrepreneurial intentions, verbal persuasion seems to be a mighty tool that may be easily used and misused. If students' ESE can be influenced by verbal persuasion, any effects measured in pre-test and post-test studies of entrepreneurship education may only stem from this source and have a more short-term characteristic. Hence, it is important to know if especially verbal persuasion with regard to venturing plays a role in the formation of ESE and entrepreneurial intentions of students. If so, measurement of short- and long-term effects for entrepreneurship education are greatly needed to see whether the influence of an entrepreneurship education on ESE is persistent. While we could not find a study that tried to measure the influence of verbal persuasion on ESE, Erikson (1999) included social persuasion into his model controlling for self-employment experience and existence of role models. He found social persuasion to be significantly related to ESE in his regression model. Interestingly, previous experiences and the existence of role models were not. The study shows: (1) that it may be interesting to include social influences into a study investigating the underlying mechanisms of ESE; and (2) that it is important to include all antecedents from SCT in one study. With regard to this study, we suggest including a measure for social persuasion as well as a more direct measure for verbal persuasion. Similar questions with regard to the measurement of vicarious experiences apply: (1) Who exerts verbal influence with regard to career decisions? (2) Is this person influencing the student to start a venture? (3) How strong is the perceived influence of this person? With regard to social and verbal persuasion we propose to deploy two different measures and also formulate two different hypotheses:

*Hypothesis 3a:* The more positive and the stronger the students' degree of social persuasion towards venturing, the stronger ESE will be.

*Hypothesis 3b:* The stronger the direct verbal persuasion towards venturing in the students' environment, the stronger ESE will be.

### Judgements of One's Own Physiological States (Emotional Arousal)

'People also rely partly on judgments of their physiological states when they assess their capabilities' (Wood and Bandura 1989: 365). Hence, the fourth way to influence self-efficacy beliefs is to improve physical status and increase stress tolerance (Bandura 1977a; Wood and Bandura 1989). Emotional arousal evoked by stressful and exhausting situations may convey information about one's competencies. Therefore reactions to such situations may as well have a strong influence on perceived self-efficacy (Bandura 1977a). Strong emotional reactions may decrease performance and distract people from effectively coping with a situation in terms of problem-solving. According to Gist and Mitchell (1992), the formation of self-efficacy also includes an analysis of task requirements for the respective behaviour, especially if the task is novel. Entrepreneurs typically have a high workload and take financial and personal risks, and therefore require a high stress tolerance (Rauch and Frese 2007). Studies show that students are aware of this fact as they associate a higher level of workload, complexity and stress with the role of entrepreneurs (e.g. Kolvereid 1996a). In addition, and this may especially be important in the case of ESE, 'fear reactions generate further fear of impending stressful situations through anticipatory self-arousal' (Bandura 1977a: 199). This may also lead to a fear level for unknown situations that exceeds the fear experienced in the respective situations in reality.

In connection with ESE, those who easily experience emotional arousal in stressful situations may perceive the idea of starting a venture as an extremely uncertain and stressful situation and judge themselves incapable, irrespective of their 'hard skills'. Therefore judgements of one's own physiological state, like knowledge about one's own stress tolerance, may play an important role in the formation of ESE and entrepreneurial intentions (Zhao et al. 2005).

Findings on the influence of judgements of one's own physiological state on ESE arc vcry scarce. To our best knowledge only Zhao et al. (2005) have used risk propensity as a proxy to measure the potential relation of this antecedent to ESE. The authors found a significant positive relationship but call for further research with more direct measures targeting stress tolerance. Using a more direct measure for stress tolerance we formulate the next hypothesis:

*Hypothesis 4:* The higher the students' general stress tolerance, the higher ESE will be.

## The Mediating Effect of ESE on Entrepreneurial Intentions

Intentions are the best predictors of behaviour, especially if the behaviour is rare, hard to observe or involves unpredictable time lags (Krueger and Brazeal 1994). Numerous studies have shown that intention models are well suited to studying entrepreneurial behaviour. Out of various intention models the theory of planned behaviour (TPB) (Ajzen 1991) dominates entrepreneurial intentions research (Krueger and Kickul 2006). Within the TPB, attitude, subjective norm and perceived behavioural control (ESE) towards a given behaviour are antecedents to behavioural intention and thus explain actual behaviour (Ajzen 1991). Other variables are typically expected to have only an indirect effect on intention via one of the three TPB factors (Krueger and Carsrud 1993). Some researchers have already given proof for this in empirical studies. Zhao et al. (2005) and Carr and Sequeira (2007) confirmed the mediating effect of ESE in the relationship of its antecedents to entrepreneurial intentions. In line with TPB theory and with previous empirical findings, we argue that any influencing factors on ESE as discussed in Hypothesis 1–Hypothesis H4 (H1–H4) along the lines of social cognitive theory (SCT) will only show an indirect effect on entrepreneurial intentions mediated by ESE:

*Hypothesis 5:* Possible effects of mastery experiences, vicarious experience, social and verbal persuasion and judgements of one's own physiological states on entrepreneurial intentions of students are mediated by ESE.

Figure 7.1 shows our overall research model, which includes all antecedents identified by SCT.

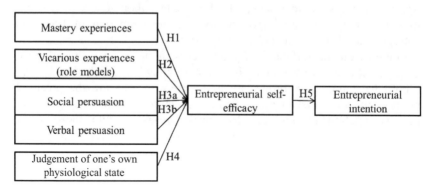

*Figure 7.1   Research model*

## DATA AND METHOD

We conducted an empirical study among 430 non-business students at RWTH Aachen University, one of the biggest technical universities in Germany with a high reputation. In all, 211 completed the survey and qualified to be included into this study. The majority of students were industrial engineers majoring in machinery construction (133 students). Other subjects included, for example, management of geo-resources, materials engineering, chemistry and other natural sciences. Only approximately 10 per cent of the sample was female, reflecting the small share of female students in engineering degree programmes. The survey was conducted at the end of an introductory course to business administration. Sixty-seven per cent of the students were within the first three semesters of their studies, 23 per cent were in semesters 4–6 and 10 per cent were in the seventh or a later semester.

### Measures

The chosen scales for mastery experience, vicarious experience, and social and verbal persuasion are formative, while judgement of one's own physiological state, entrepreneurial self-efficacy and entrepreneurial intentions were measured with reflective constructs. Except for mastery experience, all items were measured with a seven-point Likert scale.

## Mastery experiences

Students were asked to indicate whether they had ever worked for a small or new company, written a business plan, participated in a 'start your own business' planning seminar, conference or lecture, and whether they had ever participated in a new product or service development process. The questions are related to questions within previous studies on previous entrepreneurial experiences or nascent entrepreneurship (McGee et al. 2009; Zhao et al. 2005). If the student answered positively to any of the questions above, mastery experience was coded as '1', otherwise as '0'.

## Vicarious experiences

We measured vicarious experiences by deploying belief and motivation-to-comply questions (following Ajzen 2006). Wood and Bandura (1989) state that people are only influenced by observed accomplishments if they can remember them. Thus, we asked the students to judge by looking at the lives of their father, mother, other relatives, friends, famous persons and 'others' if they are positively or negatively influenced concerning their decision to start their own venture. We did not limit possible role models to people that have been self-employed before. We argue that, for example, employed parents may well convey strategies that can increase ESE. Additionally, we aimed at capturing 'inverse role models'. We also asked students to indicate the strength of motivation to comply with the respective role model by indicating whether the observation of the respective role model generally influences the student's career decisions. The belief items were recoded into a bipolar scale (–3, +3) and multiplied with the respective motivation-to-comply item. Afterwards we averaged the results to come up with a total score of influence of role models.

## Social and verbal persuasion

We also deployed belief- and motivation-to-comply questions for these constructs (following Ajzen 2006). For social persuasion we adapted a measure by Kolvereid (1996b) with three belief and three motivation-to-comply items. Verbal persuasion was measured by asking the students whether their father, mother, other relatives, friends, a professor or teacher, people in their social online network, or 'others' are actively influencing their career decision in conversations and discussions in general; whether such conversations have a strong influence on them; and whether the respective person motivates them to start an own venture in such conversations. The first two items were interpreted as motivation-to-comply items, the last one as a belief measure and therefore again recoded on a bipolar scale (–3, +3). The three items were multiplied and averaged to come up with an overall verbal persuasion measure.

### Judgements of one's own physiological state

Drawing on Zhao et al. (2005) and their call for further research with a more direct measure for stress tolerance, we included items more related to stress tolerance and how people regulate their emotions. We used six items from the self-control subscale of the Trait Emotional Intelligence Questionnaire (Petrides and Furnham 2001, 2006). Items included, for example, 'I usually find it difficult to regulate my emotions' and 'I'm usually able to find ways to control my emotions when I want to'. Internal consistency of the construct was 0.58 only, which could indicate that the measure may cover different dimensions.

### Entrepreneurial self-efficacy

We deployed a multidimensional ESE instrument (19 items) developed by McGee et al. (2009). The items cover a wide range of tasks related to planning, launching and growing a new venture. We averaged all items to come up with an overall ESE scale (Cronbach's alpha: 0.87).

### Entrepreneurial intentions

These were measured on a ten-item scale developed by Thompson (2009) (Cronbach's alpha: 0.74).

### Control variables

Previous studies have found gender effects on both ESE and entrepreneurial intentions (Wilson et al. 2007). Hence, we included gender as a control variable. In addition, we grouped the students into three groups representing the stage of their current studies. This seems important to us with regard to the timing of their employment status choice decision, and with regard to experiences gathered until the survey took place. The questionnaire was translated into German and back-translated into English by several academics to control for consistency. Furthermore, the questionnaire was reviewed by four researchers familiar with the underlying theory and three non-participating students to ensure clarity of wording and face validity.

## RESULTS

We used correlation tables and stepwise hierarchical robust regressions (STATA 11) to analyse the data. In order to control for multicollinearity, we calculated variance inflation factors (VIF) after all regressions. The maximum VIF value found was 1.35. This suggests that no multicollinearity problems are present (Diamantopoulos and Winklhofer 2001). We did not gather any data about non-respondents but tested for significant differences in the early- and late-responding group (Armstrong and Overton 1977). No significant differences were found, indicating that non-response bias was unlikely to be a major problem. Table 7.1 shows correlations for measures deployed.

All measures deployed as antecedents, except for social persuasion, are significantly and positively correlated to ESE. In addition, ESE, mastery experiences, vicarious experiences, and social and verbal persuasion are significantly and positively correlated to entrepreneurial intention. Except for our social persuasion construct, the antecedents moderately correlate with each other.

Table 7.2 shows the results of stepwise hierarchical regressions being used for hypothesis testing. Except for our social persuasion measure, all antecedents' measures are significantly related to ESE in the expected direction. Hence, both newly introduced antecedents 'verbal persuasion' ($\beta = 0.14$, $p < 0.05$) and 'judgments about one's own physiological state' ($\beta = 0.19$, $p < 0.01$) have a significant positive impact on ESE. In addition, our measures for mastery experience ($\beta = 0.15$, $p < 0.05$) and vicarious experience (role models) ($\beta = 0.20$, $p < 0.01$) have a positive impact on ESE. Only social persuasion ($\beta = -0.04$, $p = 0.54$) did not show a significant impact (overall $R^2 = 0.25$). Therefore, hypotheses 1, 2, 3b and 4 are supported, while hypothesis 3a is not supported.

To test for possible direct and mediated effects of mastery experiences, vicarious experiences, social and verbal persuasion, and judgements of one's own physiological state on entrepreneurial intentions we used stepwise hierarchical regression following Baron and Kenny (1986).

Model 4 shows direct effects of mastery experiences ($\beta = 0.13$, $p < 0.05$), vicarious experiences ($\beta = 0.13$, $p < 0.1$) and verbal persuasion ($\beta = 0.41$, $p < 0.01$) on entrepreneurial intention without the presence of the mediator. When entering ESE as a mediator (Model 5) the coefficients of mastery experience and role models decreased and became non-significant, indicating a mediating effect of ESE (Baron and Kenny 1986). In contrast, verbal persuasion remained highly significant, indicating the strong direct effect that verbal persuasion has on the development of intentions. Hence, hypothesis 5 is partly supported.

*Table 7.1 Means, standard deviations and correlations of variables used in research model*

| | Mean | SD | 1 | 2 | 3 | 4 | 5 | 6 | 7 | 8 | 9 |
|---|---|---|---|---|---|---|---|---|---|---|---|
| *Controls* | | | | | | | | | | | |
| 1. Gender (0 = m) | 0.09 | 0.29 | 1*** | | | | | | | | |
| 2. Semester | 1.43 | 0.67 | –0.03*** | 1*** | | | | | | | |
| *Main effects* | | | | | | | | | | | |
| 3. Mastery experiences | 0.55 | 0.5 | –0.18*** | –0.06*** | 1*** | | | | | | |
| 4. Vicarious experiences | –0.26 | 3.84 | 0.06*** | –0.20*** | 0.30*** | 1*** | | | | | |
| 5. Social persuasion | 3.59 | 5.97 | –0.15*** | –0.03*** | 0.09*** | 0.15*** | 1*** | | | | |
| 6. Verbal persuasion | –12.01 | 18.67 | –0.10*** | –0.09*** | 0.22*** | 0.36*** | 0.29*** | 1*** | | | |
| 7. Judgements of one's own physiological state | 5.31 | 0.78 | –0.14*** | –0.01*** | 0.15*** | 0.13*** | 0.19*** | 0.14*** | 1*** | | |
| *Mediator/dependent variable* | | | | | | | | | | | |
| 8. ESE | 4.59 | 0.71 | 0.05*** | –0.27*** | 0.26*** | 0.36*** | 0.07*** | 0.27*** | 0.24*** | 1*** | |
| 9. Entrepreneurial intention | 3.46 | 1.22 | –0.16*** | –0.23*** | 0.27*** | 0.33*** | 0.12*** | 0.49*** | 0.05*** | 0.36*** | 1*** |

*Note:* * $p < 0.1$, ** $p < 0.05$, *** $p < 0.01$.

*Table 7.2 Hierarchical regression models for mediation effect (n = 211)*

| | Standardized coefficients | | | | |
|---|---|---|---|---|---|
| | Dependent variable: ESE | | Dependent variable: entrepreneurial intention | | |
| | Model 1*** | Model 2*** | Model 3*** | Model 4*** | Model 5*** |
| *Controls* | | | | | |
| Gender | 0.05*** | 0.10*** | -0.19*** | -0.13*** | -0.15*** |
| Semester | -0.27*** | -0.20*** | -0.14*** | -0.16*** | -0.12*** |
| *Main effects* | | | | | |
| Mastery experiences | | 0.15*** | | 0.13*** | 0.10*** |
| Vicarious experiences | | 0.20*** | | 0.13*** | 0.09*** |
| Social persuasion | | -0.04*** | | -0.04*** | -0.03*** |
| Verbal persuasion | | 0.14*** | | 0.41*** | 0.38*** |
| Judgements of physiological state | | 0.19*** | | -0.06*** | -0.10*** |
| *Mediator* | | | | | |
| ESE | | | 0.34*** | | 0.21*** |
| F-Statistic | 8.41*** | 10.20*** | 12.52*** | 17.01*** | 17.49*** |
| Overall R² | 0.07*** | 0.25*** | 0.18*** | 0.33*** | 0.36*** |
| Δ overall R² | | 0.18*** | | 0.15*** | 0.03*** |

*Notes:*
*p < 0.1, **p < 0.05, ***p < 0.01; two-tailed.
Max. VIFs found: 1.29 (Model 2, 4); 1.35 (Model 5).

# DISCUSSION

This chapter aimed at further investigating antecedents of ESE and their direct and mediated effects on the formation of entrepreneurial intentions in order to better ground future studies on the link between entrepreneurship education, ESE and entrepreneurial intention by students. Based on SCT we tested the impact of the two antecedents 'verbal persuasion' and 'judgements of one's own physiological states' in a model that included measures for all main antecedents of ESE. This was important to us in order to investigate the effect of each single antecedent while controlling for the others. In addition, we deployed different measures for mastery experience and vicarious experiences compared to previous studies. Our results show that, except for our measure of social persuasion, all other antecedents significantly contributed to the explanation of ESE while controlling for the other antecedents. Therefore, all sources of self-efficacy identified by SCT are important within the entrepreneurship environment. In line with previous studies, mastery experiences (e.g. Kolvereid 1996b; Krueger 1993; Thun and Kelloway 2006) and vicarious experiences and role models (e.g. Carr and Sequeira 2007; Kolvereid 1996b; Scherer et al. 1989) were significantly related to ESE. With regard to our mastery experience measure we can state that students with some practical experience related to venturing have a higher ESE and higher entrepreneurial intentions than those students with no practical experience. Hence, we confirm prior results that internships in small or new companies, business planning lectures and product development positively contribute to the formation of ESE. It will be important for entrepreneurship education to identify the impact of specific mastery experiences and to use this knowledge to design specific modules. With regard to role models, our results also show that sources for vicarious experiences may not only stem from parents, although their perceived influence on ESE was the strongest among all sources. Additionally, the effects of the different sources were significantly and positively correlated with each other. Thus, reducing this antecedent in student samples to questions related to parents only may result in a good proxy. Yet, this may not be true for samples with older people as the influence of one's parents might diminish. In contrast to Erikson (1999), social persuasion did not have a significant effect on ESE, nor on intention. This leaves some room for speculation: as an example, students may not perceive the same social pressure from their family (i.e., in most cases, parents and siblings) with regard to becoming self-employed than more senior people who need to support a family (i.e., life partner and own children).

Prior research especially lacked knowledge on the potential impact of two antecedents on ESE: verbal persuasion and judgements of one's own physiological state. Both antecedents proved to have an impact on the formation of ESE. In line with SCT, verbal persuasion can be used to increase ESE. This is important with regard to entrepreneurship education aiming at influencing ESE and entrepreneurial intentions. Verbal persuasion may increase ESE and ultimately intention, and hence lead students to start a venture. Yet, ESE raised by persuasion only may also lead to frustration in the face of complex tasks, difficult situations and failures. This in turn may decrease students' ESE and entrepreneurial intentions in the long term. Furthermore, this result is important with regard to measuring the impact of entrepreneurship education with pre-test and post-test studies using ESE and entrepreneurial intention scales. A significant increase in ESE and entrepreneurial intention may not ultimately prove the excellence of a programme if the increase mainly stemmed from verbal persuasion.

Our measure of judgements of one's own physiological state covered a person's general stress tolerance. The results showed that indeed those students who perceive themselves to tolerate more stress have a higher ESE. This finding is important with regard to students who may possess practical and hard skills to start a venture and have interesting business ideas but fear their reactions to possible stressful situations connected to venturing. Therefore, it may be important to include modules in entrepreneurship education programmes on how to deal with entrepreneurial stress or stress in general. We underline calls for further research into entrepreneurial cognition on this construct (e.g. Krueger 2009). More complex psychological measures may reveal further insights on how students' ESE is affected by, for example, emotional arousal and on what entrepreneurship education can do to help students to better cope with stress and arousal.

Furthermore, we tested a possible direct effect of the antecedents on entrepreneurial intentions and whether ESE mediates this effect. Mastery experiences, vicarious experiences and verbal persuasion showed a direct effect on entrepreneurial intentions. While the impact of mastery experiences and vicarious experiences diminished with the inclusion of ESE, verbal persuasion still showed a strong direct effect on intentions. Previous research states that variables typically only affect intention via its three antecedents: attitude, subjective norm, and behavioural control or ESE (Krueger and Carsrud 1993). Our measure of verbal persuasion therefore seems to be closely related to subjective norm and develops its influence not only on ESE but also directly on entrepreneurial intention. Hence, using verbal persuasion within entrepreneurship education is even more critical as it influences both ESE and intention directly.

Our results also contribute to the use of the theory of planned behaviour within the entrepreneurship environment. In their meta-analysis, Armitage and Conner (2001) find that the subjective norm construct was the most weakly related antecedent to intention within the theory of planned behaviour. They conclude that this may be a function of poor measurement. Some studies using the theory of planned behaviour on entrepreneurial intentions also report that the subjective norm construct did not show a significant impact on intentions (e.g. Krueger et al. 2000). For a student sample, a measure that addresses verbal persuasion more directly may reveal a greater significance, as social pressure in terms of supporting a family may not be as present as for more senior people.

There are some limitations to this study that offer several avenues for further research. Firstly, our sample is limited to non-business students with mainly engineering backgrounds and hence a typical bias regard to gender. It would be interesting to replicate the study with other students or in a representative population sample. Our measures for mastery experiences, vicarious experiences, social and verbal persuasion, and judgements of one's own physiological state may be further improved. Especially, the role of judgements of one's own physiological state offers interesting research avenues.

It may also be interesting to include personality traits as moderators in future studies to investigate whether the effect of the antecedents varies for different types of personality. As an example, a person with a high internal locus of control may rely more on mastery experiences, while one with a low internal locus of control may need more support through role models and verbal persuasion. Theoretically, such studies will contribute to a further integration of personality traits into intention models. In addition, results could indicate that different students should focus on different modules of an entrepreneurship education to gain the best overall result.

With regard to pre-test and post-test design studies on entrepreneurship education we encourage future research to give extensive descriptions of the entrepreneurship education and the modules and pedagogical tools used. Any results on an increase or decrease of ESE and intention without such descriptions are not very useful as we do not know if the impact stemmed from mastery experiences, vicarious experiences or verbal persuasion only. In addition, two post-tests may be required to indicate short- or long-term impact of any programme. Furthermore, the development of a standardized questionnaire for pre- and post-tests would bring forward the research on entrepreneurship education. This questionnaire should not only measure changes in ESE and intention but also ask the students for perceived influences of modules and tools used. These questions should be related to and cover the antecedents of ESE derived from SCT. This would allow assessment of which sources of ESE may have been addressed in any specific entrepreneurship education programme.

Finally, prior studies have revealed an interaction effect of attitudes towards venturing and perceived behavioural control and ESE (Fitzsimmons and Douglas 2010). It would be interesting to investigate which of the antecedents of ESE also impact desirability towards venturing. Those antecedents might prove to exert an even stronger effect on intentions via both antecedents: desirability and ESE.

## NOTE

1. We subsume perceived behavioural control, self-assessed entrepreneurial skills and feasibility under ESE. The concepts are closely related (see e.g. Ajzen 1991; Boyd and Vozikis 1994) and are often used interchangeably in entrepreneurship research.

## REFERENCES

Ajzen, I. (1991), 'The theory of planned behavior', *Organizational Behavior and Human Decision Processes*, **50** (2), 179–211.

Ajzen, I. (2006), 'Constructing a TpB questionnaire: conceptual and methodological considerations', http://www.unix.oit.umass.edu/tpb.measurement.pdf.

Armitage, C.J. and M. Conner (2001), 'Efficacy of the theory of planned behavior: a meta-analytic review', *British Journal of Social Psychology*, **40** (4), 471–499.

Armstrong, J.B. and T.S. Overton (1977), 'Estimating non-response bias in mail surveys', *Journal of Marketing Research*, **14**, 396–402.

Bandura, A. (1977a), 'Self-efficacy: toward a unifying theory of behavioral change', *Psychological Review*, **84**, 191–215.

Bandura, A. (1977b), *Social Learning Theory*, Englewood Cliffs, NJ: Prentice-Hall.

Bandura. A. (1982), 'Self-efficacy mechanism in human agency', *American Psychologist*, **37** (2), 122–147.

Bandura, A. (1986), *Social Foundation of Thought and Action: A Social Cognitive Theory*, Englewood Cliffs, NJ: Prentice Hall.

Bandura, A. (1997), *Self-efficacy: The Exercise of Control*, New York: Freeman.

Bandura, A. (2000), 'Cultivate self-efficacy for personal and organizational effectiveness', in E.A. Locke (ed.), *Handbook of Principles of Organization Behavior*, Oxford: Blackwell, pp. 120–136.

Bandura, A. (2001), 'Social cognitive theory: an agentic perspective', *Annual Review of Psychology*, **52**, 1–26.

Baron, R.M. and D.A. Kenny (1986), 'The moderator–mediator variable distinction in social psychological research: conceptual, strategic, and statistical considerations', *Journal of Personality and Social Psychology*, **51**, 1173–1182.

Boyd, N.G. and G.S. Vozikis (1994), 'The influence of self-efficacy on the development of entrepreneurial intentions and actions', *Entrepreneurship Theory and Practice*, **18** (4), 63–77.

Carr, J.C. and J.M. Sequeira (2007), 'Prior family business exposure as intergenerational influence and entrepreneurial intent: A theory of planned behavior approach', *Journal of Business Research*, **60** (10), 1090–1098.

Chen, G.C., P.G. Greene and A. Crick (1998), 'Does entrepreneurial self-efficacy distinguish entrepreneurs from managers', *Journal of Business Venturing*, **13**, 295–317.

Diamantopoulos, A. and H.M. Winklhofer (2001), 'Index construction with formative indicators: an alternative to scale development', *Journal of Marketing Research*, **38** (2), 269–277.

Erikson, T. (1999), 'A study of entrepreneurial career choices among MBAs – the extended Bird model', *Journal of Enterprising Culture*, **7** (1), 1–17.

Fayolle, A. and B. Gailly (2009), 'Assessing the impact of entrepreneurship education: a methodology and three experiments from French engineering schools', in G. Page West III, E.J. Gatewood and K.G. Shaver (eds), *Handbook of University-Wide Entrepreneurship Education*, Cheltenham, UK and Northampton, MA, USA: Edward Elgar, pp. 203–214.

Fitzsimmons, J.R. and E.J. Douglas (2010), 'Interaction between feasibility and desirability in the formation of entrepreneurial intentions', *Journal of Business Venturing*, **26** (4), 431–440.

Gist, M.E. and T. Mitchell (1992), 'Self-efficacy: a theoretical analysis of its determinants and malleability', *Academy of Management Review*, **17** (2), 183–211.

Graevenitz, G. von, D. Harhoff and R. Weber (2010), 'The effects of entrepreneurship education', *Journal of Economic Behavior and Organization*, **76** (1), 90–112.

Hayward, M., D. Shepherd and D. Griffin (2006), 'A hubris theory of entrepreneurship', *Management Science*, **52** (2), 160–172.

Katz, J. (2003), 'The chronology and intellectual trajectory of American entrepreneurship education 1876–1999', *Journal of Business Venturing*, **18** (2), 283–300.

Klandt, H. (2004), 'Entrepreneurship education and research in German-speaking Europe', *Academy of Management Learning and Education*, **3** (3), 293–301.

Koellinger, P., M. Minniti and C. Schade (2007), '"I think I can, I think I can": overconfidence and entrepreneurial behavior', *Journal of Economic Psychology*, **28** (4), 502–527.

Kolvereid, L. (1996a), 'Organizational employment versus self-employment: reasons for career choice intentions', *Entrepreneurship Theory and Practice*, **20** (3), 23–31.

Kolvereid, L. (1996b), 'Prediction of employment status choice intentions', *Entrepreneurship Theory & Practice*, **21** (1), 47–57.

Krueger, N.F. (1993), 'The impact of prior entrepreneurial exposure on perceptions of new venture feasibility and desirability', *Entrepreneurship: Theory and Practice*, **18** (1), 5–21.

Krueger, N.F. (2007), 'What lies beneath? The experiential essence of entrepreneurial thinking', *Entrepreneurship Theory and Practice*, **31** (1), 123–138.

Krueger, N. (2009), 'The microfoundations of entrepreneurial learning: maximizing entrepreneurial education', in E. Gatewood and G.P. West (eds), *Handbook of Cross Campus Entrepreneurship*, Cheltenham, UK and Northampton, MA, USA: Edward Elgar, pp. 35–59.

Krueger, N.F. and D. Brazeal (1994), 'Entrepreneurial potential and potential entrepreneurs', *Entrepreneurship Theory and Practice*, **18** (3), 91–104.

Krueger, N.F. and A.L. Carsrud (1993), 'Entrepreneurial intentions: applying the theory of planned behaviour', *Entrepreneurship and Regional Development*, **5**, 315–330.

Krueger, N.F. and J. Kickul (2006), 'So you thought the intentions model was simple? Navigating the complexities and interactions of cognitive style, culture, gender, social norms, and intensity on the pathway to entrepreneurship', paper presented at the 2006 United States Association Small Business and Entrepreneurship Conference.

Krueger, N.F., M.D. Reilly and A.L. Carsrud (2000), 'Competing models of entrepreneurial intentions', *Journal of Business Venturing*, **15** (5–6), 411–432.

Krumboltz, J.D., A.M. Mitchell and G.B. Jones (1976), 'A social learning theory of career selection', *Counselling Psychologist*, **6**, 71–80.

Kuratko, D.F. (2005), 'The emergence of entrepreneurship education: development, trends, and challenges', *Entrepreneurship Theory and Practice*, **29** (5), 577–598.

Lucas, W. and S. Cooper (2004), 'Enhancing self-efficacy to enable entrepreneurship: the case of CMI's Connections', MIT Sloan School of Management Working Paper 4489-04 (May), Cambridge MA.

Mauer, R., H. Neergaard and A.L. Kirketerp (2009), 'Self-efficacy: conditioning the entrepreneurial mindset', in A. Carsrud and M. Brännback (eds), *Understanding the Entrepreneurial Mind: Opening the Black Box*, New York: Springer, pp. 233–257.

McGee, J.E., M. Peterson, S.L. Mueller and J.M. Sequeira (2009), 'Entrepreneurial self-efficacy: refining the measure', *Entrepreneurship Theory and Practice*, **33** (4), 965–988.

Mitchell, L.K. and J.D. Krumboltz (1984), 'Social learning approach to career decision making: Krumboltz's theory', in D. Brown and L. Brooks (eds), *Career Choice and Development*, San Francisco, CA: Jossey-Bass, pp. 235–280.

Oosterbeek, H., C.M. Van Praag and A. Ijsselstein (2010), 'The impact of entrepreneurship education on entrepreneurship skills and motivation', *European Economic Review*, **54**, 442–454.

Peterman, N. and J. Kennedy (2003), 'Enterprise education: influencing students' perceptions of enterprise education', *Entrepreneurship Theory and Practice*, **28** (2), 129–144.

Petrides, K.V. and A. Furnham (2001), 'Trait emotional intelligence: psychometric investigation with reference to established trait taxonomies', *European Journal of Personality*, **15**, 425–448.

Petrides, K.V. and A. Furnham (2006), 'The role of trait emotional intelligence in a gender-specific model of organizational variables', *Journal of Applied Social Psychology*, **36**, 552–569.

Rauch, A. and M. Frese (2007), 'Let's put the person back into entrepreneurship research: a meta-analysis on the relationship between business owners' personality traits, business creation, and success', *European Journal of Work and Organizational Psychology*, **16** (4), 353–385.

Scherer, R.F., J.S. Adams, S.S. Carley and F.A. Wiebe (1989), 'Role model performance effects on the development of entrepreneurial career preference', *Entrepreneurship Theory and Practice*, **13** (3), 53–71.

Souitaris, V., S. Zerbinati and A. Al-Laham (2007), 'Do entrepreneurship programmes raise entrepreneurial intention of science and engineering students? The effect of learning, inspiration and resources', *Journal of Business Venturing*, **22** (4), 566–591.

Thompson, E.R. (2009), 'Individual entrepreneurial intent: construct clarification and development of an internationally reliable metric', *Entrepreneurship Theory and Practice*, **33** (3), 669–694.

Thun, N.B. and E.K. Kelloway (2006), 'Subjective norms and lemonade stands: The effects of early socialization and childhood work experiences on entrepreneurial intent', paper presented at the Administrative Sciences Association of Canada (ASAC), Banff, Alberta.

Townsend, D.M., L.W. Busenitz and J.D. Arthurs (2010), 'To start or not to start: outcome and ability expectations in the decision to start a new venture', *Journal of Business Venturing*, **25** (2), 192–202.

Wilson, F., J. Kickul and D. Marlino (2007), 'Gender, entrepreneurial self-efficacy, and entrepreneurial career intentions: Implications for entrepreneurship education', *Entrepreneurship Theory and Practice*, **31** (3), 387–406.

Wood, R. and A. Bandura (1989), 'Social cognitive theory of organizational management', *Academy of Management Review*, **14** (3), 361–384.

Zellweger, T., P. Sieger and F. Halter (2010), 'Should I stay or should I go? Career choice intentions of students with family business background', *Journal of Business Venturing*, **26** (5), 1–16.

Zhao, H., S. Seibert and G.E. Hills (2005), 'The mediating role of self-efficacy in the development of entrepreneurial intentions', *Journal of Applied Psychology*, **90** (6), 1265–1272.

# 8. Intrapreneurial risk-taking in public healthcare: challenging existing boundaries

## Jarna Heinonen, Ulla Hytti and Eeva Vuorinen

### INTRODUCTION

Healthcare organisations across Europe face enormous challenges to meet the needs of the ageing population. This is highly prevalent in Scandinavia, particularly in Finland, where the so-called Nordic welfare society is strongly supported by government and provides citizens with access to a wide variety of public healthcare services (Henrekson 2005). A number of recent changes call for a new approach to organising healthcare services. Firstly, the public healthcare sector faces the challenge of finding new ways to organise quality and customer-oriented services to cope with shrinking budgets and the increasing demands and changing needs of the population. Healthcare organisations are expected to develop more and better services through organisational renewal and to create new, innovative services while increasing labour productivity (Valovirta and Hyvönen 2009). In addition, the emergence of private sector clinics has influenced the market for services and labour alike. As a result, public sector healthcare organisations find their working practices challenged by both reduced resources and difficulties in attracting competent staff (Åmo 2006; Eskildsen et al. 2004).

Innovative action and organisational change are, therefore, crucial for healthcare organisations and the concept of intrapreneurship is highly topical to organisations open to taking innovative steps to develop their activities and to improve their performance. 'Intrapreneurship' refers to the practice of developing new ventures and strategic renewal within an existing organisation in order to exploit new opportunities and generate economic value (Guth and Ginsberg 1990; Ireland et al. 2009). Previous research shows that entrepreneurial organisations are innovative and proactive more often than their peers, and are also able to continuously renew themselves (Antoncic and Hisrich 2001) and to enhance their efficiency and effectiveness (Morris et al. 2011). Intrapreneurship enables and enhances employees' abilities to generate more economic value and renewal within the organisation (Covin and Slevin 1991; Holt et al. 2007).

It is unclear how intrapreneurial activities might manifest themselves in the non-profit sector (Morris et al. 2011), particularly in a public sector healthcare organisation, which has a social mission that shapes its key processes and the outcomes it is tasked to achieve. Particular antecedents and outcomes of public sector intrapreneurship have been defined (e.g. Kearney et al. 2008), but the existing models seldom capture the different manifestations of intrapreneurship across different hierarchical and organisational contexts (Wales et al. 2011) and tend to neglect the role of the individual intrapreneur in intrapreneurship. We agree with Slevin and Terjesen (2011) when they suggest that it is problematic to use the concept of intrapreneurship as an individual construct, and we acknowledge the crucial role of an individual in taking risks and behaving entrepreneurially within an existing organisation. It is unclear what kind of constraints or incentives an intrapreneur may face in the public healthcare arena. The aim of this chapter is to discuss – through a single case – the risk-taking processes and their consequences for the individual in the context of a public healthcare organisation. A finer-grained understanding of the manifestations of intrapreneurship and the obstacles that face it in the particular context complements the previous knowledge on intrapreneurship and corporate entrepreneurship.

Our study contributes to the literature by illustrating the role of the individual risk-taking that is required to cross the various organisational boundaries encountered when departing from the norm and introducing activities outside the existing practice framework. Our findings will be particularly relevant for public healthcare organisations seeking to rethink and reorganise their grassroots activity to become more competitive. We argue that managers and employees would benefit from understanding that intrapreneurship requires someone to challenge existing boundaries and perhaps cross them, even though that involves personal risk-taking. It is important to understand that intrapreneurial activity is not something organised by elite groups, but an everyday activity undertaken by employees (see also Kearney et al. 2008). In addition, organisational fora and routes are needed to communicate and channel the individual initiatives towards broader organisational goals.

# THEORETICAL FOUNDATIONS: INTRAPRENEURSHIP

The study draws on the previous literature on intrapreneurship and corporate entrepreneurship. Intrapreneurship is defined here as entrepreneurship within an existing organisation regardless of size. The term incorporates emergent intentions and behaviours that deviate from the customary way of doing business (Antoncic and Hisrich 2001, 2003, 2004). This chapter focuses on creativity and developing innovation, basing its approach on the model of strategic entrepreneurship presented by Ireland et al. (2003). Similarly, Sharma and Chrisman (1999) refer to individual or team processes, which instigate renewal or innovation within an existing organisation, thereby emphasising the dynamic elements of the phenomenon. We acknowledge that (depending on the studies) corporate entrepreneurship and intrapreneurship may not be understood as exact synonyms but to represent slightly different aspects of organisational renewal or change (see, e.g., Åmo and Kolvereid 2005; Sharma and Chrisman 1999). Intrapreneurship becomes visible within an organisation through strategic renewal or the birth of new businesses and ventures (Covin and Slevin 1991; Guth and Ginsberg 1990).

Many ideas for innovation and renewal come from the bottom up, if an organisation provides its members with sufficient freedom and autonomy to pursue entrepreneurial action (Lumpkin et al. 2009). Intrapreneurship 'runs deep' within an organisation (Ireland et al. 2006a). Employees and managers both have significant (but different) roles in intrapreneurial processes (Heinonen and Toivonen 2008; Wales et al. 2011) and organisational development (Day 1994; Shane 1994) although it seems easier for more senior managers to implement their entrepreneurial ideas than it is for their colleagues at a lower level (Hornsby et al. 2009; Wales et al. 2011). Intrapreneurship involves collective action towards mutually accepted goals within an existing organisation, but it is also about individual intrapreneurs behaving entrepreneurially and throwing themselves boldly into the process of entrepreneurship (Heinonen and Toivonen 2008; see also Pinchot 1985). Underestimating the intrapreneur's agency leads studies on intrapreneurship in the wrong direction, as they are prone to forget that the true meaning and intent of the word implies the involvement of creative and passionate actors (see Hjorth and Johannisson 2006; Kuratko 2005). Both bottom-up and top-down processes in the organisation are important to intrapreneurship (Phan et al. 2009).

The phenomenon of intrapreneurship is characterised by innovativeness, proactiveness and risk-taking (Covin and Slevin 1991). In this study, we focus particularly on individual risk-taking, which since Cantillon (1734) has been viewed as a fundamental characteristic of both the entrepreneur and entrepreneurship. At the time, the term 'entrepreneur' referred to a person bearing the risk of loss to obtain profit (Antoncic and Hisrich 2003) while later risk-taking came to be related more to entrepreneurial behaviour than to a characteristic of an individual (Brockhaus 1980). Typically, such a risk is linked to financial loss and is not considered relevant in the context of intrapreneurship. Indeed, from an individual point of view intrapreneurship does not involve financial risk-taking in a sense typical of entrepreneurs. However, previous studies suggest that intrapreneurial activities reflect a bold, directive, opportunity-seeking style with elements of risk-taking (Dess et al. 1997). When innovation champions, intrapreneurs at different organisational levels, question the current working practices and behave entrepreneurially, they may take personal risks related to their career advancement and reputation (Antoncic 2003). Intrapreneurship is not about business as usual, but rather implies unusual business or business approaches (Thornberry 2001), which can affect an economy by increasing productivity, improving best practices, changing competitiveness and even creating new industries (Wennekers and Thurik 1999). The notion of risk is further emphasised as intrapreneurship is about operating at the organisational boundaries and stretching norms, structures, technologies, orientations and operations of the organisation into new directions (Antoncic and Hisrich 2003). This is something that is often considered highly desirable, although challenging to achieve in the current risk-averse public healthcare system, which relies heavily on long traditions of norms and structures with limited individual opportunities to question and revitalise existing routines and practices (Virtanen 2010). Therefore, we are interested in the intrapreneurial risk-taking of individual staff members in this particular context.

## METHODOLOGY

Methodologically, this chapter draws on an ethnographic study (Berger and Luckmann 1976; Rosen 1991; Van Maanen 1988) carried out in one Finnish healthcare organisation, a large, public university hospital and particularly its eye clinic. The hospital saw more than 440 000 hospital admissions in 2010 and has a staff of 3055 professionals. Approximately 2370 of them are nurses and 500 are doctors. The eye clinic employs 61 nurses (including practice nurses), 20 doctors (including registrars) and 16 other members of staff. The research project deals with developing understanding of the management or organisational practices that either hinder or support intrapreneurial behaviour by an individual in the healthcare organisation. All staff members were asked to respond to a survey and several staff members – both management and non-management – were interviewed. The research team also observed the everyday activities in the clinic, and organised feedback sessions and other workshops. Hence, the research material is extensive and rich, allowing us to carefully choose an illustrative case for this chapter (Siggelkow 2007).

Through the research process, we developed a strong sense of the importance of the public healthcare context (Welter 2011). To illustrate and generate new understanding of how entrepreneurial behaviour is manifested in this particular context, we focus on one single case: one nurse's account of her activities in the clinic. We became interested in her story since it exemplified an alternative way of thinking and a divergent form of activity compared to the other accounts we heard. For us, it offered the prospect of following an intrapreneur in a large public sector healthcare organisation. By analysing this account and one event – the establishment of a reception area run by nurses to deal with routine patient treatment – we have the opportunity to develop a rich understanding of what it takes to become an intrapreneur in the studied context. We will examine the barriers encountered that must be overcome in order to make ideas reality (Welter 2011). The case story is written from the perspective of the nurse, adding a particularly interesting aspect, as previous studies tend to focus on senior managers' perceptions of intrapreneurship (Wales et al. 2011). While our approach may obscure alternative, and possibly rational, explanations for the existence of organisational boundaries, we believe the individual employee perspective is important because the individual is the key actor in intrapreneurial behaviour (Heinonen and Toivonen 2008; Pinchot 1985), even though the behaviour happens within an organisational and social setting (Biniari 2012; Phan et al. 2009). Methodologically, our aim is not to generalize from the findings but to use the single case study as a very persuasive example (Siggelkow 2007) of intrapreneurship taking place in the real-world context of public healthcare (Eisenhardt and Graebner 2007).

In our case, Mary, the nurse, attempts to behave entrepreneurially, looking to create new ideas and solutions within her organisation. Mary is a single mother in her forties. She has international nursing experience gained in Germany after finishing her degree in nursing. Apart from the two years spent abroad, she has spent her whole career in the same organisation, first in dialysis and then in the eye clinic. She has covered positions other than her own when presented with the opportunity. In her work Mary takes some risk, and develops a plan on the basis of which she implements her venture by recognizing an opportunity where others see chaos and confusion (Kuratko 2009). Next, we present Mary's story.

# FINDINGS

## Mary's Story

Mary identified a problem in the organisation. There were an increasing number of patients suffering from macular degeneration, a by-product of the general population living longer, and therefore a problem likely to continue to grow. Mary was concerned by the length of waiting lists in her own hospital. First-time patients, patients with severe or acute problems, and patients requiring routine check-ups (referred to in the unit as 'control patients') were all admitted together, forming one long queue, reducing the ability of the staff to treat all the patients at the requisite pace. The doctors' time was not being well spent, administering routine check-ups alongside treating those in desperate need. 'Age-related [macular] degeneration patients come from doors and windows[1] and they are not going to decrease in number, but increase. So, I started thinking would there be a way to make this job easier.'

In public healthcare, doctors are accountable for seeing a certain number of new patients in a given time. Mary realised that patients attending the clinic to have the extent of their pre-diagnosed macular degeneration monitored (control patients) were filling reception areas and preventing the doctors from seeing as many new patients as they were supposed to. In response to the issue, Mary had the idea of opening a reception and check-up area staffed by nurses for the control patients, so freeing the doctors to focus on the first-time patients and more demanding cases. The reception offers a solution to the demands posed by the increasing number of macular degeneration patients and control visits:

> I thought about what I should do. The workload was expanding and there was work a nurse could do. It [the nurse-run reception] would help our whole clinic. If a doctor sees more new patients, we get more patients onto treatment ... The positive thing in this is clearly the fact that during one day I can see between six and eight patients who would otherwise burden a doctor ... This way it becomes possible [for the doctor] to see more new patients.
>
> Then doctors could really focus more on new patients [instead of control patients who do not always need a doctor's opinion] ... They could focus more on the more challenging patients. Then nurses, [could contribute more]

if we were trained and given a little more power to make the decision [on a patient's treatment].

First, Mary presented the plan for this new reception to her immediate supervisor, head nurse Tina, who did not take the plan very seriously and did next to nothing to support the development of the idea:

> The response was a bit like: 'Yea, well, "tap on the head". You can put some pros and cons on the paper … '. I wrote down the pros and cons and tried to suggest it to her again. She said, 'It might be a nice idea', but the idea didn't develop anywhere.

Mary persisted with the idea. Aware that the organisation had recently established a panel tasked to review initiatives, Mary started to work alone on an action plan. 'For six months I developed it; what it would be like, how should it work; what would be needed; equipment; room; something else, like additional training; mentoring …'.

Mary did not take notice of her immediate supervisor's remarks but took her action plan to the highest body deciding on new projects in the hospital. Prior to submitting the plan, she also consulted a chief physician, two nurses working closely with macular diseases and an expert doctor, and obtained clear support for her idea.

> I made an action plan and I sent all of it as an initiative and went first to our head doctor … to ask what he thought. I felt I had stepped on someone's toes; I had bypassed someone [her immediate supervisors] and taken the initiative. The request to start a macular nurse reception came from above them.

Finally, Mary received positive feedback but only after working on her project alone for six months. In the meantime, she encountered pessimistic attitudes and a lack of interest in her project. Even once the reception idea was approved and was up and running she did not get any feedback on her hard work. 'It got started sort of on the quiet. I never got any feedback from my own supervisors, or complaints, or a thank you.'

Once the reception was open, Mary formulated new plans to maximise her own and the nurse-run reception's performance. She targeted getting more training and being capable of doing even more at the reception. However, the request for more training was denied and deemed unnecessary by the doctors on her ward. This training would have helped her to interpret patients' eye scans and decide whether the patient could wait until the next scheduled check-up for an injection administered by a doctor, or whether treatment was necessary before that scheduled date.

The cons are, from my point of view that almost every time I still have to consult a doctor about the [eye] scans ... It is a bit stressful because the doctor has his/her own reception and I always burst in to ask: 'What do you think?' I have experience [so she could be trained to make the decision] but it seems here no one sees the need for that. The doctors still want me to consult them ... Often I have already made a decision before I go to consult the doctor. And these are matters of opinion. One doctor says: 'Yes, let's give another injection,' and another says, 'it's no use [to give another injection], let's keep observing.'

Mary attempted to justify the training she sought by explaining that patients visiting the eye clinic in general, and her own practice in particular, were not normally at risk of complications and not in a life-threatening condition, unlike on some other hospital wards. According to Mary, a nurse could be trained to take more responsibility. In addition, patients were coming to Mary's nurse-run reception in a transition period and as control patients. Nurses would neither be admitting them to the hospital, nor discharging them from it. The check-up is a scheduled part of their treatment and patients would have to return regardless of the decision a nurse made concerning their optical health. A doctor is required to administer the injection to the patient and a nurse would only have been making the decision on whether it was time for the injection or better to wait a little longer.

Having been granted her nurse-run reception initiative, Mary was denied any other special responsibilities on the ward. In Mary's view her supervisor, head nurse Tina, was not comfortable with nurses having too many responsibilities:

I have wanted to learn a lot more, but I haven't been given a chance. I wanted to learn the photography [of eyes] ages ago ... I have been going there on my own to learn ... I can do it but the supervisors don't want to give me a chance ... Apparently, I have so many roles, responsibilities, here that I can't take any more. Not a good explanation. The more responsibilities the better; the more I can do the more I can be utilised.

Even if they recognize the potential of entrepreneurial activity to create value, organisations may have inbuilt barriers that prevent it from occurring (Ireland et al. 2006a). This is demonstrated in our case. Next, we will analyse this account by identifying the different hurdles and boundaries Mary encountered when setting up the nurse reception. The boundaries are discussed in the context of this particular organisation, but also more generally in the context of the management and organisational practices of Finnish healthcare organisations.

**Boundary 1: Bypassing the Supervisor**

Mary came up with an idea for a new type of service, a nurse-run reception at the hospital. She first followed the ordinary line of command by presenting the idea to her immediate supervisor, head nurse Tina. Tina did not openly oppose the idea but neither was she supportive of Mary progressing it. Perhaps Tina anticipated some further challenges or problems along the way, perhaps opposition from the management or the doctors. However, Mary felt so strongly about her idea that she bypassed her supervisor and sent it to the panel reviewing new initiatives. We interpret Mary's action of bypassing the supervisor to be an example of risk-taking behaviour.

Risk, understood as the possibility of incurring financial loss, is a fundamental characteristic of entrepreneurship and innovation in existing firms. Intrapreneurial risk normally includes risk relating to career advancement and reputation (Antoncic 2003). Mary did not experience risk as a possibility of financial loss – it would not be realistic to argue that she would have experienced a salary cut or sacrificed her job had she failed in her project – but she risked her relationship with her immediate supervisor and possibly even with her immediate colleagues. Studies show that employees in organisations are subject to a socialisation process and they experience social risks of this kind, rather than the financial type, when they act in an intrapreneurial manner (Antoncic 2003).

Antoncic argues that individual risk-taking can be compounded to organisational-level risk-taking behaviour. Individual risk-taking or individual innovations – will eventually result in organisational level activities and 'impact organisational level risk-taking behavior in intra-preneurship' (2003: 16). However, risk-taking behaviour is individual even if it is eventually transmuted to the organisational level (Antoncic 2003). At the organisational level, the case organisation's top management valued individual risk-taking, since Mary's proposal was eventually accepted.

**Boundary 2: Solitude and Support**

In order to present the idea to the board, it was necessary for Mary to develop a thorough action plan. The case organisation, or in this case the lower management, offered no explicit support for Mary's new idea and instead of solving problems for the intrapreneur, built imaginary obstacles by stating that the idea was not worthy of further development (see Ireland et al. 2006a). Mary did not feel she was being supported by her supervisor. Instead, she faced discouragement, obstacles and people preventing her from realising her new ideas. Therefore, she could not ask for help from her colleagues with the plan and was forced to work on the plan alone. Mary needed to maintain a positive spirit and belief in her idea without any support or recognition from others. However, in time Mary was able to launch her nurse-run reception after the panel reviewing initiatives accepted her initiative and authorised the establishment of the reception.

She worked alone with little organisational support for taking a risk. The only official advice had been the recommendation of the head nurse that amounted to advice to keep her head down and do her job as a nurse. Acting as an individual, Mary was able to develop her idea and formulate detailed plans for her reception, but to communicate her plan within the hierarchy and to make it happen, she needed to access the official structure via the forum of the panel responsible for overseeing initiatives. Mary's independence and stubborn endeavour to achieve her goal suggest that she was willing to and capable of taking individual risk and exploiting the organisation structures even in the absence of any expressed sponsorship of her ideas.

It is expected that organisational support and organisational values have a positive impact on intrapreneurship (Antoncic and Hisrich 2001). An intrapreneurial organisation attempts to remove obstacles to problem-solving, and to ensure that different parts of the organisation are neither too protected nor too isolated that they restrain the intrapreneur from creating new ideas. An intrapreneurial organisation encourages new ideas and experimentation rather than discouraging them, and is aware that new products and services do not necessarily work instantly but may take some time to bear fruit. Hisrich (1990) also emphasises the importance of human and financial resources in the case of new ventures, and the importance of multidisciplinary teamwork. In intrapreneurship literature, the concept of 'intracapital' has been introduced, referring not only to resources but also to the freedom to make the new ideas happen (Pinchot 1985).

Literature on intrapreneurship recognizes the crucial role of organisational support and teamwork in intrapreneurship (Kearney et al. 2008; Kuratko et al. 2004, 2005). Teamwork facilitates intrapreneurship as, for example, it allows large-scale problems to be broken down into more manageable problem areas. That facilitates solutions arising from smaller decisions, meaning that an individual is likely to have a more positive attitude towards risk, as problems divided into smaller, more comprehensible segments make the risks involved appear manageable (Antoncic 2003). In addition, an optimistic atmosphere and the impression that staff can exert some influence foster risk-taking in organisations (Kahneman and Lovallo 1993). The same qualities offer a more supportive environment for handling the inevitable disappointment arising from a failed venture (Shepherd et al. 2009). Conversely, Mary's experience was of pessimism and a lack of interest in her project during the development phase. Before the plan was submitted to the board, Mary presented it to some of her peers (nurses) and doctors in her internal networks. Their positive feedback probably helped Mary decide to move forward with developing the plan and eventually submit it to the panel (see Kelley et al. 2009 on intra-organisational networking). She continued to work on her plan alone and in an atmosphere of uncertainty, but trusting that her effort would pay off.

## Boundary 3: Job Description

As a nurse in a large university hospital, Mary had her own tasks and duties within the organisation. She was, however, interested in the nationwide challenges of increasing numbers of patients with macular degeneration and the resultant huge treatment queues. She was worried by the length of the waiting lists in her own hospital and about the doctors' capacity to meet their target imposed by the public healthcare authorities of treating a certain number of new patients in a given period. Since the doctors were also responsible for seeing all the control patients, it was difficult for them to meet all the new patients as well. In addition, Mary acknowledged the current situation in the Finnish healthcare system where doctors are leaving the public sector and increasingly moving to the private sector, often citing financial reasons for doing so. Mary realised that, generally, doctors appreciate challenging cases, and in the case of eye diseases, those are to be found predominantly in the public sector hospitals. Hence, Mary's idea of nurses taking care of the control patients and doctors concentrating on the more interesting and challenging cases incorporates different interests and implies a holistic style of thinking beyond her own job or responsibilities. In addition, she felt that she would gain from the initiative herself through broadening her own job description. However, she suggested in the interview that the main motivation for her to push the idea forward was the magnitude of the problem. She needed to look beyond her own responsibilities and to stretch the scope of her own job in order to provide a justification for her initiative. Her holistic perception resonates with entrepreneurial behaviour, which takes into account the interests of various stakeholders (Gibb 1993) but on the other hand acknowledges the ambiguity related to problem-solving and decision-making. An individual nurse is not expected to be able or willing to group problems afflicting the organisation and see the 'big picture'. 'The job that we [nurses] have been trained to do ... is meeting the patient, guiding the patient, helping the doctor in the patient situation ... If one is a nurse by nature one will seek this kind of nursing work.'

Mary took a very holistic approach to her work and workplace by trying to solve wider societal and organisational problems while also improving the satisfaction involved in her own job. This is behaviour that suggests risk-taking while stretching the boundaries of her own job and simultaneously being interested in others' concerns. Kahneman and Lovallo (1993) suggest that people tend to make a series of single decisions from their own perspective without paying attention to any related future decisions or wider implications. For an individual and an organisation, the ability to accept long-term risk requires the skill to group problems and implement a procedure to evaluate outcomes and the quality of performance. This also implies a more holistic approach to decision-making.

## Boundary 4: The Hierarchy between Positions and Professions

Mary's role in the organisation is defined through her job description and particularly through the traditional division of tasks between doctors, nurses and other administrative staff. These divisions are clear and rather static in Finland. By opening her own nurse-run reception, Mary implied that she had a desire to cross hierarchical boundaries, as her new tasks were traditionally the preserve of doctors alone. 'The doctor is the king and we [nurses] come behind... It doesn't have to be like that. We could cooperate if both had a clear description of tasks. This way we [nurses] wouldn't only be here to follow the doctors.'

As a nurse, Mary was supposed to follow the guidelines, instructions and norms learned by nurses during their education and later reinforced at work. Her establishment of the reception clearly broke the unwritten rules of the game and conflicted with established attitudes. Firstly, the nurse-run reception conducted tasks considered the preserve of doctors alone. Secondly, it can be considered quite revolutionary that Mary did not take notice of her immediate supervisor's remarks but proceeded with her action plan to the most senior body deciding on new projects in the hospital. Mary also invoked examples of existing nurse practice (that of diabetes nurses, for example) in other hospitals and asked to be trained to maximise her performance and that of the nurse-run reception. However, she faced the hierarchical system of beliefs prevalent in Finnish public healthcare, as exemplified by the doctors in her ward considering obtaining further training for her to be unnecessary.

In a public sector healthcare organisation, the hierarchy is not only rigid between professions but also within those professions and between organisational positions. An individual's social identity defines individual attitudes as members of the group ponder how they should think and behave (Monsen and Boss 2009). In addition, shared cultural values are especially strong in a public hospital. Operational principles reproduce what is traditional in the healthcare sector (Virtanen 2010). In Finland, doctors have special rights to prescribe drugs (only since 2010 have nurses had some limited ability to prescribe), conduct medical examinations, diagnose, decide methods of treatment, decide hospital treatment and discharge patients from the hospital. This is in contrast to Sweden, for example, where none of these tasks is restricted to doctors alone. Similarly, in most of the other Nordic countries only prescribing drugs is restricted to doctors (Lindström 2003). In Finland, however, the subordination of nurses to doctors has a long tradition and nurses' tasks are strictly separated from those of doctors (Virtanen 2010). This clear division of duties is currently being widely debated in Finland. Access to healthcare with limited resources is closely related to the division of tasks in public healthcare and this has led to calls to transfer tasks from doctors to nurses (Ministry of Social Affairs and Health 2003).

Although Mary's reception was an innovation in the relevant university hospital, nurse practices are not wholly new in Finnish public healthcare. Pilot projects were implemented in many public hospitals in the first decade of the century that involved a particular emphasis on the transfer of doctors' tasks to nurses, promoted by special training arrangements and organisational support provided by the doctors (Lindström 2003). The lack of flexibility of Finnish legislation (compared to other Nordic countries) does not fully explain the lack of support Mary faced when she crossed existing hierarchical boundaries in our case study. A particularly conservative organisational culture favours rational decision-making and tends to be risk-averse. As an extreme case, employees are not expected to take the initiative, to fail, to make mistakes; but they are expected to follow the rules, mind their own business and watch their backs. This kind of environment is not very supportive of, for example, creativity and risk-taking (Hisrich 1990).

## Boundary 5: Culture of Equality

Mary took the initiative to get her nurse-run reception up and running. She had to present her idea to the board and to tackle certain obstacles before she was able to start to realise her ambition. Her behaviour ran counter to basic assumptions related to public healthcare organisational culture as she took steps normally considered unacceptable for a nurse. In our case the immediate supervisor, the head nurse, was socialised to her position and considered the proposal (coming as it did from a nurse) to be perhaps too innovative and with the potential to stir negative reactions towards the venture among the staff (e.g. Biniari 2012). The lower management strata in this organisation maintains the traditional division between professions, positions and group thinking among nurses (see Monsen and Boss 2009 on social identity). After being granted her wish to establish a nurse-run reception, Mary was subsequently denied the opportunity to assume other special responsibilities in the ward. Head nurse Tina felt that one nurse should not have too many responsibilities – irrespective of what the nurses themselves might have wanted – and considered it important to treat all nurses equally. Such new ventures easily offend long-standing perceptions of organisational justice and may therefore create envy among the staff (Biniari 2012). Possibly Tina wanted to safeguard Mary from such envy or from becoming over-worked. Mary's endeavour suggests that organisational assumptions need to be stretched and questioned to allow a nurse to stand out from the group.

Organisational values are drivers of individual risk-taking. Organisational culture provides values, norms and a basis for socialisation and groupthink processes. Therefore, strategic leaders usually share values and visions that support intrapreneurship (Antoncic 2003). Organisational culture affects 'individual attitude formation' and moderates one form of risk acceptance, the 'behavior-based contractual relationship' (Antoncic 2003: 14). It is suggested that the single best aspect of organisational structure that defines entrepreneurial behaviour is 'structural organicity' (Ireland et al. 2009: 31). The structure of an organisation is organic when decision-making is decentralised, there is a low degree of formality, and rules and policies are not followed too fastidiously. In addition, in an organic organisation, power is based on expertise, not position, and information is made available to everyone and the processes are flexible (Ireland et al. 2009). Although providing equal opportunities for every-one, structural organicity also allows individuals to take the initiative, stand up and to strive for peak performance. This desire to ensure equality and concern with the equal treatment of employees (regardless of merit or even individual wishes) can be seen as characteristic of the culture in Finnish public sector organisations. The principle is likely to stem from the country's Community Act, which is founded on equal treatment and opportunities of its citizens. In the workplace, this is often interpreted as equal treatment of employees irrespective of their efforts and performance, which accordingly does not encourage individual initiative and innovative behaviour (Heinonen 1999).

## DISCUSSION

In this chapter, we have investigated how intrapreneurial activities take place in a public sector healthcare organisation by looking at the risk-taking processes and the consequences for an individual employee. We investigated one nurse's accounts of her activities working in a clinic within a large public university hospital. Our ethnographic study was able to reveal five related boundaries, which had to be crossed or at least stretched before it became possible for the nurse to behave entrepreneurially within the organisation. The boundaries identified suggest that intrapreneurial behaviour implies individual risk-taking by bypassing supervisors, working alone without organisational support, thinking holistically, stretching the lead actor's job description and challenging the established hierarchy between positions and professions. Perhaps most importantly, our intrapreneur had to be prepared to question the culture of equality typical of public sector organisations.

Previous studies suggest that public sector healthcare organisations are not considered very fertile ground for intrapreneurial endeavours due to their traditional culture, norms and rigid working practices (Heinonen 1999). Although our study demonstrates that it is not easy for an individual to behave entrepreneurially within a large public sector hospital, it is certainly possible. Employees can develop the skills they need to grow, take on responsibility and exploit opportunities for renewal and change. This requires individual risk-taking, which implies the stretching and crossing of existing boundaries (see Antoncic and Hisrich 2003).

An intrapreneur is not necessarily an exceptional person and employee. Our case features an ordinary nurse who was interested in what she was doing, and the outcomes and impacts of her activity. Our study demonstrates that intrapreneurship is about doing something and making things happen. This emphasises the role of an entrepreneurial process: exploring and discovering an opportunity for change and renewal, and then exploiting it (Shane and Venkataraman 2000). The main actor involved in intrapreneurship is an individual who decides to 'step up to the plate' to make their dreams come true (Ireland et al. 2006b; see also Pinchot 1985), even when their organisation does not provide them with the best environment in which to do so.

Nevertheless, our study clearly demonstrates the role of supporting organisational structures and practices in making it possible for an employee to execute an idea. The panel reviewing initiatives was a tangible, existing organisational structure that proved to be an instrument our nurse could use to gain wider acceptance of her initiative, particularly in the hierarchy, when her immediate supervisor did not support her. This instrument made it possible for top management to become aware of initiatives and to determine whether individual initiatives could serve wider organisational goals. When that was seen to be the case, the initiative was given enough support to progress to a trial. The study further elucidates the co-evolutionary process of intrapreneurial action in which organisational structures and managerial behaviour from the top down, and individual entrepreneurial behaviour from the bottom up, can together form a structure for intrapreneurship within an existing organisation (Heinonen and Toivonen 2007, 2008). Although intrapreneurship is intrinsically employee- and action-oriented (Heinonen and Toivonen 2008), it also relies heavily on organisational antecedents, such as practices and structures (Hornsby et al. 2002; Kuratko et al. 2004, 2005). These organisational premises can be, and sometimes have to be, stretched or even overcome, which involves individual risk-taking and persistence as demonstrated by our case. Eventually, such courageous individual action not only influences one's own work through increasing job satisfaction, for example, but also has wider implications within the organisation and even for society.

## CONCLUSIONS AND IMPLICATIONS

Our chapter contributes to the literature on intrapreneurship and corporate entrepreneurship by highlighting the role of individual risk-taking and particularly the different organisational boundaries that must be stretched or crossed when departing from the norm and introducing activities outside the framework of existing practices. Our study makes the existing organisational boundaries visible and suggests that an individual needs to tackle these boundaries in order to behave entrepreneurially. The chapter contributes to developing a contextualized account by analysing intrapreneurship embedded in the public healthcare sector (Welter 2011). It also provides an individual account of intra-preneurship, which has predominantly been studied from the managerial and organisational perspectives (e.g. Hornsby et al. 2002; Kuratko et al. 2004, 2005). Previous studies on intrapreneurship have acknowledged the need to investigate the phenomenon at lower levels of the organisation, utilising informants other than managers (Wales et al. 2011). Our study tackles this research gap particularly, and contributes to the existing literature by offering fresh insights on the manifestations of intrapreneur-ship and related organisational boundaries.

Our study was conducted in one public hospital and offers an account from an individual nurse. That account forms the basis of a powerful and persuasive case study illustrating how entrepreneurial behaviour happens in the context of a public healthcare organisation (Siggelkow 2007). It would be interesting to investigate other related accounts, for example those of her co-workers and managers, to find out how they felt about the public clinic and Mary's intrapreneurial behaviour. Attempting to under-stand an entrepreneurial act embedded in its social environment, as revealed by multiple interactions between intrapreneurs and other stake-holders, does present considerable methodological challenges (Biniari 2012). Team-, group- and organisational-level activities are equally important to researchers attempting to find out how intrapreneurial behaviour occurs and how it varies in certain contexts (Wales et al. 2011).

The study also has clear practical implications for public healthcare organisations involved in the process of reorganising their grassroots activities to become more competitive in the eyes of customers and employees (nurses and doctors in our case). By making the existing boundaries visible, we pinpoint the crucial individual obstacles to intra-preneurial behaviour within a particular context. We argue that managers and employees need to understand that intrapreneurship requires personal risk-taking, and that it implies stretching and crossing existing bound-aries. It is possible for anyone to act entrepreneurially within an organisation as intrapreneurship is an everyday activity of normal employees, and does not depend on heroic behaviour. However, indi-vidual action will have to be complemented by organisational fora and methods to communicate and channel individual initiatives to match broader organisational goals. In addition, the integration of the entre-preneurial venture with those not involved in it is important in order to prevent clashes and unproductive emotional outbursts among staff.

## NOTE

1. A Finnish expression meaning 'are appearing from everywhere'.

## REFERENCES

Åmo, B.W. (2006), 'Employee innovation behaviour in health care: the influence from management and colleagues', *International Nursing Review*, **53** (3), 231–237.

Åmo, B. and L. Kolvereid (2005), 'Organizational strategy, individual personality and innovative behaviour', *Journal of Enterprising Culture*, **13** (1), 7–19.

Antoncic, B. (2003), 'Risk taking in intrapreneurship: translating the individual level risk aversion into the organization risk taking', *Journal of Enterprising Culture*, **11** (1), 1–23.

Antoncic, B. and R.D. Hisrich (2001), 'Intrapreneurship: construct refinement and cross-cultural validation', *Journal of Business Venturing*, **16** (5), 495–527.

Antoncic, B. and R.D. Hisrich (2003), 'Clarifying the intrapreneurship concept', *Journal of Small Business and Enterprise Development*, **10** (1), 7–24.

Antoncic, B. and R.D. Hisrich (2004), 'Corporate entrepreneurship contingencies and organizational wealth creation', *Journal of Management Development*, **23** (6), 518–550.

Berger, P.L. and T. Luckmann (1976), *The Social Construction of Reality: A Treatise in the Sociology of Knowledge*, Harmondsworth: Penguin.

Biniari, M.G. (2012), 'The emotional embeddedness of corporate entrepreneurship: the case of envy', *Entrepreneurship Theory and Practice*, **36** (1), 141–170.

Brockhaus, R.H. (1980), 'Risk taking propensity of entrepreneurs', *Journal of Business Venturing*, **2** (2), 509–520.

Cantillon, R. (1734), *Essai sur la nature du commerce en general* (*Essay on the Nature of General Commerce*), transl. H. Higgs, London: Macmillan.

Covin, J.G. and O.P. Slevin (1991), 'A conceptual model of entrepreneurship as firm behavior', *Entrepreneurship Theory and Practice*, **16** (1), 7–25.

Day, D.L. (1994), 'Raising radicals: different processes for championing innovative corporate ventures', *Organization Science*, **5** (2), 148–172.

Dess, G.G., G.T. Lumpkin and J.G. Covin (1997), 'Entrepreneurial strategy making and firm performance', *Strategic Management Journal*, **18** (9), 677–695.

Eisenhardt, K.M. and M.E. Graebner (2007), 'Theory building from cases: opportunities and challenges', *Academy of Management Journal*, **50** (1), 25–32.

Eskildsen, J.K., K. Kristensen and H. Jørn Juhl (2004), 'Private versus public sector excellence', *TQM Magazine*, **16** (1), 50–56.

Gibb, A.A. (1993), 'The enterprise culture and education: understanding enterprise education and its links with small business, entrepreneurship and wider educational goals', *International Small Business Journal*, **11** (3), 11–34.

Guth, W.D. and A. Ginsberg (1990), 'Guest editors' introduction: corporate entrepreneurship', *Strategic Management Journal*, **11** (4), 5–15.

Heinonen, J. (1999), *Kohti asiakaslähtöisyyttä ja kilpailukykyä. Sisäinen yrittäjyys kunnallisen yksikön muutoksessa* (*Towards Customer Orientation and Competitiveness. The Potential of Intrapreneurship in the Change Process of a Municipal Service Unit*), Dissertation, Publications of Turku School of Economics and Business Administration, Series A-5:1999, Turku.

Heinonen, J. and J. Toivonen (2007), 'Approaching a deeper understanding of corporate entrepreneurship – Focusing on co-evolutionary processes', *Journal of Enterprising Culture*, **15** (2), 165–186.

Heinonen, J. and J. Toivonen (2008), 'Corporate entrepreneurs or silent followers?', *Leadership and Organization Development Journal*, **29** (7), 583–599.

Henrekson, M. (2005), 'Entrepreneurship: a weak link in the welfare state?', *Industrial and Corporate Change*, **14** (3), 437–467.

Hisrich, R.D. (1990), 'Entrepreneurship/intrapreneurship', *American Psychologist*, **45** (2), 209–222.

Hjorth, D. and B. Johannisson (2006), 'Learning as an entrepreneurial process' in A. Fayolle (ed.), *Handbook of Research in Entrepreneurship Education*, Cheltenham, UK and Northampton, MA, USA: Edward Elgar Publishing, pp. 46–66.

Holt, D.T., M.W. Rutherford and G.R. Clohessy (2007), 'Corporate entrepreneurship: an empirical look at individual characteristics, context, and process', *Journal of Leadership and Organizational Studies*, **13** (4), 40–54.

Hornsby, J.S., D.F. Kuratko, D.A. Shepherd and J.P. Bott (2009), 'Managers' corporate entrepreneurial actions: examining perception and position', *Journal of Business Venturing*, **24** (3), 236–247.

Hornsby, J.S., D.F. Kuratko and S.A. Zahra (2002), 'Middle managers' perception of the internal environment for corporate entrepreneurship: assessing a measurement scale', *Journal of Business Venturing*, **17** (3), 253–273.

Ireland, R.D., J.G. Covin and D.F. Kuratko (2009), 'Conceptualizing corporate entrepreneurship strategy', *Entrepreneurship Theory and Practice*, **33** (1), 19–46.

Ireland, R.D., M.A. Hitt and D.G. Sirmon (2003), 'A model of strategic entrepreneurship: the construct and its dimensions', *Journal of Management*, **29** (6), 963–989.

Ireland, R.D., D.F. Kuratko and M.H. Morris (2006a), 'A health audit for corporate entrepreneurship: innovation at all levels: part I', *Journal of Business Strategy*, **27** (1), 10–17.

Ireland, R.D., D.F. Kuratko and M.H. Morris (2006b), 'A health audit for corporate entrepreneurship: innovation at all levels: part II', *Journal of Business Strategy*, **27** (2), 21–30.

Kahneman, D. and D. Lovallo (1993), 'Timid choices and bold forecasts: a cognitive perspective on risk-taking', *Management Science*, **39** (1), 17–31.

Kearney, C., R. Hisrich and F. Roche (2008), 'A conceptual model of public sector corporate entrepreneurship', *International Entrepreneurship Management Journal*, **4** (3), 295–313.

Kelley, D.J., L. Peters and G.C. O'Connor (2009), 'Intra-organizational networking for innovation-based corporate entrepreneurship', *Journal of Business Venturing*, **24** (3), 221–235.

Kuratko, D.F. (2005), 'The emergence of entrepreneurship education: development, trends, and challenges', *Entrepreneurship Theory and Practice*, **29** (5), 577–597.

Kuratko, D.F. (2009), *Entrepreneurship: Theory, Process, Practice*, 8th edn, Mason, OH: Southwestern/Cengaga Publishers.

Kuratko, D.F., J.S. Hornsby and M.G. Goldsby (2004), 'Sustaining corporate entrepreneurship: modeling perceived implementation and outcome comparisons at organizational and individual levels', *Journal of Entrepreneurship and Innovation*, May, 77–89.

Kuratko, D.F., R.D. Ireland, J.G. Covin and J.S. Hornsby (2005), 'A model of middle-level managers' entrepreneurial behaviour', *Entrepreneurship Theory and Practice*, **29** (6), 699–716.

Lindström, E. (2003), 'Terveydenhuollon eri ammattiryhmien välisen työnjaon kehittäminen Suomessa ja muissa Pohjoismaissa' ('Division of tasks among health care professionals in the Nordic countries'), Sosiaali- ja terveysministeriön monisteita (The Ministry of Social Affairs and Health handouts), 2003:12.

Lumpkin, G.T., C.C. Cogliser and D.R. Schneider (2009), 'Understanding and measuring autonomy: an entrepreneurial orientation perspective', *Entrepreneurship Theory and Practice*, **33** (1), 47–69.

Ministry of Social Affairs and Health (2003), 'Kansallinen projekti terveydenhuollon tulevaisuuden turvaamiseksi – Hoidon saatavuus ja jonojen hallinta' ('National project to secure future of health care – access to care and waiting list management'), Sosiaali- ja terveysministeriön työryhmämuistioita (The Ministry of Social Affairs and Health handouts), 2003:33.

Monsen, E. and R.W. Boss (2009), 'The impact of strategic entrepreneurship inside the organization: examining job stress and employee retention', *Entrepreneurship Theory and Practice*, **33** (1), 71–104.

Morris, M.H., J.W. Webb and R.J. Franklin (2011), 'Understanding the manifestation of entrepreneurial orientation in the nonprofit context', *Entrepreneurship Theory and Practice*, **35** (5), 947–971.

Phan, P.H., M. Wright, D. Ucbasaran and W.-L. Tan (2009), 'Corporate entrepreneurship: current research and future directions', *Journal of Business Venturing*, **24** (3), 197–205.

Pinchot, G., III (1985), *Intrapreneuring: Why You Don't Have to Leave the Corporation to Become an Entrepreneur*, New York: Harper & Row.

Rosen, M. (1991), 'Coming to terms with the field: understanding and doing organisational ethnography', *Journal of Management Studies*, **28** (1), 1–24.

Shane, S. (1994), 'Are champions different from non-champions?', *Journal of Business Venturing*, **9** (5), 397–421.

Shane, S. and S. Venkataraman (2000), 'The promise of entrepreneurship as a field of research', *Academy of Management Review*, **25** (1), 217–226.

Sharma, P. and J.J. Chrisman (1999), 'Toward a reconciliation of the definitional issues in the field of corporate entrepreneurship', *Entrepreneurship Theory and Practice*, **23** (3), 11–27.

Shepherd, D.A., J.G. Covin and D.F. Kuratko (2009), 'Project failure from corporate entrepreneurship: managing the grief process', *Journal of Business Venturing*, **24** (3), 588–600.

Siggelkow, N. (2007), 'Persuasion with case studies', *Academy of Management Journal*, **50** (1), 20–24.

Slevin, D.P. and S.A. Terjesen (2011), 'Entrepreneurial orientation: reviewing three papers for further theoretical and methodological development', *Entrepreneurship Theory and Practice*, **35** (5), 973–987.

Thornberry, N. (2001), 'Corporate entrepreneurship: antidote or oxymoron?', *European Management Journal*, **19** (5), 526–533.

Valovirta, V. and J. Hyvönen (ed.) (2009), 'Julkisen sektorin innovaatiot ja innovaatiotoiminta. Esiselvitys sektoritutkimuksen neuvottelukunnalle' ('Public sector innovations and innovative activity. Pilot study'), *Osaaminen, työ ja hyvinvointi* 11/2009.

Van Maanen, J. (1988), *Tales of the Field: On Writing Ethnography*, Chicago, IL: Chicago University Press.

Virtanen, J.V. (2010), *Johtajana sairaalassa. Johtajan toimintakenttä julkisessa erikoissairaalassa keskijohtoon ja ylimpään johtoon kuuluvien lääkäri- ja hoitajataustaisten johtajien näkökulmasta* (*Being a Manager in a Hospital Setting*), Dissertation, Series A-2:2010, Turku School of Economics, Turku: Uniprint.

Wales, W., E. Monsen and A. McKelvie (2011), 'The organizational pervasiveness of entrepreneurial orientation', *Entrepreneurship Theory and Practice*, **35** (5), 895–923.

Welter, F. (2011), 'Contextualizing entrepreneurship – conceptual challenges and ways forward', *Entrepreneurship Theory and Practice*, **35** (1), 165–184.

Wennekers, S. and R. Thurik (1999), 'Linking entrepreneurship and economic growth', *Small Business Economics*, **13** (1), 27–55.

# 9. Critical resources and capabilities for successful entrepreneurship: the case of agriculture

## Jorunn Grande

## INTRODUCTION

This chapter explores entrepreneurial efforts, ability to change and resources of critical importance to new value-added ventures on farms. Policymakers, researchers and practitioners as well as advisory services seem to perceive increased entrepreneurial efforts on farms to be an important tool in offsetting the prospect of declining income and employment in the agricultural sector (Alsos et al. 2003; De Wolf et al. 2007; Vesala et al. 2007). A challenge is however that previous research struggles to identify significant improvements in income levels on farms arising from such efforts (McNally 2001; Rønning and Kolvereid 2006). Also knowledge on which are critical factors to improve performance appears limited (Barbieri and Mshenga 2008; Evans 2009; McElwee 2008). Engagement in new diversifying ventures may be a challenging task for all types of firms, hence the success of value-added farm ventures is not guaranteed. Farm firms may in particular encounter trouble due to the type of industry, traditions and their liability of smallness. Nevertheless, their ability to cope with this new situation and perform necessary changes is of great importance both for their own survival and for sustaining economic development in rural communities.

To investigate these issues the chapter takes on an explorative approach looking at three Norwegian farm cases. Furthermore, a theoretical framework with pillars within the resource-based view (RBV), the dynamic capability (DC) and the entrepreneurial orientation (EO) perspectives underpins the study. These theories have in recent years received increased attention within the general management and entrepreneurship literature due to their importance in explaining business change and sources of value creation in firms. The RBV elicits which types of resources appear to be most critical to these firms, that is, that they are valuable, rare and contributing to forming unique and hetero-geneous resource bundles. Such unique resources may give the firm a competitive advantage and thus be an important source to superior profit. Next, the DC perspective provides a better understanding of which types of processes and routines are most critical in forming and supporting changes needed for developing successful new ventures. DC involves adaption and change because these build, integrate and reconfigure other resources and capabilities (Helfat and Peteraf 2003). Finally, investiga-tion of a firm's EO shows which types of entrepreneurial decision-making styles and processes are seemingly dominant or lacking in these types of firms.

The agricultural setting should provide an interesting context yielding further insight into the fields of RBV, EO and DC. The literature shows that effective patterns of both EO and DC might vary within different business contexts (Lumpkin and Dess 1996; Teece et al. 1997). From being a heavily subsidized sector the farm sector is now facing tougher market challenges due to reduced domestic protection and increased competition. It is a mature industry with little room for market expansion through traditional production and economics of scale. Traditionally large co-operatives have taken care of the market relations and single-farm enterprises may have had little experience with sales and product development. Based on the challenges discussed above this chapter investigates the following research questions: (1) Which are critical resources and capabilities to farm firms engaged in new value-added ventures? (2) Why are these resources and capabilities important? and (3) How might the farm context have influenced this situation?

The rest of this chapter is organised as follows. Firstly, the theoretical perspectives guiding the study are presented. Then the explorative case methodology and selection of cases are discussed, followed by a presen-tation of firm context and description of the cases. Next, the analysis maps and investigates the importance of various resources, capabilities and entrepreneurial orientation in these three ventures. Finally, the conclusion presents important findings and implications.

## THEORETICAL BACKGROUND

### The Resource-based Perspective

According to the RBV, firm resources vary in their level of importance for generating added value to the firm (Barney 1991). It postulates that only firm resources that are valuable, rare and inimitable (VRI) have a potential to gain a lasting superior performance to the firm (Barney 1991, 2002). This means that the resources must possess some kind of value or capacity enabling the firm to pursue certain opportunities or to avoid threats in the environment (Newbert 2007). The RBV also assumes that firms are heterogeneous with respect to these resources and capabilities, and that these resources and capabilities are not always easy to move or copy between firms. In order to sustain these advantages over time they must also be inimitable and non-substitutable (Barney 1991; Dierickx and Cool 1989). This notion allows for differences in firm resource endowments to exist and persist over time (Newbert 2007). In this way the firm's unique resource bundle provides a foundation for developing new firm strategies and lasting competitive advantages.

Previous studies of the farming sector suggest that the availability of physical assets such as land and buildings are important for development of new business ventures (Alsos and Carter 2006). This relates to Miller and Shamsie (1996) who divided resources into two main groups, property-based and knowledge-based resources: 'Some resources cannot be imitated because they are protected by property rights, such as contracts, deeds of ownership or patents. Other resources are protected by knowledge barriers – by the fact that competitors do not know how to imitate a firm's processes or skills' (Miller and Shamsie 1996: 521). This seems to fit the situation on farms which have a lot of resources tied up in properties and through legal systems such as production quotas. In this study it is thus of particular interest to see how the resource situation at the originating farm has influenced the development of a new venture.

**Developing Dynamic Capabilities**

Dynamic capabilities enable firms to alter and renew their resource base (Ambrosini and Bowman 2009). Exploring new markets and developing and selling new products and services often demand quite different use of resources and might also require changes in how the firm is organized and operates (Easterby-Smith et al. 2009). How do farm firms manage to reshape their business platform and adapt to changes in an efficient way? In these situations RBV has been criticized for falling short by focusing too much on resource possession and too little on the dynamics of resource exploration.

To capture and strengthen the attention to these processes the DC approach has thus emerged as a useful supplement to the RBV (Eisen-hardt and Martin 2000). Teece et al. (1997: 515) define DC as 'the firm's ability to integrate, build, and reconfigure internal and external competence to address rapidly changing environments'. Furthermore, Helfat et al. (2007: 4) explain DC as 'the capacity of an organisation to purposely create, extend and modify its resource base'. DCs are critical in the sense that they create change and renewal of the firm by enabling it to alter its resources base. Examples of DCs mentioned in the literature are business networks, strategic orientation, educational routines and research (Eisenhardt and Martin 2000; Teece et al. 1997); resource acquisition, resource reconfiguration and integration, learning network and strategic path aligning (Borch and Madsen 2007). Prior research suggests that DCs are important for the creation and evolution of new business ventures (Newbert 2005). However, there seems to be little knowledge about the link between resources and the mechanisms in which they are used in creating new value for firms (Sirmon et al. 2007; McKelvie and Davidsson 2009).

## Entrepreneurial Orientation

Entrepreneurial alertness and activities enable firms to discover and explore resources that form their unique resource bundle. Both the RBV and its extension into the DC perspective have been criticized for insufficiently integrating creativity and the entrepreneurial act (Alvarez and Busenitz 2001; Arthur and Busenitz 2006). More knowledge about entrepreneurial processes – that is, how ideas are generated and new resources are explored – is thus a valuable supplement to the RBV by suggesting alternative uses of resources that have not previously been discovered (Alvarez and Busenitz 2001). This means that entrepreneurial attitudes and activities will be important aspects to explore when investigating critical factors to the performance of new ventures in farm firms.

   The concept of entrepreneurial orientation (EO) has become a well-known and widely used framework for investigating the entrepreneurial 'mind' of firms due to its possible influence on strategic processes and performance (Rauch et al. 2004). This frame of mind may be reflected through the firm's organisational culture, decision-making style and processes. EO is thus used to characterise a set of related processes including a variety of activities within the firm. These may be summarized in the following key dimensions described by Lumpkin and Dess (1996): (1) a propensity to act autonomously; (2) a willingness to innovate; (3) a willingness to take risks; (4) a tendency to act aggressively towards competitors; and (5) a proactive approach towards market opportunities. The key argument is that firms that act more autonomously, and are innovative and take risks and so forth, are better equipped to sustain their performance than their peers with fewer such efforts. Research shows that firms with a high EO score tend to perform better than firms with a lower EO score (Wiklund 1999; Zahra and Covin 1995).

Studies have however shown that the relationship between EO and performance might be contingent on other environmental and/or organizational factors (Covin and Slevin 1989; Lumpkin and Dess 1996). For instance, turbulent environments and limited access to financial capital are likely to negatively affect risk level and thus indirectly influence the relationship between EO and performance. This means that all of the dimensions above may not be present or important in a new venture.

**Integrating Perspectives**

The respective scientific perspectives of EO, RBV and DC all provide interesting views and in-depth insights into how new value may be revealed and created in firms. Through investigation of firms' entrepreneurial orientation we get signals of their creativity and ability to renew and explore their own resource bases aligned to the needs and opportunities in the market. Their entrepreneurial alertness and mind also make them in better shape to discover and explore unique resources. Furthermore, investigation of resources through the RBV gives a foundation for understanding which type of resources appears most critical to the firm, that is, valuable, rare and contributing to the formation of unique and heterogeneous resource bundles. Finally, the DC perspective provides a better understanding of the processes and routines that are critical in forming and supporting these changes. In some respects the concepts might partly overlap and compete (Grande 2008), but most importantly, the EO, RBV and DC perspectives each have their unique hallmarks providing in-depth insights into what constitutes the source of profit in firms.

## METHOD

An in-depth and longitudinal study of three Norwegian farm businesses engaged in new value-added businesses was undertaken to explore the importance of resources, dynamic capabilities and entrepreneurial orientation in the performance of these new ventures. A case study research design was set up with the farm business as the unit of analysis. The cases were selected according to Yin's (2003) suggestions about contrasting cases, making sure that they represented different firm sizes, type of operations, farmer's background, location and so forth. The three cases originate from farms with very different resource endowments, which give the study a potential for rich information about possible resource advantages and disadvantages. In one way all these firm cases may be considered successful since they have been able to start as well as run the business initially. However, they have chosen very different paths in developing their business, and they also differ quite a bit with respect to size and ambition of growth.

The cases were investigated through farm visits and several interviews in the period from 2006 to 2009. First, semi-structured face-to-face interviews directed toward the business manager and/or owner were performed in 2006 to 2007. The interviews were taped and then transcribed after each interview, a process that enabled further in-depth interpretation immediately following the interview. Web pages and newspaper articles were also used as supplementary information. After preliminary work and analyses of the data the respondents were contacted again to verify unclear information and to get supplementary information where needed. The firms were interviewed two years after the initial interviews, during autumn 2008 and spring 2009, to supply additional information about their further development. The process of interviewing and analysing was performed as a parallel and interactive process. The analysis and results presented in the following are based on both initial and follow-up interviews. Table 9.1 gives a brief description of the three cases.

## PRESENTATION OF CASES

The presentation of the three farm cases gives a brief view of the characteristics and resources attached to the farms and their owners/managers, their background and reasons for engaging in the new ventures. Tables 9.2, 9.3 and 9.4 give a chronological overview of important resources, decisions and events for each case.

**The Meat Case**

The Meat case is located fairly close to populated areas and in an agricultural area consisting of mainly farms that are above country average in size. The new venture involves producing and selling differentiated meat products based on the farmed animals. The new business venture also includes a farm store for direct sale to consumers. It is

*Table 9.1   Brief description of cases*

|  | Meat case | Jelly case | Cheese case |
|---|---|---|---|
| Type of new venture | Meat processing and farm shop | Jellies, juices and health care products based on local berries and herbs | Cheese factory and farm shop |
| Start of new venture | 2001 | 2004 | 1998 |
| Number of full-time employees | 2.5 (1.5 at the farm) | < 1 | 3 (+2 at the farm) |
| Traditional production | Milk and meat | None (land rented) | Milk and grain |
| Size of farm | Large | Both very small | Average |
| Location | Agricultural production close to populated areas | Coastal community, agriculture in decline, distant from populated areas, tourists in summer | Agricultural production area, close to populated areas |
| Farm resources | Rich | Limited | Good |
| Education | Agricultural school | University: one in horticulture, one a nurse | University: teacher and polytechnic engineer |
| Involved persons | Couple, wife manager of new business | Collaboration between two women | Couple, wife manager of new business |

funded on a conventional farm operation including quite a large milk production in addition to beef and pig production. The new business venture is registered as a separate firm and owned by the couple, but the wife is the head manager. The husband is head of the board and runs the conventional farm operation together with one employed person. Their history as farmers goes back to the mid-1980s, when they took over the farm property from his parents. At that time the farm was an average sized farm with respect to milk quota and acreage. Later they expanded the milk production, and added pigs and beef cattle to the operation. The new value-added venture in meat processing is thus the last one in a series of several diversification activities at the farm.

*Table 9.2   Chronology of important decisions and events for the Meat case*

| Year | Event/decision | Critical factors |
| --- | --- | --- |
| 2000 | Planning new business | Governmental farm policies |
| 2001 spring | Firm established, investments in processing and buildings | Governmental support Expertise from family/ relatives |
| 2001 autumn | First sales, farm shop opened | Expertise from family/ relatives |
| 2002 | Started using room for meeting and parties Making and serving food for these | |
| 2002–04 | Started and ended participation in farmers market | Time-consuming, problem with cooling and perishable products |
| 2004 | Started selling at two local fairs | Hired workers |
| 2006 | Use of wholesaler for distribution | Need to add storage capacity |
| 2007 | Ended use of wholesaler | Problem with perishable products and due dates, low profitability |
| 2007 | Started own distribution | Time, experience, knowledge |
| 2008 | Ended participation at local fairs Participated in two courses Business as usual | Time-consuming, focus marketing Time Two employees |

*Source:*   Author.

## The Jelly Case

The Jelly case was established in 2003 and is founded on two small farms and the use of natural resources from its surroundings. The new venture is organised as a separate firm situated on one of the farms. Here it produces and sells jellies, jam and healthcare products based on local berries and herbs. It is owned and operated by two women in their mid-thirties who inherited the two separate farms from their parents. Also, the farms are located quite far from populated areas in a coastal community with relatively small farms. The women grew up on their respective farms, but have lived and worked outside the community until

*Table 9.3   Chronology of important decisions and events for the Jelly case*

| Year | Event/decision | Critical factors |
|---|---|---|
| 1997 | First woman moved back to the community, took over the parents' farm, initiated business | Feeling responsibility for keeping the farm in the family |
| 2001 | Second woman moved back to parents' house/small farm in the community | Desire to move back, prepared to be 'self-made' |
| 2001–03 | Developing business idea together Several ideas: some stopped due to legal issues and governmental regulation. Finally idea about using local berries and herbs developed. | Close personal relationship, one a strong urge to start own business Ideas based on agricultural policies, past work experience and education. |
| 2003 summer 2003 Nov./ Dec. | Starting the business, plan for farm shop Starting juice and jelly production First sales related to Christmas season | Local resources: wild/garden berries, perceived competition. Support from rural development agency |
| 2004–05 | Two entrepreneurship courses, one designed for women | Expenses paid by local authorities Critical in developing self-esteem |
| 2004 autumn | Rebuilding farm house establishing, and opened farm shop | Old farm building, one husband carpenter |
| 2005–06 | Informal agreement about renting juice press | Equipment from horticultural school |
| 2006 | Decided not to join wholesaler | Demanded increased production. Perceived too risky. Control growth |
| 2006–08 | Not building kitchen/production facilities, renting production facilities sustained | Avoid risk, keep flexibility |
| 2007 | Joined network of 16 local food producers | Organizing/network building skills |
| 2008 autumn | Two regional prizes | Persistent quality, local resources |
| 2008 autumn | New web pages and web shop | Marketing bureau, new knowledge needed |

*Table 9.4    Chronology of important decisions and events for the Cheese case*

| Year | Event/decision | Critical factors |
|------|----------------|------------------|
| 1996–98 | Developing idea, planning the new business | External courses, study tours, owner proactivity, external network, milk as input, spare buildings |
| 1998 | Starting the business Includes rebuilding old farm house, producing cheese for sale | Financing from rural development agency, own developed product, food safety authorities |
| 1998 | Establishing local network of local artist and small-scale producers | Quality of services and products offered to consumers Person as driving force |
| 2001 | Expanding storage capacity and production facilities | Support from rural development agency Need hired employees to handle increased production |
| 2001 | Several prizes for excellent products and innovative capacity | Excellence in production and quality |
| 2004 | One of the products receives the special denomination 'Norwegian speciality' | |
| 2003–08 | Limiting the production. Advisers eager to expand the new business – keeping own pace Increase in production due to increased efficiency | Want to keep a hand on productions and sales herself Hired workers, good health |
| 2007–08 | Person in family seriously ill | Employees' ability to run the operation |
| 2008 | Technical and administrative improvements | Son IT expert, external resources: IT supplier |

a few years ago. The decision to move back home was motivated by a felt responsibility for keeping the farm in the family and also an urge to establish a business venture. The owners/founders had not coordinated their plans, but explained that it has been natural for them to cooperate since they were close friends from childhood and had great trust in each other. Both women are married and have small children living at home.

**The Cheese Case**

The Cheese case was established in 1998 and was one of the first farms in Norway to start producing cheese at the farm. Since then it has developed several types of cheeses which are sold at the farm shop, local supermarkets and through speciality food shops around the country. The farm is average in size and has a traditional production of milk and grain. It is located fairly close to populated areas in an area surrounded by other grain and/or milk-producing farms. In recent years several farms in this area have engaged in value-added business and the area has become increasingly a popular tourist attraction. The owner/manager of the Cheese case has been central in developing a local network of small-scale producers, handicraft and other tourist attractions. The cheese production business is run as a part of the traditional farm and owned by the couple together; however, the wife is in charge of managing it. The owner/manager grew up on the farm and inherited the farm together with her husband from her family in 1983. Prior to taking over the farm they had both been university educated and had worked and lived outside the farm. They have received several prizes for their products and are perceived as very successful by other business owners and rural developers.

# EXPLORING FIRM RESOURCES (RBV)

## Physical Firm Resources

The RBV explains that firms need to possess valuable, rare and unique resources that are difficult for others to copy in order to sustain a superior competitive advantage (Barney 1991). The analysis indicates that the existing resource endowments at the farms may contribute to such resources. The two cases based on conventional meat and milk production use the output from this production as a major input in their new ventures. These resources might be considered valuable, but not rare, immobile or difficult for others to imitate. However, the access to these resources at a certain quality and price seems to have been beneficial compared to firms that may not have this opportunity. By producing their own raw material they are able to make better use of the special quality in these products. As expressed by the owner of the Meat case: 'we know what we feed our pigs and that this gives a special quality of the pork which the customers really appreciate', and also, 'it is the type of meat they got in the old days and which our customers are not able to get in the supermarket today'. For the Cheese case the access to sufficient quantities of milk of a certain quality and freshness is necessary to make good-quality cheese. The existing resource endowment seems thus to have been important for selecting both type and size of engagement. This indicates that the size of the farm in terms of farmed land and conventional production of milk and meat may be important for opportunity recognition, growth and revenue generation in the new ventures. This is in line with Barbieri and Mshenga's (2008) arguments and findings related to agro-tourism at United States (US) farms. They argue that larger farms, based on acreage and number of employees, have a greater potential for revenues since these assets enable firms to offer a greater variability of products.

A location relatively close to populated areas has enabled the Meat and Cheese cases to attract consumers to the farm shop more easily and thus sell a considerable share of sales directly to consumers. In both agricultural and general business economies, distance to market has traditionally been considered an influential factor for the profitability of firms, due to lower transportation costs and easier access to consumers. Thus, the findings above are in line with the concept of 'location rent' (also called Von Thünen rent), which is described as a surplus to the producer earned due to the location of the production (Barlowe 1986; Hanink 1997). This also supports earlier work of De Wolf et al. (2007), who found that farms engaged in new business ventures often depend on the adjacent market for selling their products. Finally, by attracting consumers to the farm it also seems easier to develop the farm setting, buildings and landscape as an important part of the product, thus adding further value and uniqueness less easily copied by others. Higher profit margins are also earned on products sold at the farm store.

## Human Resources

The involved persons' competence and personal characteristics may be perceived as a unique resource related to the RBV. All farm entrepreneurs seem to make good use of their prior knowledge and experience. Earlier studies have focused on the level of education (university education) as an influential factor to new venture performance on farms (Barbieri and Mshenga 2008). The present study indicates that the type of education (subject or vocational type) is equally important for the new ventures. As woman B in the Jelly case explains: 'As a nurse I saw that old people liked the traditional recipes on cosmetics, soaps and lotions. These were very good for problematic skin. I learned a lot about this when I was as a nurse working with farmers.' Also, the owner of the Cheese case explains that experience as a teacher has been a very valuable experience when working with people and in communication with the consumers. The owners of the Meat case have no university education, but their practical education in agronomy and in home economics at vocational school as young people may have built a foundation for their new venture through agrarian attitudes, accepting farm values and traditional foods. This suggests that different types of vocational education, and not necessarily many years of university education, might be important for getting entrepreneurial ideas and carrying them through.

The personal characteristics and attitudes of the owners and managers of the investigated cases seem to be equally as important as formal education and practice. All cases show that they can act independently and think differently from the mainstream within agriculture. However the cases still seem to differ in how strongly they go on pursuing their ideas. For instance the Jelly case owners/managers seem to need to discuss and have more support from others to carry through their ideas, while the Meat case owners/managers just act instantly if they have a strong belief in an idea. They seem to be quite quick to initiate projects instead of taking on a 'wait and see' attitude. Next, the Cheese case seems to stand out as being the most professional in all aspects. The founder and manager acts very professionally, she presents herself as very sincere and determined in all her business relations. This might be due to having the longest experience since the start-up of the new venture in 1998, but it might also stem from her educational background and work practice outside agriculture.

In total, this suggests that the cases have not succeeded in establishing their new ventures based on better resources alone, but rather through applying unique knowledge to make better use of these resources. This supports and adds to earlier findings in Blundel's (2002) study of two artisan cheese makers. He found that his study objects depended heavily on core tacit knowledge in order to reproduce traditional and sometimes geographically specific practices. This is also similar to what has been observed in our cases. Their new bundling of resources may thus represent the advantages that shape their portfolio of difficult-to-trade assets as prescribed by the RBV (Alvarez and Busenitz 2001).

## EXPLORING ENTREPRENEURIAL ORIENTATION (EO)

### Innovative Capacity and Idea Generation

A joint feature of the founders/managers seems to be their creativity and continuous search for new ideas. All of them therefore appear to be well equipped with business ideas and possess innovative capacity, even if these may originate from different sources and have different purposes. As the wife in the Meat case explains about her husband: 'I have to keep him busy all the time otherwise he will come up with some new ideas and give us even more work.' The businesses seem to be clever in making small adjustments in developing their business, both as a response to consumer needs and also as a means to making their production more effective. Several of them have received special awards for their products. Especially, the Cheese case has been successful in making unique and remarkable products for several years and stands out as the most innovative with regard to product as well as production processes. When the founders started out with this type of cheese production, it had not been done in the country in more recent times. Also, the most successful products seem to be those invented on the farm, by adapting traditional recipes to new food trends and tastes. The Meat case has renewed the old 'butcher's shop', which has almost disappeared in Norway due to harsh competition from supermarkets in recent decades. Even if it is an old concept, the owners have been able to spot and grasp this opportunity and also give it a unique link to the farm setting through traditional recipes, branding and sales through the farm shop.

**Risk-taking Propensity**

The cases with a rich physical resource base are seemingly more willing to take on risk, indicating a tendency that the firms adjust their risk level to the risk they can 'afford'. The farm with the largest resource endowment in terms of farmed land and animal production (the Meat case) tends to be more risk-taking and proactive compared to the two other cases. They started up with quite heavy investments right away, and explained that they took on quite a risk at the start: 'then it came about that we built and opened the shop in 2001. We admit to have gambled a bit then. We really did not know if anyone would show up at all' (Wife), 'it was not that easy to know' (Husband fills in). This risk attitude might be due to the personal characteristics of the owners, but might also arise from a better financial situation. Being based on a larger traditional production indicates access to and a possibility to generate larger income streams. The Jelly case, however, which had the least initial resources, seems to be more risk-averse. The two founders/owners seem to have developed the venture more carefully and stepwise in a way that fits their risk profile and financial situation. However, more agile risk attitudes might also be related to the personal ambitions of the owners. Due to differences in farm resources and knowledge they therefore seem to have adopted different approaches for developing the new ventures.

**Proactivity and Autonomy**

All cases show that they can act independently and think differently than the mainstream within agriculture. According to Lumpkin et al. (2009: 63) autonomy 'may not be an issue among independently owned and managed entrepreneurial firms, because such founders are already acting autonomously'. According to this statement we could also assume that all the cases must possess strong autonomy since they have all created a viable new venture that is still in operation. The cases seem however to differ in how strongly they pursue their ideas: that is, they differ in the level of autonomy they display. For instance the Jelly case owners/ managers seem to need to discuss and have more support from others to go through with their ideas, while the Meat case owners/managers just act instantly if they have strong belief in an idea. For instance, woman A in the Jelly case explains: 'we also discuss with our colleagues in two other similar firms at times. They are not competitors, since one of them has a slightly different product and the other one operates in another part of the country.' The strong autonomy and independence of others of the Meat case can be exemplified by the attitude of the owners/managers towards integrating new knowledge and developing ideas: the husband explains, 'It's no good that everybody should do the same things; if your neighbour succeeds on a venture it does not mean that you should do the same thing. You have to look further away and get your ideas and competence elsewhere.' Also the Cheese case showed strong autonomy in the manager's endurance in learning the craft of cheese-making and continuous product development. She was the first to start cheese-making on farms in recent times and thus tested and pushed new governmental regulation on these issues. Altogether, this endurance of independent spirit and autonomy has enabled the farm firms to shape their uniqueness and competitive advantage.

**Competitive Aggressiveness and Market Relations**

Competitive aggressiveness and a description of being fierce competitors (Lumpkin and Dess 1996) does not seem to fit these ventures. Even if one of the cases (the Cheese case) seems to handle the marketing side very well, the description of 'fierce competitor' does not seem to fit the manager at all. The manager of the Cheese case has worked her way to the markets and made agreements very wisely but through more peaceful and polite negotiations. Two of the cases seem however to lack a particular strategy against potential competitors, and in fact they claim to have no competitors at all. They believe that emphasising their own brand gives them sufficient advantage in case new competitors show up. They seem not to dwell on the risk and what to do if others copy them, but express that 'others must understand that there will be no profits if they start similar types of business' (husband, Meat case). These attitudes might seem a bit naive and strange, but make sense when compared to earlier findings. Prior research has detected that farmers lack knowledge in several areas such as product development and market orientation (Alsos and Carter 2006; Kvam et al. 2002). Competition and market relations are also expected to pose challenges to local food producers in Norway due to a mature food industry dominated by a few powerful wholesalers (Dulsrud 1999).

## EXPLORING DYNAMIC CAPABILITIES

### Integrating Knowledge and Physical Resources

Integrating external experience and knowledge has been critical in product development, production processes and marketing in all cases. The farm couple in the Meat case explained that initially they knew very little about meat processing, product development, food safety issues and regulations related to developing this type of business. Also, the Cheese case manager explained that she spent a lot of time on learning and integrating new knowledge by taking courses and visiting cheese factories abroad. She explained: 'We invested a lot of time and effort the first years before starting commercially. I looked to Sweden because they have had a lot of experience there. Spent a lot of time testing the cheese production and did not start any sales before we were 100% satisfied with the production'. In this way she learned the craft of making cheese herself and spent a lot of time testing production processes and a variety of cheese types before her first sales. Devoting time to this seems to have been of great benefit in the further development of the firm. This might also be seen as a product development capability which includes a mix of attitudes, knowledge and competence allowing further changes and continuous renewal of the firm.

A limited resource base seems to have made the Jelly case more explorative in the initial phase with regard to which type of resources to integrate and use. From the very beginning the owners/managers have needed to integrate external resources as input to a much greater extent.

They have converted old buildings into a shop and thus partly use the farm buildings and premises as a resource in their new venture. However, due to their resource constraint they exploit adjacent local resources to a greater extent and rest on prior work experience in the product development and in managing the business. Earlier studies also indicate that resource scarcity may stifle entrepreneurial efforts in the very early stage (Kodithuwakku and Rosa 2002). However, the Jelly case shows that creative use and integration of external local resources may partly compensate for lack of resources.

The cases seem to differ considerably when considering the methods of learning and integrating of new knowledge. All firm owners have engaged in entrepreneurial coursework prior to establishing the new venture, but have since then used different ways of acquiring external knowledge. While the Jelly and the Cheese case owners/managers explain that they often participate in courses and other arenas where small-scale producers meet, the owners of the Meat case express quite a sceptical view on the courses that are offered to rural entrepreneurs. On integrating new knowledge, the wife in the Meat case explains: 'It is wrong to say that we have nothing to learn from taking external courses, but we have the competence we need. Courses are courses, they often seem a bit narrow focused. We have been lucky to know people with that competence.' In this way they show a great independence, but this attribute might hamper them in a situation where they need to renew their competence base. The owners/managers with the highest level of education (the Jelly and Cheese cases) seem more proactive in seeking new knowledge through formal courses and using external resources. These two cases also seem to be more frequently in touch with local and regional advisory services. In total this might suggest that their different educational background and work experience influences their way of learning and integrating knowledge, and thus also the type of DC that develops in terms of appropriate learning capabilities and new product and process development, as is also suggested by Zahra et al. (2006) and McKelvie and Davidsson (2009).

**Network and Strategic Alliances**

The owners/managers of these cases seem to have relied on both formal and informal (social) networks in developing their new ventures. In this way they have been able to reduce costs, increase access to consumers, and get information on product development and marketing, as well as discussing ideas. As an example, the Cheese case participates in and has been an important part in developing a local network of artisan firms, artists and historic sites in the community. Joint efforts through this network in marketing and sales have resulted in an increased stream of better-paying customers to the farm shop. During the summer there might be busloads of tourists several days a week coming to watch, experience and shop. Another example of a less formal but still important connection is an agreement the Jelly case has had with a horticultural school in product development and processing. Woman B in the Jelly case explains: 'We have an agreement with a horticultural school about using a berry press. This is very cost and time efficient for us. The people over there are also very useful for discussing this with.' Even if many relations are informal, these contacts level out some of the disadvantages the ventures may have connected to market knowledge and product development. These findings then support George et al. (2001), who argue that appropriate networks might keep businesses updated on product development, new technology, consumer trends and market development.

However, challenges in some areas suggest that their existing network may not be sufficient. Even if earlier work has found that consolidation and fostering of social networks are important to the success and well-being of farm businesses (Meert et al. 2005), these may not be sufficient or appropriate to farmers who engage in new ventures. The domination of a few formalized networks, and dependence on family and acquaintances in the investigated cases, suggest that they tend to stick to their previous social network and rely on less professional relationships. The seeming lack of appropriate networks within marketing and distribution for two of the cases signals that they might suffer in establishing appropriate new networks for their venture.

## SUMMARY AND PROPOSITIONS

Figure 9.1 illustrates the relationships explored in this chapter. It suggests that a firm's final performance (P) may be created through several internal sources of competitive advantage and profit, and through the interaction between these sources.

The result of this study might be summarized in the following propositions:

*Proposition 1: Related to resources and RBV*

- Unique farm premises and competence may increase the value-creating potential in conventional farm products when applied in new value-added ventures (R→P)

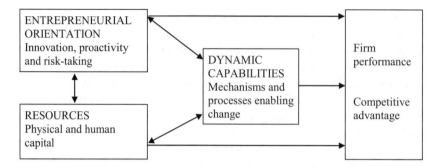

*Figure 9.1   Research model and explored relationships*

- Human capital resources such as past experience and education may influence idea generation capacity (R→EO)
- Human capital resources such as past experience and education may influence knowledge integration and learning (R→ DC)

*Proposition 2: Related to EO*

- A high idea generation and innovative capacity has a positive influence on performance in new farm ventures, because it enables them to more easily explore the uniqueness of their own resource base and increases their chance of offsetting lack of resources (EO→R→P)
- A high idea generation and innovative capacity has a positive influence on performance in new farm ventures, because it enables them to more easily spot new market opportunities and improve product efficiency (EO→DC→P)
- A relatively low risk profile, limited proactivity and competitive aggressiveness might reduce potential profits in new farm ventures by being too conservative in market penetration and sales (EO→P)

*Proposition 3: Related to DC*

- A high integrative capability (DC) ensures efficient value creation from entrepreneurial activities by supplying needed new competence (learning) and resources (DC→R→P)
- High integrative capacity may level out disadvantages related to initial lack of resources and knowledge (DC→R)
- Human resources such as educational type and level, and work experience are likely to influence the firms' method of knowledge integration (R→DC)

- The ability to build appropriate networks and strategic alliances (DCs) may benefit new value creation in farm firms by reducing costs, increasing access to consumers and information on product development and marketing (DC→P)
- Path-dependency, lack of knowledge and experience may reduce the appropriateness of DC related to building strategic network and alliances (R→DC)

## CONCLUSION

Through the lenses of the RBV, EO and DC perspectives this chapter has explored resources, entrepreneurial activities and capabilities critical for change in farm firms engaged in new value-added ventures. Three farm cases have been explored, yielding findings contributing to both theory and practice.

The investigation of resource use shows that the farm cases with traditional productions have had a significant transfer of these resources to their new venture. Due to property rights, legal entrance and knowledge barriers these may be considered valuable and unique resources. Such resource richness may thus give greater access and potential to develop valuable and unique resources.

An assessment of entrepreneurial activities and attitudes indicates that all three cases are good at idea generation and innovativeness in product development. This has enabled them to more easily spot new opportunities in the market as well as increase their chance of offsetting lack of resources. The study confirms that farm firms struggle with market relations. The cases appear rather modest on competitive aggressiveness and proactivity against market opportunities. None of the cases seem to be extreme risk-takers, but rather low or medium types of risk-takers. This might reduce their potential profit by being too conservative in market penetration and sales. However, by concentrating on local markets and keeping a low profile in marketing they might be able to develop at a pace that fits their capacity and knowledge background.

In all three cases, learning, integration of external resources and knowledge seem to have been crucial DCs for nourishing change and success in the new venture. In this way the cases have managed to supply needed external resources and knowledge in order to act on ideas and developing their business. However, the analysis indicates that they may benefit from improving their skills on building strategic alliances and network.

Finally, by integrating these three theoretical concepts – RBV, EO and DC – the study supplies valuable insight in how they may be interlinked. By investigating these issues through only one of these perspectives, important pieces may be missing. The theoretical discussion and empirical findings demonstrate that together these perspectives may provide a more complete picture on how a firm's internal factors may interact and leverage several bases of competitive advantage in new value creation processes. The investigated cases have not achieved profits based on better resources alone, but rather through exploring the potential uniqueness and better use of these resources. In order to launch a new idea, rural farm firms will benefit from developing and applying DCs to facilitate necessary changes. Without entrepreneurial attitudes and alertness these firms would be neither dynamic nor adaptive.

Even though the study leads to interesting findings, it has limitations. The case study approach limits the possibility of making generalizations. Thus, further replications are needed in order to increase the validity of the findings. The investigation of these three cases, including three different resources situations, has given rich information about possible outcomes and links. However, this also has limited comparisons with respect to equalities in the resource base and possible links to EO, DC and performance. Parts of the analysis are also based on retrospective information, which might have highlighted some information more than it should.

The study has several implications for policymaking and for farm and rural business owners. The explored cases indicate that both entrepreneurial efforts and unique resources are critical in creating new profitable ventures in micro-rural firms such as farms. Micro-rural firms have great differences in their physical as well as in their human resource bases which will affect their needs in relation to support systems. In line with earlier work by De Wolf et al. (2007) and McElwee (2008) our results suggest that increased competence and skills among farmers is essential in enabling them to carry out and perform on entrepreneurial ideas and activities. Building entrepreneurial skills may increase their awareness of possibilities and threats in the environment and may aid them in exploring their own uniqueness. However, this study also shows that rural entrepreneurs learn in different ways. A greater focus on how these firms learn and integrate new knowledge is therefore pertinent.

# REFERENCES

Alsos, G.A. and S. Carter (2006), 'Multiple business ownership in the Norwegian farm sector: resource transfer and performance consequences', *Journal of Rural Studies*, **22**, 313–322.

Alsos, G.A., E. Ljunggren and L.T. Pettersen (2003), 'Farm-based entrepreneurs: what triggers the start up of new business activities?', *Journal of Small Business and Enterprise Development*, **10**, 435–443.

Alvarez, S.A. and L.W. Busenitz (2001), 'The entrepreneurship of resource-based theory', *Journal of Management*, **27**, 755–775.

Ambrosini, V. and C. Bowman (2009), 'What are dynamic capabilities and are they a useful construct in strategic management?' *International Journal of Management Reviews*, **11** (1), 29–49.

Arthur, J.D. and L.W. Busenitz (2006), 'Dynamic capabilities and venture performance: the effects of venture capitalists', *Journal of Business Venturing*, **21** (2), 195–215.

Barbieri, C. and P.M. Mshenga (2008), 'The role of the firm and owner characteristics on the performance of agritourism farms', *Sociologia Ruralis*, **48**, 166–183.

Barlowe, R. (1986), *Land Resource Economics: The Economics of Real Estate*, 4th edn, Englewood Cliffs, NJ: Prentice-Hall.

Barney, J.B. (1991), 'Firm resources and competitive advantage', *Journal of Management*, **17**, 97–120.

Barney, J.B. (2002), *Gaining and Sustaining Competitive Advantage*, 2nd edn, Upper Saddle River, NJ: Prentice Hall.

Blundel, R. (2002), 'Network evolution and the growth of artisanal firms: a tale of two regional cheese makers', *Entrepreneurship and Regional Development*, **14**, 1–30.

Borch, O.J. and E.L. Madsen (2007), 'Dynamic capabilities facilitating innovative strategies in SMEs', *International Journal of Technoentrepreneurship*, **1** (1), 109–125.

Covin, J.G. and D.P. Slevin (1989), 'Strategic management of small firms in hostile and benign environments', *Strategic Management Journal*, **10**, 75–87.

De Wolf, P., G. McElwee and H. Schoorlemmer (2007), 'The European farm entrepreneur: a comparative perspective', *International Journal of Entrepreneurship and Small Business*, **4**, 679–692.

Dierickx, I. and K. Cool (1989), 'Asset stock accumulation and sustainability of competitive advantage', *Management Science*, **35**, 1504–1511.

Dulsrud, A. (1999), 'Markedstrender og utvikling i distribusjonsmønsteret' ('Trends in marketing and distribution'), in O.J. Borch and E.P. Stræte (eds), *Matvareindustrien mellom næring og politikk*, Oslo: Tano Aschehoug, pp. 104–133.

Easterby-Smith, M., M.A. Lyles and M.A. Peteraf (2009), 'Dynamic capabilities: current debates and future directions', *British Journal of Management*, **20** (s1), S1–S8.

Eisenhardt, K. and J.K. Martin (2000), 'Dynamic capabilities: What are they?', *Strategic Management Journal*, **21**, 1105–1121.

Evans, N. (2009), 'Adjustment strategies revisited: agricultural change in the Welsh Marches', *Journal of Rural Studies*, **25** (2), 217–230.

George, G., D.R. Wood Jr and R. Khan (2001), 'Networking strategy of boards: implications for small and medium-sized enterprises', *Entrepreneurship and Regional Development*, **13**, 269.

Grande, J. (2008), 'Linking entrepreneurial orientation and dynamic capabilities: research issues and alternative models', in P. Kyrö and A. Fayolle (eds), *The Dynamics between Entrepreneurship, Environment and Education*, Cheltenham, UK and Northampton, MA, USA: Edward Elgar, pp. 220–244.

Hanink, D.M. (1997), *Principles and Applications of Economic Geography*, New York: John Wiley & Sons.

Helfat, C., S. Finkelstein, W. Mitchell, M.A. Peteraf, H. Singh, D. Teece and S. Winter (2007), *Dynamic Capabilities: Understanding Strategic Change in Organizations*, Malden, MA: Blackwell.

Helfat, C.E. and M.A. Peteraf (2003), 'The dynamic resource-based view: capability lifecycles', *Strategy of Management Journal*, **24**, 997–1010.

Kodithuwakku, S.S. and P. Rosa (2002), 'The entrepreneurial process and economic success in a constrained environment', *Journal of Business Venturing*, **17**, 431–465.

Kvam, G.T., B. Brastad, E.P. Stræte and O.J. Borch (2002), 'Regional nyskaping i matsektoren' ('Regional innovation in the food sector'), *Landbruksøkonomisk forum*, **19**, 5–16.

Lumpkin, G.T., C.C. Cogliser and D.R. Schneider (2009), 'Understanding and measuring autonomy: an entrepreneurial orientation perspective', *Entrepreneurship Theory and Practice*, **33**, 47–69.

Lumpkin, G.T. and G.G. Dess (1996), 'Clarifying the entrepreneurial orientation construct and linking it to performance', *Academy of Management Review*, **21**, 1–8.

McElwee, G. (2008), 'A taxonomy of entrepreneurial farmers', *International Journal of Entrepreneurship and Small Business*, **5**, 465–478.

McKelvie, A. and P. Davidsson (2009), 'From resource base to dynamic capabilities: an investigation of new firms', *British Journal of Management*, **20**, 63–80.

McNally, S. (2001), 'Farm diversification in England and Wales – what can we learn from the farm business survey?', *Journal of Rural Studies*, **17** (2), 247–257.

Meert, H., T. Van Huylenbroeck, M. Bourgeois and E. Van Hecke (2005), 'Farm household survival strategies and diversification on marginal farms', *Journal of Rural Studies*, **21**, 81–97.

Miller, D. and J. Shamsie (1996), 'The resource-based view of the firm in two environments: The Hollywood film studios from 1936–1965', *Academy of Management Review*, **38** (3), 519–543.

Newbert, S.L. (2005), 'New firm formation: a dynamic capability perspective', *Journal of Small Business Management*, **43** (1), 55–77.

Newbert, S.L. (2007), 'Empirical research on the resource-based view of the firm: an assessment and suggestions for future research', *Strategic Management Journal*, **28**, 121–146.

Rauch, A., J. Wiklund, M. Frese and G.T. Lumpkin (2004), 'Entrepreneurial orientation and performance: cumulative empirical evidence', paper presented at 23rd Babson College Entrepreneurship Research Conference, Glasgow, 4–6 June.

Rønning, L. and L. Kolvereid (2006), 'Income diversification in Norwegian farm households: Reassessing pluriactivity', *International Small Business Journal*, **24**, 405–420.

Sirmon, D.G, M.A. Hitt and R.D. Ireland (2007), 'Managing firm resources in dynamic environments to create value: looking inside the black box', *Academy of Management Review*, **32**, 273–292.

Teece, D.J., G. Pisano and A. Shuen (1997), 'Dynamic capabilities and strategic management', *Strategic Management Journal*, **18**, 509–533.

Vesala, K., J. Peura and G. McElwee (2007), 'The split entrepreneurial identity of the farmer', *Journal of Small Business and Enterprise Development*, **14**, 48–63.

Wiklund, J. (1999), 'The sustainability of the entrepreneurial orientation–performance relationship', *Entrepreneurship Theory and Practice*, **24**, 37–48.

Yin, R.K. (2003), *Case Study Research. Design and Methods*, Applied Social Research Methods Series, Vol. 5, New York: Sage.

Zahra, S.A. and J.G. Covin (1995), 'Contextual influences on the corporate entrepreneurship performance relationship – a longitudinal analysis', *Journal of Business Venturing*, **10** (1), 43–58.

Zahra, S.A., H.J. Sapienza and P. Davidsson (2006), 'Entrepreneurship and dynamic capabilities: a review, model and research agenda', *Journal of Management Studies*, **43** (4), 917–955.

# 10. Grasping the entrepreneurial opportunity process with diaries

**Leila Hurmerinta and
Eriikka Paavilainen-Mäntymäki**

## INTRODUCING OPPORTUNITIES AND WHAT IS YET TO BE GRASPED

In the entrepreneurship research tradition, many researchers have considered that the true nature of entrepreneurial behaviour is demonstrated in the process, where entrepreneurs search, identify, evaluate and capitalize on opportunities (e.g. Baron 2006; Brännback and Carsrud 2008; Chen et al. 2009; Kaish and Gilad 1991; Smith et al. 2009). This process, or chain of events, has yet to gather a consensus understanding within academia, and the variations in terminology and conceptualizations are manifold. For example, Baron and Ensley (2006) discuss pattern recognition in relation to opportunities; Casson and Wadeson (2007) treat different types of opportunity as different projects within the firm; Baum and Bird (2010) discuss creative, practical and analytical intelligence and opportunities; and Chen et al. (2009) discuss the creation, recognition and exploitation of opportunities. Moreover, studies on the topic have accumulated and continued to accumulate increasingly during recent years, but only a handful have tried to tackle opportunities from preliminary weak signals and inventive ideas to final materialization (e.g. Baron and Ensley 2006; Chen et al. 2009). Existing studies, both on the academic side and on the managerial side, address the topic either by focusing on a small cross-section of the entire process, such as the identification of an opportunity, or are conceptual papers looking to form some comprehension of the subject. In the existing studies, opportunities are often defined as something tangible or separable from the context, such as opening a niche market, inventing a new product, or the implementation of a new law. However, this chapter contends that opportunities are much more abstract, dynamic and complex. They can be comprehended as sudden inspirations or epiphanies, where an entrepreneur identifies an opportunity and understands its potential applicability in an instant. This provides a sound basis for the research described here, which attempts to address the propositions and implications of earlier research on opportunities, namely capturing the opportunity process together with its dynamics, logic and potential patterns within firms, by focusing on the behaviour and perceptions of the entrepreneurs. The chapter is positioned within the research traditions of entrepreneurship, organizational behaviour and innovation.

The context of the study constitutes Finnish small enterprises operating in the food industry. Food industry small and medium-sized enterprises (SMEs) have long remained robustly domestic operators, adhering to local tastes, positioning themselves close to primary production as well as the end consumers, and limiting international exposure due to stringent food safety regulations, national protectionism and product perishability. During recent years, Finnish food SMEs have acquired an interest in developing their operations to become more competitive, and adopted bolder strategies to achieve growth, international market share, visibility and profitability. At the same time, international food chains and imported foodstuffs and groceries have gained a firmer foothold in Finnish food markets. In this increasingly competitive and crowded marketplace, opportunities have played an essential role in creating new inputs and insights to the somewhat traditional industry sector (Ahola 2008; Kaipio and Leppänen 2005; Mäki 2008; Wrang 2008; Wrang et al. 2008).

The chapter begins with a brief theoretical discussion on opportunities and the opportunity process in the context of firms' growth, development and internationalization. Methodological choices, and especially the diary as a primary data collection method, are then discussed. This is followed by research findings and finally conclusions and implications.

## CONCEPTUALIZING OPPORTUNITIES OF GROWTH, DEVELOPMENT AND INTERNATIONALIZATION

During the past four decades of active entrepreneurship research, an excessive amount of research has accumulated and a steady research stream has been formulated and found its place in the management research tradition (see e.g. Blackburn and Kovalainen 2009). Opportunities have always played an implicit but central role in entrepreneurship, whether connected to the source and reason for companies to be established (e.g. Cornelissen and Clarke 2010), company development to

take place (e.g. Companys and McMullen 2007), technological developments to emerge or new entrepreneurs to advance (e.g. Baron 2006). In
the traditional writings of Schumpeter (1934) and Kirzner (1973),
opportunities, though under different names and titles, had an impact,
whether equilibrating or disequilibrating, on the development of entire
economies and market systems. Opportunities have, however, lacked a
clear and unified conceptualization among researchers, for which there
are multiple, understandable reasons: the topic can be seen as too
complex to obtain a single definition, too challenging to grasp with one
particular approach, it is highly contextual and related to the personality
and characteristics of the entrepreneur, and is strongly situational. As
such, one can justifiably ask, is there really any point in trying to tackle
this issue in order to formulate one generally acceptable and usable
definition?

Despite a multitude of studies that have grasped the topic of opportunities and all the grandeur built around them, researchers still lack genuine
knowledge about what opportunities are really formed of and how they
can be searched, recognized, explored, evaluated, analysed, exploited and
materialized (e.g. Ardichvili et al. 2003). The sources of opportunities, as
well as the mechanisms for how their preliminary weak signals are
turned into something tangible – be it a product, service, system, business
model or a strategy – and made profitable, persists in the nature of a
black box. In the existing literature, the focus has been on detecting and
categorizing opportunities as such, but an issue that has not yet been fully
tackled is the actions that are connected to opportunities. An opportunity
is not really an opportunity unless entrepreneurs act to realize it.
Opportunity is an outcome of the entrepreneurial process (Alvarez and
Barney 2010). In this sense, it might be advisable to study the combination of opportunities and their practical exploitation. In addressing the
issue, a working definition was developed for this study: an opportunity
is an instance where the entrepreneur identifies potential and realizes its
practical applicability.

Alvarez and Barney (2010) suggest that an integrated approach to
opportunities is not always possible. They have presented two different
approaches to opportunities that also influence the pattern of the opportunity process. Entrepreneurs may discover objective opportunities that
already exist in the market (the critical realism of discovery opportunities), or may create opportunities that do not exist without the human
input of entrepreneurs (the evolutionary realism of creation opportunities). While learning is a central feature of forming and exploiting both
discovery and creation opportunities (Alvarez and Barney 2010: 567), the
mechanisms of the process are different. In creating opportunities,

knowledge is formed during the process so that decision-making is incremental and experimental, while when discovering opportunities the evaluation and exploitation of opportunities is based on previously learned techniques allowing for normative decision-making. The working definition and the role of action in opportunities are depicted in Figure 10.1.

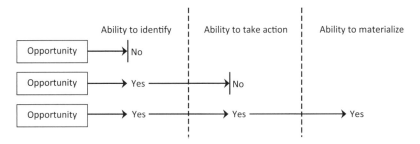

*Figure 10.1   The relationship between opportunities and actions*

Whatever the opportunity is, an entrepreneur has first to identify it – its existence or the potential for creating it. Next they should act either to analyse and evaluate the opportunity or to start to explore it. Finally, exploitation in the form of materializing or developing the opportunity makes it real. All these phases demand special skills and characteristics from the entrepreneur, summed up as ability.

In recent years, opportunities, for example as an element of entrepreneurial behaviour, have attracted increased attention and interest in academia (see e.g. Mainela et al. 2011 for a recent publication). New publications on the topic have mushroomed and conferences have been filled with sessions addressing opportunities.[1] On the crest of the wave, this chapter also aims to address opportunities. The aim of this study is to introduce the opportunity concept and the process of how entrepreneurs identify, evaluate and capitalize on opportunities.

In order to work around the existing research challenges in relation to opportunities and yet learn from them, it is necessary to conduct further research, studies that try to dig deeper than what is observable with the naked eye and tackled with traditional methods. Methodological experimentation is one of the alternatives at the researcher's disposal that can, in the best-case scenario, provide them with the depth, breadth and diversity of data they are seeking to unravel the complex and unresolved characteristics of opportunities (Balogun et al. 2003). This is closely related to the observation made by Balogun et al. (2003: 198) that there is a 'growing need for researchers to be close to the phenomena of study, to concentrate on context and detail, and simultaneously to be broad in their scope of study'. Diaries represent a newer approach in business research that could possibly provide some fresh insights on opportunities. The following sections outline the diary approach and how it has been applied in this research.

## METHODOLOGICAL APPROACH AND RESEARCH SETTING

The methodology in this chapter can be considered experiential and quite new to business research. As entrepreneurs themselves have indicated, it is often difficult to tell where new ideas and the so-called winning formulas for business originate, and how they truly transpire; it is also a challenge for the researcher to collect data on them. To overcome this challenge, the researchers decided to apply an approach known as the diary method, familiar from the realm of sociology (e.g. Corti 1993; Weil 2006), to collect data related to opportunities and the opportunity process in real time.

### Diaries as Data Collection Tools

Research topics that have a time dimension and require sensitivity in uncovering their dynamics are especially suitable for the diary approach. Diaries have a long tradition in data collection and data creation (Bolger et al. 2003). They have been applied in several fields, but are as yet a little-used tool in the business research discipline.

Diary studies can be closely linked to ethnography, since the approach allows context to exert a strong presence in the data (e.g. Bolger et al. 2003; Balogun et al. 2003; Hall 2008; Kenten 2010). The informants in diary research are active data providers and creators instead of passive participants (Balogun et al. 2003), and a trusting relationship needs to be built (e.g. Plowman 2010) between the diarists and the researchers; diaries by nature deal with personal experiences rather than public facts. Additionally, while conducting narrative diary studies, the researcher can take into consideration the essence of time and provide a timeline and a process context for the content (see e.g. Hurmerinta-Peltomäki 2003).

Wheeler and Reis (1991) and Bolger et al. (2003) analysed diary methods and classified diary studies according to the frequency and structure of the diary entries. Diaries can be positioned in three categories, the first being interval-contingent designs, where the diarists are expected to make diary entries at predetermined, regular intervals. The second is signal-contingent designs, where the diarists are prompted to make a diary entry at fixed and/or random intervals, for example with the help of a signalling device such as a digital watch or a pager. The third class comprises event-contingent designs, where the diarists are expected to make a diary entry every time the studied event occurs in the diarists' context; this is particularly suited to studying topics that occur infrequently and over time, and cannot be traced on a fixed, regular basis.

Diaries enable feelings, attitudes, experiences, impressions, sensations and emotions to be captured that the informants may not be able to describe in interviews, which are retrospective accounts of past events (e.g. Kenten 2010). In particular, complex, processual, implicit, personal, close to unobservable and somewhat nebulous research topics are usually the targets of diary research (e.g. Bolger et al. 2003). Further, when studying a topic that is not thoroughly covered in existing research, and where emergent findings are expected, or at least hoped for, the diary approach is a viable alternative. It does not force theory or research-related concepts on the informants or the data they are providing. The diary approach is especially valuable in studies where the researcher attempts to be objective and detached from the data creation process, and it enables the diarists to use their own words and bring their own voices to the fore (e.g. Balogun et al. 2003). The diarists are not merely reporting what they have experienced; they are also selecting what they report, as well as creating their experiences and interpreting them. In this way diarists are both observers and informants in the studies, and along with the researcher play an active and central role (e.g. Alaszewski 2006; Zimmerman and Wieder 1977). Alaszewski (2006) even calls the diarists para-researchers and self-observers. This is particularly suitable in the context of opportunities, as researchers have thus far not been able to put forward a consensus definition of opportunities. So the diarists also define in their diaries what they consider as and have observed to be opportunities, which at the same time provides the researcher with a more truthful and realistic image of the topic than does the existing literature.

The study employs the self-reported event-contingent solicited diary approach, which is presented in detail in the following section together with the data analysis.

## Data Collection and Analysis

The empirical study in the focus of this chapter is part of a larger research project concentrating on the domestic and international opportunities of Finnish food sector SMEs. The dataset collected for the research project included multiple open-ended personal interviews with entrepreneurs, a nationwide survey of food sector SMEs,[2] secondary data from public and private sources, and diaries from interviewed entrepreneurs. This chapter reports on the diary material and is based on three diary narratives, supported by interviews and discussions with entrepreneurs during the research process. The entrepreneurs who took part in the qualitative data collection in the research project were selected by an independent regional food sector association, and a total of five agreed to participate. However, the diary method is quite new and unfamiliar to entrepreneurs so we were finally able to utilize only three entrepreneurs' diaries. The entrepreneurs contributing to this study are the company founders, owners and/or chief executive officers (CEOs) of their firms representing the processed food, bakery and honey production sectors. None of the firms had personnel of more than 20; the managers' business experience ranged from 10 to 25 years; and the oldest of the companies had been in business since the late 1960s. The entrepreneurs knew each other from other connections and the atmosphere in the project was quite open. All were willing to commit to the project for the entire research period, that is, 1.5 years. In terms of keeping the diary, the entrepreneurs were asked to write one for a period of approximately six months. Opportunities can be considered to emerge quite irregularly and unpredictably, and this was seen as an adequately long time span for some to arise, as well as sufficiently limited to hold the project together and keep the entrepreneurs motivated and committed to the writing task. The first interviews were conducted in 2011 from early January to late February, so the earliest diaries stretched from January to late June 2011, and the latest from February to early August 2011.

The approach selected for this study is the self-reported event-contingent solicited diary approach that follows the guidelines presented, for example, by Bolger et al. (2003), Balogun et al. (2003), Patterson (2005) and Kenten (2010). It was chosen on the basis, according to Balogun et al. (2003: 209), that 'It would be wrong to suppose that an intimate journal in management research needs to be as comprehensive as an individual's personal diary, since research-oriented diarists are likely to be prompted to record impressions of only certain types of events or issues.'

The diary approach was initiated by interviewing the entrepreneurs, which yielded a primary understanding of the firms, the entrepreneurs themselves and the food sector business and markets. All were eyeing up international markets to grow their business, yet at that time had no international experience at the organizational level. At the end of the interview, the entrepreneur was asked to keep a diary for half a year reporting on experiences, feelings and thoughts related to opportunities. The researchers provided the entrepreneurs with notebooks and flash drives, between which they could choose, together with written instructions on what issues the entrepreneurs were expected to reflect in their diaries.

The instructions were that the entrepreneurs should 'write freely, either in the form of a diary or as short notes or log entries, about how you search, create, observe, analyse and exploit business and internationalization opportunities in practice, as part of your daily business activities and routines'. The entrepreneurs were also asked to consider opportunities from the perspective of their experiences, observations, insights, feelings and emotions, challenges they had faced, critical situations, events and changes; as well as questions that arose during the period over which the diary was kept and that they would like the researchers to pay particular attention to and provide the entrepreneurs with some support and consultation on. The diarists were also advised to mark the date of each entry. All in all, the instructions were to provide the entrepreneurs with a theme that they should cover in depth.

The instructions aimed mainly to provide some guidance and reassurance for the entrepreneurs on what to write about, how often to make entries and what format they could use. In addition, the instructions aimed to ensure that the diaries would have at least some level of comparability as well as the breadth and depth to provide the researchers with rich and profound data and understanding on the complexities and dynamics of opportunities in the SME context. As the researchers did not have a clear picture beforehand of the nature of the opportunities or the entrepreneurial opportunity process, the aim was also to provide the entrepreneurs with a frame and an idea as to what we were looking for. Thus, the pre-established definition of opportunities was not very strict, rather suggestive (Bolger et al. 2003).

During the diary period, the researchers met with the diarists a couple of times in research project meetings, where the researchers presented queries on how the diary writing was proceeding and whether the diarists had any questions or need for clarification with regard to keeping the diary. These meetings also served as reminders about the ongoing diary-writing, and connected the diaries to the rest of the research project. Additionally, the entrepreneurs had the opportunity to hear each other's experiences of writing the diary.

At the end, the diaries were collected from the diarists, either by taking photocopies of the notebooks or by copying the Word files from the flash drives. It was agreed that all the diary data were to be treated confidentially, the entrepreneurs were anonymized, the diary material was to be used solely for research purposes, and the researchers would not disclose the material to any third parties.

The diary data were already in a written text format, which expedited the analysis process. The data analysis was based on a loose coding frame, where the researchers aimed to grasp an understanding of opportunities and how they emerge as a process. Thus, the nature of opportunities (complexity, contextuality, situation specificity, dynamics) answering the 'what' question, and the opportunity process (logic, pattern, dynamics) answering the 'how' question were analysed. Diary data provide the researcher with the potential to formulate a timeline, a sequence or a story for the opportunity process based on the diary logs and entries. The two approaches to opportunities, namely discovery and creation, were taken into account in analysing the process.

## THE RELATIONSHIP BETWEEN ENTREPRENEURS AND OPPORTUNITIES BASED ON DIARIES

### Case Descriptions

We had three cases all looking to international markets, constrained at the time of research by there being different kinds of opportunity processes, at different phases (Figure 10.1). The manager of the processed food company (firm A) had while working for another firm spotted international market potential for her company's products. Although the idea of international markets had already matured in her mind, she had not had time for careful planning and market research. The research project was seen as an opportunity to learn about international markets and marketing. The company was still at the identification phase, and no real action had been taken towards materialization. Opportunity was seen as a combination of new ideas and the ability to realize them: 'I have ideas, but what is then really possible …'. The manager of the bakery business (firm B) strongly aspired to grow nationally and internationally, a clear growth vision. He actively took part in research projects and seminars to discover the true potential for international markets and the capacity to realize that potential in practice. The bakery was at its active identification stage, and the manager already had an idea of where to establish the next bakery: 'opportunities are new ideas that arise from markets'. The honey production company's (firm C) vision was to develop profitability through new products and markets; the main concern was how to realize that vision. The manager had gradually become aware of the distorted image of honey as a fattening food product. He understood the need to rectify the image and thereby enlighten potential customers on the composition of honey products; systematic product development with a partner was initiated, followed by a range of projects (market scanning, marketing, cost-efficient logistics, etc.) as sub-opportunity processes, all of which aimed to achieve the main vision and materialize the primary opportunity potential (new product). Thus, it could be characterized as a creation opportunity still on its way to being materialized as a real opportunity. The manager stated that opportunity means you are 'looking for new paths and if you fail, at least you have learned something'. The three entrepreneurs could be characterized according to their activeness and systematics related to opportunity processing, and the phase of the opportunity process they stood at as the research was conducted (Table 10.1):

*Table 10.1*   *The activeness and systematics related to opportunity processing, and the phase of the opportunity process at the time of research in case companies*

|        | Activeness and systematics      | Phase of opportunity process |
|--------|---------------------------------|------------------------------|
| Firm A | Neither active nor systematic   | Identification phase         |
| Firm B | Active but not so systematic    | Identification phase         |
| Firm C | Active and systematic           | Materialization phase        |

Firms A and B had perceived the internationalization of their current products, but no evaluation of opportunity potential had been conducted at that point. We characterized firm C more as a creator of its own opportunity. A synthesis based on diaries supplemented with interviews and discussions is presented as follows.

## Synthesis of Case Results

Opportunities and the opportunity process were interwoven, and thus an analysis separating these two issues proved to be impossible. An opportunity related to 'Aha!' experiences but also to events. When analysing opportunities in greater depth it seemed that every time entrepreneurs reported 'Aha!' experiences, these were preceded by a combination of different events and actions. The opportunity is thus not merely an event or action but a combination thereof, indicating that an event needs a reaction or action from the entrepreneur to proceed towards materialization of the opportunity. Thus, some kind of complexity and dynamics in opportunities was observed.

An idea suggesting an opportunity seemed to arise from participation in events, such as seminars or meetings, or just from discussions: somebody said something that made you think, which gradually grew into a perception, or even resulted in a decision. The entrepreneurs had 'feelers' out all the time and the social context was essential in discovering opportunities (opportunity identification) (cf. Alvarez and Barney 2010). The entrepreneurs might use words like 'I was wondering', 'it attracted a lot of ideas' and so on that refer to the mental process documented in the diary. It became evident that business can also be in the form of thinking; writing your thoughts down in a diary is one way to materialize them. We think business, not only do it. The entrepreneur may approach opportunities in a rather analytical and even critical way, already processing and evaluating them efficiently as events unfold. Can they be realized? What are the risks? Profit potential? Risks should always be manageable and not threaten other business. But the entrepreneurs believed in themselves. Thus, the identification and evaluation of opportunity potential are partly simultaneous processes (cf. Ardichvili et al. 2003). An event or project might appear each day that was worth mentioning, although opportunity or materialization potential varied.

While evaluating opportunity potential there was a strong emphasis on explaining the history underlying the thoughts before elucidating them. It did not become clear whether the aim was to convince the researchers or the entrepreneur themself of the justification for their written thoughts – why some potential was perceived, or why not. The questions 'what to do?', 'how to do it?' and 'why do it?' and the answers showed up in the diaries. Although diaries enable the reflection of feelings and emotions they were rarely reported; behaviour, on the other hand, was.

It became clear that opportunities were related to learning, and the entrepreneurs often reported what they had learned from events and discussions (cf. Alvarez and Barney 2010). It is ultimately an iterative process around an opportunity, which does not necessarily produce one that merits the realization of its opportunity potential. Creating an opportunity demands a social context to help the entrepreneur evaluate its potential. The social network is then the most important context as the natural platform for business and opportunities, both as a source of and a basis for testing the entrepreneur's own ideas and getting feedback from their peers, whether laymen or other entrepreneurs. They cannot afford to invest much time or effort in an idea that does not also fully convince others, and here the entrepreneurs often need the support of and a gentle push from their peers. This is in line with Corbett (2005), who suggests that studies on learning and opportunity identification processes should be emphasized.

Based on the discussion found in the diaries, it was surprising and perhaps a little worrying to see how often and in what number opportunities actually emerge serendipitously from pure coincidence. This is somewhat in line with the literature focused on serendipity (Dew 2009; Pina e Cunha et al. 2010). The entrepreneurs each outlined several issues that turned out to be unexpected sources of opportunities: occasional meetings with other entrepreneurs and participation in seminars around topics that were not precisely in their core focus; discussions with family members, friends and relatives not connected to the business in any way; customers they bump into by chance in their shops; meeting people and observing events and trends in unexpected places such as while engaging in hobbies and on holiday, and taking part in research projects organized for example by the Finnish Funding Agency for Technology and Innovation (TEKES), or regional food sector unions and associations. Usually the opportunity emerged from a social context.

Time and timing play an important role in opportunity processes, which are sometimes very slow. The notes not only relate to events, happenings, decisions or behaviour but also to silent moments: 'nothing has happened, let's see …'. The opportunity needs its time and moment to emerge. It also became evident that entrepreneurs clearly waited for something to happen; they did not necessarily actively search for something but were sensitive towards new ideas that might arise. Time is usually a scarce resource for entrepreneurs, which led them to rely more on their own analytic and often intuitive thinking instead of investing their time more in the profound research of opportunities. The lack of time also restricts their realizing opportunities: 'Opportunities do exist, but I can catch them only when I have time.'

Another interesting finding was the time and place where opportunities and ideas might emerge, which could be anywhere. The entrepreneurs considered it crucial to carry some form of note-keeping media with them, a notebook or a mobile phone, or even scribbled something on the corner of a newspaper. A common observation was that ideas could not be forced into existence; a measure of peace and quiet was required. On the other hand, the entrepreneurs were able to come up with new ideas and spot opportunities at a very fast pace. The entrepreneur's mind was working on many things at the same time, all the time, and this pressure forged diamonds – usable opportunities. Opportunities do not respect time or place.

Figure 10.2 summarizes and illustrates issues connected to opportunities, as well as their momentary nature for an entrepreneur to grasp in a particular instance, if the circumstances and capabilities are favourable and the entrepreneur is primed for action to materialize the opportunity. The figure is based on diaries supplemented by perceptions based on interviews.

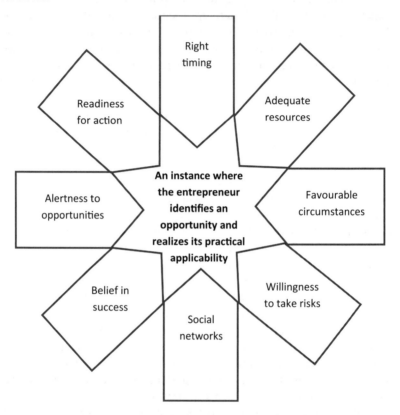

*Figure 10.2   Summary of issues contributing to momentary opportunity
            exploration and exploitation*

## CONCLUSIONS AND IMPLICATIONS FOR FURTHER RESEARCH

The contributions of the study are manifold. From the perspective of the existing research, the study is able to shed light on the black box of opportunities and the opportunity process within small firms. The diary data gave the researchers the opportunity to uncover the reality witnessed by the entrepreneurs in terms of opportunities. While the process nature of the opportunity process clearly came out in the diaries, we might wonder whether a researcher can ever gain this kind of insight to an entrepreneur's mind through a diary. Theoretically, this research clearly suggests that opportunities need a social context in order both to emerge and to be evaluated. The opportunity process is a social construct: a contextually bound iterative learning process. It is stimulated by a range of events that develop it further towards accomplishment. In this respect, the study is the first attempt of its kind to address the opportunity process as a whole, and explain the process with detailed descriptions and the personal accounts of those involved. Time plays many roles in opportunities; it is a scarce resource influencing the nature of the opportunity process, but opportunities as such are not bound by time or place.

The managerial contribution of the chapter is built around the diaries. The entrepreneurs felt that they learned about themselves as business people while observing and making notes of their own actions. They also felt that keeping a diary eased and structured their thinking processes and made them somewhat more analytical in relation to their daily activities, as they were instructed to make notes and list benefits and disadvantages related to different opportunities. The diary entries helped them recognize their own routines, as well as their strengths and features in terms of managing a firm with limited resources in highly competitive and turbulent markets. Participation in the research process also made the entrepreneurs think explicitly about opportunities, and in a few cases made them more aware of the role and nature of opportunities in terms of their company and business. They also believed that the diaries could help them communicate and justify their ideas and decisions to their employees, partners and family members holding a stake in the enterprise. The entrepreneurs also highlighted the importance of their peers and stakeholders in giving them valuable feedback on their ideas, and how the diaries further acted as tools for self-reflection. The entrepreneurs considered continuing to keep a diary after the research project as a helpful exercise for themselves. In addition to this positive feedback, the entrepreneurs also brought to light challenges related to writing a diary. They expressed that the lack of time to write and inexperience in expressing their thoughts in writing were most challenging. This is also found by Corti (1993) and Kenten (2010). The entrepreneurs would have preferred to dictate their thoughts to a digital recorder, for example while driving from place to place. This approach would also have eased their expression and possibly provided the researchers with even richer data.

Some of the entrepreneurs felt the need to edit their text before handing it over to the researchers, as they were highly critical of what they wrote and to some extent uncertain about the clarity of their 'scribblings'.

The limitations, or challenges, and implications of this study relate to the method and the research context. The first challenge was that the entrepreneurs tended to cast a critical eye over their notes; they were already analysing them as they wrote. One of the entrepreneurs rewrote his diary, not giving us the original notes but a developed version thereof, incurring the risk of double hermeneutic in analysing the results (see Giddens 1984; Noorderhaven et al. 2007). This meant he dropped out notes that he probably perceived to be less useful or important to us, or something that was not meant for us (see also Bolger et al. 2003). That may also have led to very short notes losing some or all of their information value. While the instructions were pretty clear, the problem lies more in how to gain the diarists' trust in you as a researcher and in themselves as entrepreneurs and experts in their field. That might be the only way to enable them to express themselves freely. It is clear that differences in personality between the entrepreneurs are reflected also in their diaries: while one is used to writing short reports with bullet points, another prefers to process their thoughts into a narrative. It was therefore challenging to make the diaries comparable with each other (supported by, e.g., Corti 1993).

Areas of development could include interim interviews or open discussions with the entrepreneurs, added to their writing or rather dictating their diaries. This could create more consistency in the research project and the entrepreneurs might benefit more from the diary. On the other hand, we wished to have authentic descriptions of the process that were secured from researcher intervention. Another issue is the trustworthiness of the diary; the researchers cannot guarantee that the entrepreneurs have made their entries as consistently as they can appear in the diary (for more on the timing of diary entries, see Bolger et al. 2003). Also, writing down your own thoughts and actions with the knowledge that others – that is, researchers – were to read them seemed a little uncomfortable for some of the entrepreneurs. They appeared sometimes to put too much effort into thinking about the linguistic form or quality of what they wrote rather than the actual content which was of research interest. The fact that the diary method is a valid way in which to gather relevant information was emphasized to the entrepreneurs. Contextual issues, such as culture and the industry, may also have influenced the usability of the diary approach, but with regard to the studied entrepreneurs these issues did not seem to have had any impact on writing the diaries. The diary method transpired to be a fruitful and rich source of data, providing the researchers with interesting narratives that could easily be transferred to and repeated in other contexts where the studied subject is complex and would benefit from frequent on-site real-time observation and recording.

## NOTES

1. For example, the 14th McGill International Entrepreneurship Conference hosted by the University of Southern Denmark in Odense, Denmark, 16–18 September 2011.
2. The Sapuska – Added Value for International Food Markets programme run by the Finnish Funding Agency for Technology and Innovation (TEKES), http://www.tekes.fi/programmes/Sapuska.

## REFERENCES

Ahola, M. (2008), 'Suomalaisten pk-elintarvikeyritysten markkinapotentiaali Skandinaviassa' ('The market potential of finnish food sector SMEs in Scandinavia'), Finpro Report.

Alaszewski, A. (2006), *Using Diaries for Social Research*, Thousand Oaks, CA, USA and London, UK: Sage.

Alvarez, S.A. and J.B. Barney (2010), 'Entrepreneurship and epistemology: the philosophical underpinnings of the study of entrepreneurial opportunities', *Academy of Management Annals*, **40** (1), 557–583.

Ardichvili, A., R. Cardozo and S. Ray (2003), 'A theory of entrepreneurial opportunity identification and development', *Journal of Business Venturing*, **18** (1), 105–123.

Balogun, J., A.S. Huff and P. Johnson (2003), 'Three responses to the methodological challenges of studying strategising', *Journal of Management Studies*, **40** (1), 197–224.

Baron, R.A. (2006), 'Opportunity recognition as pattern recognition: how entrepreneurs "connect the dots" to identify new business opportunities', *Academy of Management Perspectives*, **20** (1), 104–119.

Baron, R.A. and M.D. Ensley (2006), 'Opportunity recognition as the detection of meaningful patterns: evidence from comparisons of novice and experienced entrepreneurs', *Management Science*, **52** (9), 1331–1344.

Baum, R.J. and B.J. Bird (2010), 'The successful intelligence of high-growth entrepreneurs: links to new venture growth', *Organization Science*, **21** (2), 397–412.

Blackburn, R. and A. Kovalainen (2009), 'Researching small firms and entrepreneurship: past, present and future', *International Journal of Management Reviews*, **11** (2), 127–148.

Bolger, N., A. Davis and E. Rafaeli (2003), 'Diary methods: capturing life as it is lived', *Annual Review of Psychology*, **54** (1), 579–616.

Brännback, M. and A. Carsrud (2008), 'Do they see what we see? A critical Nordic tale about perceptions of entrepreneurial opportunities, goals and growth', *Journal of Enterprising Culture*, **16** (1), 55–87.

Casson, M. and N. Wadeson (2007), 'The discovery of opportunities: extending the economic theory of the entrepreneur', *Small Business Economics*, **28** (4), 285–300.

Chen, C.-M., T.-C. Lin, Y.-C. Liou and Y.-C. Liu (2009), 'Social capital, knowledge-based view and entrepreneurial opportunity', *International Journal of Management and Enterprise Development*, **7** (2), 163–182.

Companys, Y.E. and J.S. McMullen (2007), 'Strategic entrepreneurs at work: the nature, discovery, and exploitation of entrepreneurial opportunities', *Small Business Economics*, **28** (4), 301–322.

Corbett, A.C. (2005), 'Experiential learning within the process of opportunity identification and exploitation', *Entrepreneurship Theory and Practice*, **29** (4), 473–491.

Cornelissen, J.P. and J.S. Clarke (2010), 'Imagining and rationalizing opportunities: inductive reasoning and the creation and justification of new ventures', *Academy of Management Review*, **35** (4), 339–557.

Corti, L. (1993), 'Using diaries in social research', Social Research Update 2, March, University of Surrey.

Dew, N. (2009), 'Serendipity in entrepreneurship', *Organization Studies*, **30** (7), 735–753.

Giddens, A. (1984), *The Constitution of Society*, Cambridge: Polity Press.

Hall, G. (2008), 'An ethnographic diary study', *ELT Journal*, **62** (2), 113–122.

Hurmerinta-Peltomäki, L. (2003), 'Time and internationalisation: theoretical challenges set by rapid internationalisation', *Journal of International Entrepreneurship*, **1** (2), 217–236.

Kaipio, H. and S. Leppänen (2005), 'Distribution systems of the food sector in Russia: the perspective of Finnish food industry', Publications of the Center for Markets in Transition (CEMAT) of Helsinki School of Economics, Helsinki.

Kaish, S. and B. Gilad (1991), 'Characteristics of opportunities search of entrepreneurs versus executives: sources, interests, general alertness', *Journal of Business Venturing*, **6** (1), 45–61.

Kenten, C. (2010), 'Narrating oneself: reflections on the use of solicited diaries with diary interviews', *Forum: Qualitative Social Research*, **11** (2), Art. 16, http//nbn-resolving.de/urn:nbn:de:0114-fqs1002160.

Kirzner, I.M. (1973), *Competition and Entrepreneurship*, Chicago, IL: University of Chicago Press.

Mainela, T., E. Pernu and V. Puhakka (2011), 'The development of a high-tech international new venture as a process of acting: a study of the lifespan of a venture in software business', *Journal of Small Business and Enterprise Development*, **18** (3), 430–456.

Mäki, S. (2008), *Elintarvikealan Pk-Yritysten Toimintaympäristö 2008* (*The Operating Environment of Food Sector SMEs 2008*), Kuopio: Publications of Savonia University of Applied Sciences.

Noorderhaven, N.G., J. Benders and A.B. Keizer (2007), 'Comprehensiveness versus pragmatism: Consensus at the Japanese–Dutch interface', *Journal of Management Studies*, **44** (8), 1349–1370.

Patterson, A. (2005), 'Processes, relationships, settings, products and consumers: the case for qualitative diary research', *Qualitative Market Research: An International Journal*, **8** (2), 142–156.

Pina e Cunha, M., S.R. Clegg and S. Mendonça (2010), 'On serendipity and organising', *European Management Journal*, **28** (5), 319–330.

Plowman, P.J. (2010), 'The diary project: revealing the gendered organisation', *Qualitative Research in Organizations and Management: An International Journal*, **5** (1), 28–46.

Schumpeter, J.A. (1934), *The Theory of Economic Development: An Inquiry into Profits, Capital, Credit, Interest and the Business Cycle*, Cambridge, MA: Harvard.

Smith, B.R., C.H. Matthews and M.T. Schenkel (2009), 'Differences in entrepreneurial opportunities: the role of tacitness and codification in opportunity identification', *Journal of Small Business Management*, **47** (1), 38–57.

Weil, S. (2006), 'Review: Andy Alaszewski (2006), "Using diaries for social research [16 paragraphs]"', *Forum Qualitative Sozialforschung/Forum: Qualitative Social Research*, **7** (4), Art. 25, http://nbn-resolving.de/urn:nbn:de:0114-fqs0604259.

Wheeler, L. and H.T. Reis (1991), 'Self-recording of everyday life events: origins, types, and uses', *Journal of Personality*, **59** (3), 339–354.

Wrang, E. (2008), 'Suomalaisten elintarvikkeiden mahdollisuudet kansainvälisillä markkinoilla. Esimerkkejä mahdollisuuksista: Pohjoismaat, Ranska, Saksa, Iso-Britannia' ('The opportunities of Finnish food products in international markets. Examples from opportunities in the Nordic countries, France, Germany and United Kingdom'), Finpro Report.

Wrang, E., M. Ahola, T. Kuuri-Riutta, S. Paananen and N. Herlin (2008), 'Varsinais-Suomen maakunnan alueella toteutettava selvitys- ja kehitystyö koskien elintarvikealalla toimivien pk-yritysten kilpailukyvyn kehittämistä ja kansainvälistymisen edistämistä' ('Report on the development of competitiveness and enhancement of internationalisation of food sector SMEs in the Varsinais-Suomi region'), Finpro Report.

Zimmerman, D.H. and D.L. Wieder (1977), 'The diary: diary-interview method', *Journal of Contemporary Ethnography*, **5** (4), 479–498.

# Index